In Sickness and in Wealth

Also by this Author

Behind a Painted Smile

A Garland of Lies

Highway of Regret

A Circle of Deceit

Mum's the Word!

The Shame of the Name

In Sickness and in Wealth

Phoebe Neve

Front cover design by Patrick Stephen

ISBN: 978-1-917778-19-0

There are people who have money
and people who are rich." – **Coco Chanel**

Introduction

When I first had the idea to write about my father-in-law, Norman, and his quest to become a millionaire, it was to put together a list of his quirky, money saving ideas. I had visions of creating a small, humorous book that one might buy as a Christmas stocking filler. But as I began making my list it stirred up so many memories and I felt the need to explain Norman's often misguided logic behind his antics. This then had me thinking about the knock-on effects and repercussions of his actions that so often affected members of his family. Once I started, I just could not stop! So, this is my account of life with a man on a mission to be wealthy.

Chapter 1

Who wants to be a millionaire?

Have you ever wondered what it must feel like to be a millionaire? I certainly have. Many of us will have imagined what it would be like never having to count the pennies or having to think twice about the cost of anything, knowing it is just a pipe dream. It is an impossible dream that even those with good incomes, saving a little each week for a rainy day, will never achieve. Very few of us are destined to become millionaires unless Lady Luck is on our side when picking six numbers on a lottery ticket or our premium bonds come up trumps. So, we resign ourselves to never being rich, though today, a million pounds is no longer considered a fortune and is merely the cost of a decent semi-detached house in some areas of the country.

But what if it was possible to amass a million pounds in the bank simply by living a more frugal lifestyle and making some sacrifices? Who would be prepared to make such changes in their life to achieve that wealth? Well, most folk may give it a passing thought. But exactly what sacrifices would have to be made?

Would you be prepared to inflict the consequences of your frugality on your nearest and dearest to reach your goal? Would you be prepared to make the ones who love you do without what we all now consider to be the necessities in life? And would you be prepared to forfeit the love of your family, especially your children and grandchildren, in return for a healthy bank balance?

To be blessed with a loving partner, children and grandchildren are priceless gifts. So, would sacrificing the love of those who should be your nearest and dearest be a good swap for a million pounds? Well, my father-in-law, Norman, obviously thought so and did just that!

Chapter 2

From rags to riches

Norman vowed to himself that one day he would be a millionaire, determined that nothing and no-one would ever hinder his quest to be wealthy. And it didn't! Born in 1929, in West Yorkshire, like so many other children at that time, he came from a large, poor family. There had to have been a defining moment or event in his life that sparked off his determination to escape poverty and become a wealthy man, but exactly when or what it was that brought about his life changing decision escaped my knowledge for years.

Millions were born into poverty back then but had happy and loving childhoods. And it is normal to want a better life for ourselves and our offspring, but that wasn't what Norman ever wanted. He wanted a million pounds in the bank just for the status of being a millionaire. This money was never intended to benefit anyone in any way.

When I married Norman's only son, Chris, my mother-in law, Margaret, told me soon after our wedding that Norman was determined to become a millionaire and that he wanted his wealth to be handed down through future generations. In future years he wanted his family to be known for its wealth. At that time in his life, he had already managed to save a very tidy sum by investing in a stocks and shares and was well set in his odd behaviour when it came to discovering ways to save money.

Well, whatever it was that sparked Norman's ambition, which was to become an obsession, it lasted throughout his lifetime. Nothing and nobody ever got in his way when it came to reaching his goal of becoming a millionaire. Those magic numbers printed on a pile of passbooks and insurance policies were his life's goal and he did achieve this by the time he was in his eighth decade.

Over the years, I and other members of Norman's extended family laughed at his money saving tricks and habits. But behind the laughter there was always sadness and pitiful comments. Norman may have achieved his goal in life by making him one of the wealthiest men in his hometown, but he will always be the poorest man I have ever met!

Chapter 3

From Glamourous to Grouch

Norman's long-suffering wife, Margaret, was born in 1930 and came from a typical Catholic family. Her family's wealth was in the love they had for each other and not financial. She was one of seven children. Sadly, twin boys died as babies and another brother died in his youth. But having got to know Margaret's parents and surviving siblings I'm sure it was still a happy and loving home.

From some very reliable sources I have been told many tales about the teenage Margaret and her cheeky antics. And like any other teenage girl she liked to dress up and have fun with friends, going dancing or skating at the local roller rink. Margaret was also quite a glamourous young lady who loved to wear make-up and like other young girls of that era her appearance was important to her. She was a normal fun-loving young woman who had left school aged fifteen and initially gone to work in the textile industry, later working in other occupations before finding her true calling as a nurse.

With hindsight, Margaret was probably intelligent enough to have gone on to further education. But due to her family's financial situation, which was like so many others at that time, it was probably never an option open to her. Back then, it was costly to send someone to university with only the ones from financially secure families continuing in further education or those academically good enough to win a scholarship. And I suspect at that stage in her life Margaret hadn't shown any signs of being interested in staying on at school. It was only later in life did she find her true vocation. And by then she had met and married Norman.

So, the couple had met at the local roller-skating rink in Batley. In 2017, after Margaret's death, Norman told me that he'd seen this very attractive young woman skating past him and decided he was going to go speak to her. I have often wondered what his chat up line was. Whatever it was he must have charmed Margaret because they became an item or as it was better known, they started courting. Back then she could never have imagined the lengths her future husband would be prepared to go to just to achieve his ambition. She may even have thought it a positive aspect of Norman's personality, him being someone who wanted to get on in life and who wasn't afraid of hard work.

But Margaret's fate was sealed when she fell pregnant with Norman's baby. Like so many more couples in that era who had either thrown caution to the wind or simply been unlucky, it was expected that the couple would marry.

However, I'm told that Margaret's mother had concerns for her daughter on hearing that she was carrying Norman's baby. She warned her pregnant daughter about marrying Norman as she didn't think he would ever amount to much. Now did Margaret tell her future husband what had been said about him, or did he hear his future mother-in law saying those words to Margaret? I suspect this was the defining statement that started Norman's quest to prove to everyone that he could be as good, if not better than others and he would prove himself to be a worthy husband. Coupled with Norman revealing to me in his last months that as a young lad a teacher had told him he would never amount to anything, but he was an astute young man. Was that comment what initially set him on his path to craving wealth?

It was 1949 when Norman got the shock news that he was to become a father. He was twenty years old and in a serious relationship with Margaret but that must have thrown a real spanner in the works. At that time, it was expected of a young man to step up to the mark and make an honest woman of their pregnant girlfriend. So, his marriage to Margaret was hastily arranged with him having little or no choice in the matter.

Like so many other young couples, their wedding had to be swiftly arranged to avoid the baby being born out of wedlock. And just to make things a little more complicated, Norman wasn't of the Catholic faith. Margaret may not have been bothered about Norman's religious views, but her mother certainly was! It had to be a wedding in the local Catholic church, early in the morning, but without a full Catholic service. The couple were not allowed onto the church altar. Back then, being pregnant before marriage was often considered something to be ashamed of and a topic of local gossip.

I'm told that the cost of the low-key wedding was paid for by the bride's parents with Margaret's older brother, Austin, chipping in to pay the cost of the wedding taxis. It was tradition for the bride's parents to foot the bill for a wedding and a reception, but I doubt on this occasion that Margaret's parents had any choice than to cough up if they wanted their daughter married before her baby bump became too obvious. Even Norman's wedding suit was paid for by his future in-laws. So, he was penniless as he started married life, in debt to his in-laws and having to live under their roof. Add to that the fact that his mother-in-law had already made it known that she didn't think Norman would ever amount to much, this may well have been the moment when Norman's pledge to himself that he would be a wealthy man was ramped up a bit, hating the fact he was a poor man who was now indebted to his in-laws. And I can understand him wanting to prove to everyone that he was worthy of their respect and determined to get it.

I know that the couple were embarrassed about their "shotgun" wedding when years later I asked how long they had been married. Norman was swift to reply, "Too many!" to cover up the truth. But there was no escaping the truth when it was there silver wedding anniversary. Chris was only four months away from his twenty fifth birthday. It didn't take much working out. How times have changed!

So, the fun-loving Margaret was suddenly the mother of a baby boy and saddled with Norman "Till death do us part." Their lives had changed dramatically but the young couple had tied the knot and presumably intended to provide a happy home for their child, and it could still have been a good life even with a limited income. And maybe they could have been blessed with more children. But Norman didn't want to scrape by in life like his parents had. He wanted money and lots of it, but not for spending. I suspect he will have made sure there would never be a second child. Sadly, marrying Norman was the end of her fun-loving ways and the beginning of Margaret's conversion from being a glamourous young woman to becoming a grouch who was married to Ebenezer Scrooge's twin brother.

Chapter 4

All work and no play!

Nobody could ever say that Norman didn't work hard to achieve his dream of being a millionaire. He was restricted to manual work due to his poor spelling and writing skills. I saw evidence of this when I found a note that Norman had left on their kitchen table. The note said, *Maggot gon denised.* He was telling Margaret that he had gone to the dentist! And his maths left much to be desired. But he certainly wasn't afraid of hard, manual work or putting in long hours, expecting to be rewarded well for his toil.

Norman told me once he was making money by the age of ten. He was happy to do any work that he could get paid for out of school hours and weekends, including one job that I found rather unsettling to hear about. He told me that he got paid to hold down the back legs of sheep while the local farmer cut their throats! When he told me this it explained why Norman had no time for pets, be it for himself or those belonging to others. I had always assumed it was the cost of keeping a cat or a dog that stopped him and Margaret from having a pet but anyone who can help with such a gruesome task is probably void of having any affection for a furry creature. But I may be wrong.

After Chris was born in March 1950 no other children ever came along to disrupt Norman's plans to be rich, or what he considered rich. This will most certainly have been down to contraception and not good luck. Did Norman ever realise that he was already a wealthy man simply by having a wife and child? Doubtful! He was already measuring wealth by the amount of cash he had in the bank and nothing more.

After their hastily arranged marriage, the couple lived with Margaret's parents for a couple of years. This was the house where Chris was born which meant they had child minders at hand. The couple did eventually rent a house for a few months, but it was damp and not worth making it their permanent home, so they had to move back in with Margaret's parents again. Then, after another change of address, they managed to buy a terrace house only a stone's throw away from Margaret's parents for three hundred pounds. This was their home for many years. So, now they were on the property ladder.

By this time Margaret had started working as a nursing auxiliary but then decided she wanted to train as a nurse. Norman was happy to encourage his wife in her new career as it would mean a far better salary for Margaret if she qualified as a nurse. And a better salary equalled more money to put in Norman's savings pot. How the change of circumstances would affect their young son would never have crossed Norman's mind. Childcare was still needed, and it was because of those childcare arrangements that Chris formed a strong bond with his grandparents who were like surrogate parents. But I was told by Margaret's aunt that she had at one time been bribed into looking after Chris when he came home from school. What was her reward? They gave her a sideboard that she had always liked. Yes, a sideboard! And I believe there were others who helped and took charge of Chris out of school hours.

These precious years could have been spent bonding with their son. They were wasted, as Norman juggled two jobs, his wife spending her time working and studying for her new career. So, it was often down to Margaret's mother to deal with her young grandson's cheeky, boyish antics. On one occasion the parish priest had the poor woman on her knees, repeatedly chanting "Hail Mary" to atone for Chris's behaviour. He had thrown a three-legged stool at the priest who had come calling on his grandmother and then called him a "black bugger!" I can only imagine the horror his poor grandmother must have felt as she watched on in awe at her grandson's disrespectful behaviour.

Norman had various jobs before eventually settling into a full-time job in a local carpet mill as a maintenance fitter, but he often had various part time money-making activities on the go. He was happy to help the local gravedigger on occasions for a bit of cash in hand. Playing Hawaiian guitar in a country and western group was another string to his bow, as was building dry stone walls for neighbours or a stone porch. He could turn his hand to almost anything if there was a pound or two to be made and Norman was always there to make it! Weekends were never considered a time for family but to simply add more coffers into his pot. And if Norman enjoyed playing in a band, I've often wondered why he didn't keep his Hawaiian guitar and take some pleasure playing it at home? Or was it simply just another way of making extra cash?

When Chris reached seventeen, he gave up what he thought was a boring apprenticeship to join the army. It was around this time Norman was able to buy a brand-new bungalow. The two bedroomed property was in a quiet area at the other end of town from Margaret's parents but by then of course they didn't need a childminder. From then on, apart from fleeting visits home while on leave from the army, Chris's relationship with his parents was by letter until 1971 when he returned to civvy street.

Even in later years, after a full week's graft working as a maintenance fitter in a local carpet mill, Norman was always eager to work overtime at weekends. The younger employees didn't want the extra hours, often leaving Norman doing the work of three men. But of course, he expected three times the pay and he got it. This being before health and safety rules were strictly adhered to, meaning Norman was often alone in the mill at weekends, working on the boilers. Should he have had an accident of any kind no help would have been at hand. But money came before his safety every time.

He did have a couple of days off for Christmas, but New Year's Day was just another working day to Norman. When other employees were still taking their festive holidays, he was grafting away for double time, leaving himself no time to relax and make merry with his family. Though never in over fifty years did I ever see Norman come anywhere close to making merry. He struggled to be cheerful unless it involved talking his money or about making money. In later years, even when he had his three young granddaughters living close by, getting paid double time on Sundays was more important than spending time with them. Was all his toil and sweat worth missing out on quality time with his wife and family? I would say not, but he may have begged to differ.

Chapter 5

'Nip a currant in two!'

We all know that Yorkshire men are renowned worldwide for being a bit tight with their cash, but Norman could have taught even the most frugal Tyke how to save that little bit more. The expression "to nip a currant in two" didn't apply to Norman. He could nip a currant into four with great ease and into eight at a push. Basically, Norman was as tight as cramp! He had plenty of simple tricks up his sleeve to save that extra penny. Though I'm reliably informed that Margaret could be equally as thrifty and wasn't opposed to asking a family member if she could have their empty Harvey's Bristol Cream bottle so she could get it filled with wine from the wood. That was cheap 'n cheerful sherry sold by shops at a fraction of the price paid for a quality brand. The Harvey's bottle would then be put on display to offer visitors a tipple at Christmas.

In January 1972 Chris and I had seen an advert in the local newspaper about a pair of semi-detached bungalows that were going to be built locally. We had already planned our wedding for August of that year and had started searching for a suitable house to buy. We had also considered putting our names on the council housing list as a backup should we not find any suitable property. So, when we saw the advert for a brand-new bungalow at the price of £3,250, we were down at the estate agents the following morning. We scrutinised the plans and decided that as we had the required deposit we should sign up for bungalow. The building work was due to be completed by July. So, we were all sorted with a home to start our marriage and wedding arrangements for the coming August were already in place. What could possibly go wrong?

Then the builder of our prospective home realised that he had undervalued the selling price and started playing silly beggars, hoping to get more cash out of us before he completed the bungalow. For weeks it was stalemate as we stood our ground, refusing to pay him more. So, our new home wasn't anywhere near completion and our wedding was only weeks away. Chris told me that his parents had said we could live with them until the bungalow was completed and I reluctantly agreed as there was no way we could be accommodated at my parents' home.

Living with my in-laws was a very stressful time for all. I hated every second of it and I've no doubt so did my in-laws. At the time I was a quality controller in the new texturising department at a local woollen mill. Each weekday morning when I arrived at work, I would put on my ear defenders and take a walk into one of the noisiest areas of the crimping room and let rip with some very crude expletives! The men working on the crimping machines had to wear defenders, due to the high-pitched noise, so they couldn't hear anything that I screamed. It was my way of releasing the frustration and tension of living under Norman's rules. How his wife put up with it I will never know. But she did. It was a shock to my system discovering and having to live with Norman's eccentricity. I quickly discovered Norman's penny-pinching antics

So, why pay for electricity to light up your home when it's quite possible to get through life without turning the lights on, except in certain circumstances? How? Well, once Margaret had started earning decent money in her new nursing career, they had been able to buy a brand-new bungalow without a mortgage. The couple did have a mortgage initially, but Norman worked out just how much interest he would be paying back over twenty-five years. With that weighing heavily on his mind he paid off the £2000 that he owed within a couple of years. Their bungalow had the good fortune of having a streetlight directly outside the front of the property. When dusk descended, the streetlamp gave off sufficient lighting to be able to illuminate their lounge and kitchen, or so Norman thought. Watching television in the dark then became the norm for the couple. The only time a light needed switching on was when paying a visit to the bathroom and I suspect Norman will have managed to wee in the dark, when at all possible, but he would surely have needed a light on for a bowel movement.

So, during the cold, dark winter months, imagine being huddled in front of a meagre flicker of a gas fire flame, sat in the dark, waiting for 9.00pm to come around so you could go to bed dressed in more clothes than normal folk wear throughout the day. For Margaret this was the end to every busy day at work. Yet by just flicking on a few switches, she could have spent the evening relaxing in a warm bath and later watch television in a comfortably warm lounge, before retiring into a cosy, warm bed. It never happened. For Norman it was just another day of saving a few more pence, so he could rest easy in his cold bed.

Sitting in a cold temperature didn't seem to bother Norman as he proved many years later when Margaret had to spend some time in hospital having lifesaving surgery for cancer. It was December, so obviously the temperature outside was naturally cold. One afternoon during Margaret's hospital confinement her elder sister, Ellen, made an unexpected visit to see Norman to ask if he needed anything, knowing that he had never done any shopping in the past. The outer porch door to his bungalow wasn't locked so she entered and knocked on the inner door but got no reply. When she tried that door and found it too was unlocked, she entered the very chilly hall of the bungalow. Finally, she knocked politely on the lounge door to warn Norman of her presence. Getting no reply and there being no sign of life, she walked warily into the lounge. What did she find? Well, she thought she had walked into a fridge and that she had found a corpse in the armchair!

Norman had fallen asleep, but what frightened the poor woman was how cold it was in the room and her first thought was that Norman had died of hyperthermia! She gingerly shook him, fearing the worst before Norman opened his eyes, startled. She told me later that she had given him a rollocking about not having the fire on and the ridiculously cold temperature in his home, which was obvious by the fact that she could see her own breath as she spoke. I knew exactly what she meant because I once had to call at the bungalow on a very cold day and it was colder inside their home than outside. I could see my breath as I spoke and within minutes of being in their lounge I was feeling chilly to say the least. It's one thing keeping the heating low, but that was seriously cold. Why did Norman want to sit in such an uncomfortable atmosphere? And more importantly why did Margaret, who as a nurse would know the dangers of hyperthermia, agree to sit wearing multiple layers of clothing instead of putting the fire on full?

And when Margaret did return home from her stay in hospital, she was very frail. Having a part of her stomach removed had badly affected her ability to eat normally. She needed a very soft diet and one suggestion I made was for Norman to buy a microwave oven. Norman was still working at that time, so Margaret was alone during the day. How easy would it have been for her to have baked a potato in the microwave and then add butter or cheese? And she could have heated soup without messing up pans or having to stand over an oven or hob. But my suggestion was never acted on. Margaret had also lost weight and would surely have felt the effects of sitting in a cold room far more than Norman. Yet she never complained.

On summer evenings the sun would shine directly into Norman's lounge making it difficult to see their old television screen clearly. Most folk would solve the problem by having blinds fitted to the window or even pulling on a curtain to block the bright sunrays. Neither was an option Norman would consider. Having blinds fitted would cost money and would only be useful for a small part of the day and not every day. Their lounge curtains had been expensive and to my knowledge were never, ever pulled on as it would spoil the pleating. So, they were only for show. How did Norman overcome the problem of his impaired viewing? He taped pieces of cardboard along the top of the television and down one side to block the sun rays. What visitors thought when they saw his makeshift sun reflector is anyone's guess. Years later when they moved into a council flat the cardboard still functioned as a sun deflector! Now, there is one question you will be asking yourself. Why would anyone move out of a nice stone bungalow and into a top floor council flat? All will be revealed later.

Never turning on the television until the programme that they wanted to watch was just about to start was another way of saving a penny or two. And when the programme ended Norman turned the television set off again and the couple sat in silence until they were ready to watch something else. But Norman didn't just turn the television off between programmes, he unplugged it every time. Heaven forbid that he may have wasted the smallest amount of electricity by leaving the red standby light on! I'm sure most folk are like me and put the television on robotically without a thought to what is on or if it is being watched by anyone and never think to switch it off between programmes or if slipping upstairs for a few minutes. I wonder how many pennies Norman saved over the years by doing that? But did he ever work out the cost of wearing the carpet away as he trudged back and forth from sofa to television to change channels or turning the set on and off? It was years before he bought a set with a remote control. In fact, his television became so outdated, he painted the set with matt black paint to make it look more modern! The fact that it still needed time to warm up when it was switched on mattered not if it meant not having to spend money on a new one.

After many years he had no choice than to buy a new television when Margaret's health was deteriorating with Parkinson's disease, and she was struggling to see the screen on their old set. So, at Norman's request we took the couple along to our local Tesco store to look at the vast selection of televisions on display. Now, Norman slipped up here because the reason Margaret was struggling to see was because she needed her eyes testing and a pair of new spectacles. She had suffered with bad eyesight for decades before her illness and in earlier years had worn spectacles with jam jar bottoms for lenses. But Norman was adamant that he wanted a big screen television and chose a model that was all singing, all dancing. He wouldn't listen to me telling him that all the features on the set were of no use to him if he didn't have internet access! But he knew best and bought the ultra-modern television. When it came to having to re-tune the set from time to time, Norman hadn't a clue how to get into the menu and follow instructions. On this occasion he really had wasted his money.

Back in 1968 when they moved into their new bungalow it had central heating built into it, which was a luxury. No radiators were needed as each room had air vents in the walls. Hot air was blown through the vents working just like fan heaters. On the very few occasions that the heating was turned on, the bungalow warmed up very quickly. But due to lack of use, the vents filled up with dust and this was blown about the rooms by the fans when Norman felt compelled to flick the dreaded switch to “On”. This was just another waste of money and totally unnecessary to him. Though his home was built with such an efficient heating system it was rarely fired up and never allowed to function properly. It was nothing less than a visit from The Queen that could prompt Norman to flick on the heating switch, no matter how cold it was. Slight exaggeration there on my part but you’ll get my gist.

I was on a couple of occasions privileged to have experienced the rare luxury of the heating being turned on. There were occasions, like the few Christmas Days when along with our three girls, Chris and I were invited to dine with my in-laws. But for the rest of the year Norman’s or his wife’s comfort didn’t warrant such a reckless act. A Canon Gas Miser fire in the lounge was the only source of heating allowed. And just to make sure the fire lived up to the name of being a gas miser, Norman worked out exactly how low he could keep the flame alight before it became dangerously close to dying out and gas escaping. A marker pen was used to make a new line on the fire’s high/low setting dial that just kept the flame flickering. In truth, there was less flame than a lit candle and more heat was generated from striking the match to light the gas than what came from the fire. When the original battery powering the ignition button died it was never replaced. A box of matches was far cheaper.

I also found out an interesting fact after we had moved out of Miser Mansion, as I had come to call it. When we moved into our new home Norman was quick to fit our new gas fire. He told me that he had fitted their gas fire himself, refusing to pay a qualified gas fitter to do the work. The health and safety laws back then were nothing like those of today. Norman used washing up liquid rubbed onto the copper pipes he had plumbed to check for any gas leaks. I later discovered this is not a foolproof method of checking for escaping gas. But him cutting corners to save a few pounds may well explain something that often happened to me while living at Miser Mansion. Whenever I was alone in Norman’s home, I often turned up the fire to “High” to take away the constant chill in the room. If I sat on their old sofa which was pulled up as close as it could possibly be to the fire, I always found myself feeling sleepy. This I put down to the simple pleasure of being warm instead sitting in a chilly room. But what if it was toxic fumes escaping that caused my drowsiness? Norman's plumbing may well have been dangerously unsafe.

Another strange thing that happened may also have been down to Norman's poor gas fitting skills. A few weeks after moving into our bungalow, Chris and I jumped out of bed in the middle of the night when we heard a loud bang. A quick scan of our home and we found the cause. The lounge wall had a feature fireplace the length of the room and a gas fire in the centre of it. Directly above the gas fire there was a huge crevice running down the middle of the wall. The large canvas picture that had taken pride of place was hanging from just one picture hook, the other hook had fallen out of the wall. What caused this, we never knew and later tried to disguise the obvious fault with Polyfilla. And to sell our bungalow nine years later we covered the fault with a larger picture. Was the damage to the wall caused by some fault in Norman's dodgy plumbing skills? I am sure it was.

So, during the freezing winter months, extra jumpers, long woollen socks and fingerless gloves became normal lounge wear as Norman and his wife sat in the dark, in near arctic temperatures, their breath almost freezing as they exhaled. Their bedroom was equally as cold which prompted Margaret to sleep in a long-sleeved winceyette nightie, a thick cardigan and woollen socks. That must have saved him a few pence as they fought off frostbite! I once had the misfortune of bumping into Margaret in the middle of a cold November night when we had to live under their roof. She was coming out of the bathroom in the wee small hours as I was about to enter. She had more clothes on than I wore for work!

Bedtime was always 9.00pm on the dot! The television was switched off and all plugs in the house were checked in case anyone had forgotten and left one in the socket. Now sadly, due to circumstances beyond our control, when I married Chris, we had to live with my in-laws for three months and on one occasion Chris was working away from home, and I was watching television with my in-laws (deep joy). I was sitting in a chair at the back of the chilly lounge while they huddled up on the sofa in front of the fire. Not that anyone could feel any real heat coming from the tiny flicker of a flame. At 9.00pm on the dot, Norman jumped up from their little sofa, turned off the gas fire and pulled out the television plug as he usually did. When I said I wasn't going to bed so early, Norman was not pleased at knowing I would be using another few coppers worth of electricity that evening and reluctantly allowed me to turn the television back on. As for the fire, I was getting acclimatised to the cold and left it turned off. I didn't want to upset Norman too much. He wasn't at all pleased at us having to live with him, disrupting his strict routines and he made it blatantly obvious. And it certainly wasn't through choice when I married Norman's son that I went to live with them. I was very unhappy at the situation we all found ourselves in.

It goes without saying that Norman was obsessed with turning off all traces of power, even the red power switch on the electric cooker when it wasn't being used. God forbid if anyone forgot! I did on a few occasions and boy did I know it. If looks could have killed, I wouldn't be writing this! Living in his home I discovered some of his other ways to save money on electricity. Never buy a fridge, a washing machine or a hairdryer. Totally unnecessary luxuries in Norman's eyes. What did it matter that his wife had long hair (no frittering away cash on regular trips to the hairdresser) and had to spend many hours kneeling beside the fire and its faint flicker of a flame to dry her newly washed locks. Margaret wore her hair in a tight bun for most of her life. What else could she do with her ever-growing hair without having to visit a hairdresser? Had she ever fancied a complete change of hairstyle it would have meant regular visits to a salon and the cost of a hairdryer. Well, that was unlikely to happen, so Margaret was stuck with having hair like Rapunzel unless Norman tried his hand at giving her a Vidal Sasson trim with the kitchen scissors!

As for Norman, never once, in over fifty years, did I ever see any evidence that he had visited a barber's shop. Margaret chopped the back of his hair with the kitchen scissors and the rest of his straggly, long hair became a Bobby Charlton comb over held in place with lashings of liquid paraffin! Yes, liquid paraffin! Between them they must have saved a pretty penny over the years with their DIY hairstyles. But it was not the look one expects of a wealthy man or woman. I had brought my own hairdryer with me when I moved into Miser Mansion. This went down like the proverbial lead balloon whenever I used it. Thank goodness there were no smart meters back then. Norman would have spent his life watching the damn thing.

Who needed a fridge on warm summer days when standing a bottle of milk in a bowl of cold water was supposedly enough to stop it curdling in the bottle? It didn't of course. Did Norman simply enjoy drinking his cup of tea with little white floaters of sour milk? Perhaps the curds enhanced the flavour of his tea that was often made with re-used tea leaves? Yes, that's right. Re-used tea leaves!

And it wasn't just the tea leaves that Margaret and Norman had been swilling around in their cups that were re-used. In the late 1980's, Margaret had an old aunt who would often call at their bungalow when she knew our three girls were having tea there. Going for tea once a week was to appease Margaret more than Norman or our girls. Now, this old aunt fancied herself as a tea leaves reader and would drink her cup of tea, then upturn the cup into a saucer. After amusing the girls with her psychic powers, Norman would take her cup and scrape out the leaves to use again! In later years they switched to using teabags. Teabags were far less messy to re-cycle and Norman could squeeze four cups a day from one bag! Years later when Margaret had passed away, Norman gave up having milk and sugar in his tea. Milk was off the menu from then on. He often made porridge for his breakfast with just oats and water. Yum Yum!

Another thing I was at first baffled about when living with Norman was how HP sauce suddenly tasted so different to when I was living at home. Why? Because, it was watered down after the first dollop had been poured. As were bottles of vinegar. Norman would pierce a hole in an old pill bottle and fill it with diluted vinegar. One bottle would last for years! Both were made tasteless, but it saved a couple of pence every few weeks and that was all that mattered.

Who needed a washing machine when your wife could spend a few minutes swilling out your smalls in a bowl of water? Water that had been boiled in the kettle because the water heater was only switched on once a week, on Saturday evening. For larger items she lugged an old suitcase to the local launderette, hail rain or shine! And, as the water tank was only heated up on Saturdays, everyone was expected to bathe that night with the minimum of hot water. Once the tank had run out of hot water that was it for another week. Whoever had the last bath was lucky to get above three or four inches of water. I wonder if Norman ever calculated the cost of boiling endless kettles each morning for us to wash before going to work and again in the evening as he and Chris washed away the grime from their day's grafting. Or me washing my hair more than once a week.

Telephones were luxury items that other people had and on the few occasions Norman or Margaret needed to use one they happily went to their next-door neighbour to make a call, without offering to pay for the privilege.

Newspapers were another luxury that Norman enjoyed but refused to buy. In his later years he was always happy to accept a copy from his neighbour when he had read it or when she was still mobile, he sent his wife to the local library to read the latest headlines and check out that evening's television programmes.

But one memorable occasion I will never forget was on a dreadful winter's night in the 1980's. It was early evening, and snow had been heavily falling all day. It was freezing outside and the sort of evening when one is glad to be inside, curtains drawn, fires and heating on full belt. "You wouldn't throw a dog out in this weather" is often a phrase that sums up the kind of evening it was. So, there I was with my husband and kids and our cats, all glad to be home for the night, cosy and warm, watching television. No sane person would have wanted to venture out into such a snowstorm without a very good reason. Or would they?

Around 7.00pm that evening I heard a knocking sound on our side door and went to see what was causing it, expecting the culprit to be the strong blizzard. Wrong! I saw a white figure through the frosted glass panel and looked through the spy hole. I could just make out that it was Margaret doing a very good impression of the Abominable Snowman. I opened the door to the elements expecting her to have brought us some bad news.

Someone must have been ill or had died or why else would anyone venture out in such appalling weather? Wrong again!

After brushing a layer of snow from her face and stamping her feet to leave a pile of snow in my kitchen, she revealed the urgency of her visit. Norman wanted to know what programmes were on television that night! We lived relatively close to my in-laws, so the stupid woman had trudged through the wind and snow to read the TV listings in our Daily Express! I was speechless and sorely tempted to give Margaret the newspaper to take home and tell her to shove it up Norman's arse! But more fool Margaret for even considering venturing out and bracing the elements. She was allowing him to get away with his ridiculous money saving regime and had put herself at risk of slipping and falling in the treacherous conditions. Why?

Getting the last squeeze out of a tube of toothpaste was also a must for Norman, with the help of a pair of pliers, before cutting open the tube and scraping out the dregs of paste. Then and only then would a new tube be put out for use and that had to be used sparingly!

Toilet roll, the cheapest and thinnest brand of course, had to be used sparingly. Only the minimum number of sheets per visit and it was bad luck if you got caught short with a bowel movement and found just the last two flimsy sheets of bog roll available. A new roll would only be put out when the last sheet had been used. I made a point of always having a tissue or two to hand when I lived at Miser Mansion. Say no more.

On a more pleasant note, as I've mentioned nipping a currant in two, it reminds me of Margaret's Christmas cake recipe. Now, traditional festive cakes usually consist of large quantities of dried fruit and much more. But not in Norman's book. Margaret religiously made her festive cakes but as with everything else in their lives, only the smallest amount of ingredients and dried fruit were used. I've seen more currants in a teacake than found in one of her cakes (slight exaggeration there)! On the few occasions that I was ever given one of Margaret's cakes, the top half would be practically fruitless with a smattering of raisins and the odd slither of a glace cherry at the bottom. It always seemed such a waste of time and effort to me, but Norman was happy and that's all that ever seemed to matter.

Constantly living with these penny-pinching ways gave Margaret a completely different outlook on life to everyone around her, except Norman. Apparently, there was a time after Margaret had retired when she wanted to write to the Prime Minister of the day to complain about the state pension. Only she didn't want to tell the P.M. that pensioners were getting a raw deal and to increase their weekly payments. No, no, no! Margaret thought that the pensioners were getting too much money! Yes! You read it right. Too much state pension! Unbelievable! Just how out of touch with the real world were my in-laws?

It was Margaret's older sister, Ellen, who had to point out the simple fact that most pensioners didn't live the miserable, frugal existence that Margaret and Norman did. And did she realise that most folk were just getting by on their pensions and not living in the lap of luxury? How deluded and out of touch with the real world had Margaret become? But what I found most hypocritical about Margaret was the fact she had a very generous NHS pension as well as her state pension. Some would say she should have given that back to the NHS if she thought the state pension was more than enough to live on. I would agree!

In the 1980's when bus fares began to rise, Norman got out his trusty pen and paper (an old used envelope) and calculated how much he was spending on bus fares travelling to and from work. Appalled at the yearly figure, he worked out how much he could save if he bought a second-hand bicycle for transport. Once he'd seen the savings he could make, there was no turning back. Each morning, hail, rain or shine he mounted his mighty push iron and peddled to and from work. The journey was not flat terrain, and he was not a young man. But with every strain on his weary muscles, he will have been counting the pounds he was saving.

Now, Norman was quite handy around the home when it came to doing a bit of DIY. But he always spoiled the fruits of his work by cutting corners, thinking he was saving money. He was wrong on that score! One instance in the early 1970's was when he offered to do the tiling for us after we had new kitchen units put into our bungalow. He refused to use tile spacers insisting that matchsticks worked equally as well and used the tile adhesive sparingly even though we were paying for it all. Well, his tiling wasn't bad, and I thought he had saved us the cost of paying anyone else, until I picked up our kettle to make a cuppa. The small area that was directly behind the kettle's usual place on the worktop had been bodged up with bits of tiles and not a full one! Why? We had at least a handful of complete tiles left over so what made him use bits that had not been neatly cut. I was devastated as I could not avoid seeing the damned mess whenever I moved the kettle. He had not saved us a penny by using those bits as we still had tiles left over!

Sometime later, Norman also volunteered to wallpaper our kitchen as he had a week's holiday and as we were both working full time his offer was a little too tempting. So, regrettably we let him do it. After all it wasn't as if there were any full walls to paper, just the few feet above and around our new kitchen units. So, off we went to work on that Monday morning leaving Norman to crack on with the wallpapering. We had chosen a blown vinyl paper that needed no matching and then we only had to paint it. Simple! Well, I thought so, but Norman was to prove me wrong.

I arrived home from work that evening and walked into our kitchen, expecting to see bare plastered walls now covered with white blown vinyl. Yes, Norman had cleaned up any mess and gone home before I arrived but what did I find? Well, how can I describe the sight before me? Yes, the blown vinyl had been pasted to the walls but was full of air bubbles! And to make it all look much worse, Norman had used screwed up sheets of newspaper instead of a cloth or brush to smooth out the wallpaper and air bubbles. So, what should have been white was now a smudgy black mess and he hadn't flattened out the air bubbles, leaving big creases in the paper. Why didn't he use an old cloth to smooth the paper out instead of newspaper? It looked dreadful!

When Chris came home later that evening he too was underwhelmed at the sight of our kitchen. He suggested we paint the paper as originally planned and maybe it wouldn't look too bad. Really? No way was I wasting more money on paint to try and rectify Norman's poor work. There was only one solution and that was to rip it all off and start again. And we did. Only the second time we used a very plain wallpaper that needed no painting and had no air bubbles. "If you want a job doing, do it yourself!" sprung to my mind. When Norman did get to see the finished kitchen, he didn't say much as I had jumped in first and told him I'd changed my mind about the décor. The subject was never mentioned again.

So, with hindsight, maybe I should have thought twice about letting Norman loose in our kitchen after the bodged tiling. I'd seen the state of his decorating in his own home. Either he bought cheap and watery emulsion paint for his walls, or he watered down good paint to make it go further. Whatever he did his walls always looked as if they needed at least another coat of paint to cover up the patches that had been lightly brushed over. Did Margaret not notice the slapdash finish? Did she dare criticise his work?

And just to punish myself once again, I allowed Norman to hang some woodchip wallpaper on the walls of our lounge when we moved house in 1981. It was very fashionable at the time! It was easy to hang and with no pattern to match there was no wastage of paper for him to worry about so off he started, paste brush in hand, while I set about painting in another room. What could possibly go wrong?

About an hour or so later I walked into our lounge to see how Norman was cracking on. Yes, he'd finished one full wall and had almost completed another and not an air bubble in sight. But. . . the third strip of woodchip on the first wall appeared to be different and was immediately noticeable. Norman caught me staring at it and explained why it was so different. He'd only pasted it to the wall the wrong way round with the raised woodchip to the wall and smooth backing on the outside. "You'll not notice it when it's painted!" Oh yes, I would! So, rather than pull the strip off and hang another the correct way he'd chosen to soldier on and save a couple of pence! Unbelievable but typical of him. I bit my tongue and left the room until he'd finished. That night I pulled the offending strip off the wall and pasted one back on the correct way. That really was the last time I allowed Norman to do any more DIY jobs around our home. With Chris working away all week, from then on, I took charge of decorating and hired a man who knew what he was doing for any other jobs around the house.

Chapter 6

Waste not want not!

Norman wasn't one to let sentiment get in his way when it came to saving a bob or too. One such occasion proved this. It was a late December morning and the employees of the carpet mill where Norman worked were going to have their staff Christmas dinner that day. Tickets had been bought for the festive three course meal with all the trimmings, to be served in the canteen. Norman of course would never have considered paying for a dinner when he could bring a packed lunch from home (two slices of very thinly sliced bread with a wafer-thin slice of cheese was considered more than adequate). Unfortunately, one of the young men who worked alongside Norman had a nasty accident that morning. The poor man had fallen a fair height from a ladder, was badly injured and needed to be taken to hospital. The caring and compassionate Norman, being very concerned about his young friend's welfare, was eager to escort him, alongside the paramedics, to the waiting ambulance. Then, as the poor man was being lifted on a stretcher into the ambulance, a very distressed Norman leaned in close to the injured chap and asked if he could have his Christmas dinner ticket as he would no longer be needing it! What do they say? Every cloud has a silver lining! One happy Norman skipped to the canteen that day for his free Christmas dinner. Result! The cheese butties will probably have been kept for the following day!

Having had the misfortune of living in Norman's home for weeks after getting married, I was privy to many of Norman's penny-pinching tricks but something I saw one day summed up his mentality perfectly. So, there I was one morning, standing by their kitchen sink when I noticed an eggcup in the corner of the kitchen windowsill. The eggcup had in it a very small, oddly shaped item, covered with water. I was intrigued as to what it was all about but was alone in the house. That evening as Margaret was pottering about in the kitchen, curiosity got the better of me and I asked about the egg cup. Her matter-of-fact response left me speechless. Wait for it. . . "Oh, Norman peeled too many potatoes last night." And????? Well, it seemed Norman always peeled the same number of potato pieces for their meals. The previous evening, he had messed up big style and peeled one tiny piece too many! Shock! Horror! So, rather than add the extra piece of potato to the pan, it was to sit in an eggcup filled with water for the next few days (the couple had the same meals on set days each week) until the next lot of potatoes were peeled. One asks if it would have killed either he or Margaret to force an extra forkful of potato down their throat? Obviously, being so reckless in his potato peeling was a big issue and no way could the morsal of spud be thrown away. Unbelievable? Need I say that while I had the misfortune of living under their roof, Chris and I bought our own food which was quite different to the bland, repetitive and miserly portions my in-laws dined on.

Around the time they bought their new bungalow I'm told that Norman had also bought a car. I suspect it was one of their ways of letting others know they had got a few pounds in the bank. It was a Triumph Herald convertible. This was not the most practical of cars, but Norman liked to drive around with the top down even when it was freezing and poor Chris had to sit in the rear seat. And later he ditched the convertible and bought a Ford Prefect, a very popular car at the time. This was when Margaret was training as a nurse and the car proved useful for giving her lifts home from work. But when it came to parking up his cars, Norman refused to put any vehicle down their tarmac drive, thinking it would damage the surface, so he parked on the roadside. Now isn't that defeating the object of having a drive?

But it didn't take long for Norman to think that having a car was an expensive and unnecessary luxury and it was sold as soon as Margaret's work situation changed. But he did keep his driving licence for a few years until the cost of his licence renewal increased to three pounds. That put an end to him ever driving again.

Slowly, Margaret became almost as bad as her husband for penny pinching. She was well and truly brainwashed into going along with his miserly lifestyle. As she climbed up the ladder of success in her nursing career it occasionally meant Margaret had to dress appropriately for out of work functions and not wear her usual clothing bought from second-hand shops or jumble sales. One memorable occasion was after she had retired early due to having stomach cancer. A public meeting was to be held about the surgeon who had operated on Margaret. It was to be attended by news reporters from local television stations and Margaret was going to be featured making a short speech about the surgeon who had been put on a sabbatical. This was the surgeon who had acted swiftly by operating within days of her cancer diagnosis and saved Margaret's life, so she wanted to sing his praises to those that mattered. And of course, if she was going to be in the television spotlight then Margaret had to look the part. That must have caused Norman sleepless nights thinking about the cost of buying his wife some new clobber.

I watched our local television news programme, in awe as Margaret made her speech. There she was, dressed from head to toe in a striking outfit, colour co-ordinated down to the very last detail with shoes to match. She looked a true professional and a force to be reckoned with as she spoke. Naturally, I was shocked at how much her attire must have cost and if it had given Norman a heart attack? But two days later when I commented on her smart outfit I wasn't really surprised at her response. The new clothing had all been bought from good old Marks and Spencer. The day after the meeting Margaret had returned every item to the store and got a full refund! I've often wondered how many times she will have bought clothes for earlier work-related occasions and then swiftly returned them. Marks & Spencer were known for their generous returns policy, but this was taking things a little too far.

But just to prove that Margaret was slowly getting to think like Norman, on one occasion she had been searching a charity shop for clothes and found a blouse that she liked. Choosing not to try it on in the shop she bought the blouse and took a chance on it fitting when she had got it home. Well, it wasn't as nice as she thought when she tried it on. So, the following day, off Margaret trotted back to the charity shop for a full refund. And how much had she frittered on the blouse? Ten pence! Yes, the vast sum of a ten pence refund was requested. Or in Margaret's case she will have demanded a refund regardless of how little it was. It probably cost her more in boot leather walking back and forth to the shop!

In 2024 Norman was still wearing Chris's old socks that he was issued with when in the army. He left the army in 1971, so these socks were over 53 years old! They had been darned so many times that there can't have been much of the original socks left. But think of the savings Norman had made over the decade by accepting not disposing of his son's old socks.

Norman could even tell you how much money he had saved over the years by never having any home insurance or any other type of insurance. He always claimed it was a waste of money, and he probably thought his strict rules about turning off all power sockets reduced his house fire risk. But Norman wasn't too concerned about possible fire risks when he had replacement double glazing fitted! The old wooden windows frames were no longer energy efficient and painting them cost money. So, he found some cowboys who had been door knocking in the area, touting for business, to fit new UPVC ones at a very cheap price.

Now, any respectable company would have advised Norman against having no openings in the large, bow window in the lounge and a large kitchen window. Norman was convinced that windows that opened let out the heat! What heat I asked myself? The cold air that might have leaked out would be degrees colder than that outside! He wasn't bothered that the design of their bungalow meant if a fire was to spread to the hall, they would be well and truly trapped in the kitchen or lounge. But in his warped mind it was never going to happen. The new windows would pay for themselves in no time, or so he thought. Well, I'd never seen such shoddy workmanship when I first saw the newly installed windows. The Chuckle Brothers could have done a more professional job. But hey, they were cheap and cheerful! The emphasis being on cheap. And Norman could rest easy knowing he hadn't wasted any cash on having windows that opened.

As I've already mentioned, over the years Norman took pride in avoiding the need for any household insurance for the building or contents in their bungalow. Any items that Norman considered to be of value were always hidden up in the loft when they went away on holiday. But what good thief would have wanted to steal an old television and there were no other valuables worth taking as far as I could see. Though in later years he did splash out and buy Margaret a couple of rings that he thought were an investment. Did I mention going away on holiday? That's another story! But I am reliably informed that Norman did once throw caution to the wind and cough up for home insurance when he acquired, free of charge, two antique brass lamps that he fitted outside the porch door. What prompted this I don't know, but it paid off for Norman when both lamps were stolen! He was happy to make a claim on the insurance, and always claimed it was gypsies who had been in the area who were the culprits.

In his final years Norman began hoarding useless stuff. Chris discovered old bread wrappers were kept but not just one or two that may be useful, but dozens crammed into a cupboard. Then he found piles of used tin foil that we had used to wrap up his pork steaks and sausages. All the pieces were coated with dried blood from the meat, but Norman continued to re-use them. That would account for his many bouts of diarrhoea. Then he started saving the foil wrappers from Tunnocks chocolate tea cakes that we got him every week. Loads more wrappers and the foil cups from individual apple pies were all kept. Why? Hoarding useless stuff seemed to have become the norm with our Norman. I can't think of any reason for this especially as there would be no money being saved by accumulating rubbish. But waste not want not was Norman's motto!

Chapter 7

Owt for Nowt!

After our honeymoon in Scarborough in 1972, we reluctantly returned to live at Miser Mansion. One day I noticed a new set of pans displayed on top of the kitchen cupboards. Later that day I passed an innocent comment to Margaret about how nice the pans were. I was more than shocked by her response. Why? The new pan set had been bought as a wedding present for us by Chris's uncle Austin and his family! That was the first I'd seen or heard about the pans that had been dropped off prior to our wedding. Now, I ask myself this, if I hadn't commented on the pans would I have ever been told they were ours? Why would anyone remove the packaging and put something on display in their home that wasn't meant for them? And why were we never informed about such a lovely wedding present?

Dead men's clothing! Many of us would flinch at the thought of wearing it but not our Norman. When a close neighbour died and the deceased's wife was gathering all his clothing for the local charity shop, Margaret happily took the bundle of old clothes off her hands. Norman was straight in there like a rat up a drainpipe. He was thrilled with his new wardrobe full of badly fitting clothes, all a size too big for him but costing not a penny. And the fact that the deceased hadn't yet had his funeral was of no importance. Some of the clothing may even have still been warm (shudder)!

Norman never cared that his fellow workmates laughed at him and didn't believe that he was a wealthy man. But what did he expect when he would go to his work's supply stores and beg for free light bulbs and batteries for home? Even Norman couldn't shave or have a bath in the dark! Well maybe he could, but the storeman was always obliging, probably thinking that Norman was lying about his wealth and taking pity on him. And who could have blamed him?

Razor blades were not something to spend money on either. Over the years Norman spent very little on buying razor blades mainly because he would cadge his son's used disposable ones. Spending a bit of time sharpening the ten a penny used razors on a stone in the garden was a small price to pay for the savings he made. All he needed was soap and water and a piece of old newspaper stopped the cuts on his face from bleeding after using the blunt razors. But think of how much Norman saved with each shave.

Now, getting something for nothing is fine, but would you stoop so low as to rummage about in a pile of rubbish dumped in a hedge bottom, in full view of anyone passing on foot or by car? Our Norman would and did so. On one of their many walks, he spotted a pile of rubbish in a hedgerow, and something caught his eye. Sifting through the pile, he'd spotted a vacuum cleaner, a Dyson no less. Well, I should imagine the person that dumped it had done so because it didn't work but this didn't put Norman off. He skipped home with the broken Dyson over his shoulder. It took a lot of stripping down and tinkering with but eventually he got the vacuum to work. How efficient it was I don't know but the original owner must have thought it wasn't up to much. What do they say? One man's junk is another man's treasure. Owt for nowt!

Norman had a very nice semi-detached stone bungalow that was mortgage free which he liked to brag about to workmates. Yet he wasn't prepared to fork out cash for a nice new three-piece suite when their tatty old two-seater sofa was on its last legs. Then the couple dropped lucky once again. Margaret's sister, Ellen, was having a new three-piece suite delivered and had her old one to dispose of. Norman and Margaret were happy to give it a good home, thrilled at the used Dralon suite that then took pride of place in their lounge in front of their old gas miser fire. That free suite, which was almost like new in comparison to their tatty old one, lasted Norman until his dying day, though in later years new covers were bought to hide stains from bodily fluids in the fabric.

And Margaret wasn't without bare faced cheek when it came to not spending money. Our youngest daughter, Melanie, aged fourteen at the time, had joined an amateur dramatics group. Every year the budding thespians put on a variety show in a local town hall. Margaret had encouraged Melanie to take to the stage and used her free bus pass to accompany her granddaughter to rehearsals once a week, but I had to go taxi them both home later in the evening. Now, when it came to show week, the group would do three or four evening performances. I, of course was ferrying my daughter from the town hall each night and if needed I would assist by selling ice-creams at the interval. But for the Friday performances me and my mother always bought tickets so that I could enjoy the shows as a member of the audience. What did Margeret do? She offered to make tea in the interval along with a few elderly members of the society who were regular helpers after they had given up performing in shows. This meant she didn't have to buy a ticket but got to see every performance! But if that wasn't cheeky enough, one of her neighbours expressed a wish to see one show, so Margaret invited her neighbour to go along and help make the tea just so she didn't have to pay for a ticket either! Owt for nowt every time!

Chapter 8

Ration and restrict!

Eat to live, not live to eat! This statement certainly applied to Norman and Margaret. He certainly knew the meaning of portion control. From my first visit to his home for tea as his prospective daughter-in-law, meals were carefully rationed. Egg and chips were regularly on the menu with each person getting the same amount of chips on a plate. Eight chips to be exact! Never seven or nine, always eight served with one fried egg and one slice of bread carefully carved from a small loaf. Norman had carving bread down to a fine art. Each slice was just thick enough to remain intact though almost transparent. I found all this very odd as my mother would serve up a dinner plate full of chips with two eggs and beans. Bread was always in abundance at mealtimes. Seeing Norman's offerings, served on a side plate that was marginally bigger than a saucer, left me in awe. Not forgetting the diluted vinegar and HP sauce to enhance the flavour of my meal.

To finish off my gut busting meal I was offered a cup of tea and a ginger biscuit. And I do mean one biscuit not biscuits. These were something else that were strictly rationed. One biscuit per cuppa, never two or three. Ginger biscuits were a luxury item, one packet would last Margaret and Norman a week. Until they had to entertain me. That really threw a spanner in the works.

And as a treat each evening, while they watched television in the dark, the couple would indulge in the luxury of chomping on Rileys Toffee Rolls. But not too many of course, just a couple each and no more. On more than one occasion I heard Norman telling Margaret that she had had enough toffees for the night, claiming they were bad for her teeth! Did she ever insist that she was going to have an extra toffee? Not while I was there. Norman was probably worried that if his wife slipped a couple of extra ones in it would mean the bag of toffees wouldn't last the week. This was an example of ration and restrict at its best!

Many years later when we had our three daughters, Margaret began to invite our girls round to her home for Christmas dinner, served at 12.00pm on the dot. We didn't get an invite as that would have meant having to purchase a joint of pork that was marginally bigger than a pork chop! So, Chris and I sauntered off to the pub for a festive drink with friends.

Presents from my in-laws were rare and always opened in their presence on Christmas day and not when the girls got up to see what Santa had left them. Initially, the girls were each given a £10 note, but not until after Christmas dinner, to spend on something sensible. There were rarely any gifts, lovingly gift wrapped, in the girls' stockings or Santa sacks.

Years later (and I'm not sure how we came to be talked into going) Chris and I did get invited for Christmas dinner. The girls were grown up and our eldest two were happy to go to the pub with us for a festive drink. Margaret must have accepted that we didn't want an early lunch and cooked our food in readiness for us all sitting down for 3.00pm. So, after a few lagers down our throats, we'd all march up the hill to Miser Mansion, praying that there would be heating on when we arrived. Then, sat in silence around the carefully decorated table (more about the decorations in a later chapter), we'd try not to shiver too much as we eagerly awaited our meal. Did Norman pull out all the stops on our family get together? As if! We'd even supply a bottle of wine to go with our festive meal, but Norman even rationed that out, giving us just sufficient to cover the first inch of the wine glass.

Now most hosts would serve a main course meal on a dinner plate. But you must remember this was Norman's idea of a big meal and not a normal person's opinion. We'd have our starter, a tin of grapefruit segments shared six ways. I always passed on that course, not liking grapefruit at the best of times. And then after our delicious starter, Norman would come into the lounge with plates in his hand. But these were more the size of side plates and certainly not the average dinner plate. What delicious offering were we about to receive?

Each plate would have a dollop of mashed potato, flattened down with a fork so that it spread across half the surface of the plate and looked like the topping of a cottage pie. Four sprouts were carefully placed beside a few small roast potatoes and baton carrots accompanied by a sliver of roast pork. Wow! They really pushed the boat out for us. Now, I hate sprouts so always passed mine to Chris, only to find that on one occasion I had no roast potatoes on my plate. Can you imagine what I was left with? Not a lot! But I didn't care as I really don't like traditional dinners anyway, which is just as well. Two good forkfuls and my plate was empty!

We'd wait with great expectations for our Christmas pudding only to be served with a small slice of apple pie and custard for dessert. The pathetic offering went down in one good spoonful but was followed by a real treat. Margaret would offer us all an After Eight mint. Just the one mint of course as our stomachs were stuffed with the huge meal we'd just eaten. If we were ever offered any Christmas cake it was small finger sized pieces, barely a gob full. They were so small that it took four pieces to make up what I would call a normal slice and hardly worth the effort.

This annual event went on for a few years with the meals staying pitifully small. I personally always felt that Norman would rather have not had to feed or accommodate us. Each year, the time we spent having dinner at my in-laws got less and less, until one year we had devoured our festive feast in under forty minutes. Our legs couldn't carry us back home fast enough to get stuck into some real food.

We never felt we were truly welcome and one regular tradition that always sticks in my mind is my being snubbed each year as Norman handed out Christmas cash to his family. Whatever amount he considered generous, it used to be a £10 note, which over the years did slowly increase, was carefully handed to each of our daughters, then the same amount was handed to Chris, walking past me to do so. It was so blatantly obvious that he didn't consider me family. Chris of course would tell me the cash was for us both, but actions speak louder than words and Norman's actions always spoke volumes. His cash was for close family, so I never received any.

Then, one year we threw a real spanner in the works for Christmas dinner. Our eldest daughter, Joanne, had got married and so naturally she and her husband wanted to spend the day together. So, Norman had an extra mouth to feed which meant having to buy a slightly bigger joint of pork or he'd have to slice the usual sized joint a bit thinner. Then he had an extra few sprouts and a couple of potatoes to account for. The apple pie had to stretch eight ways, and the custard made a little thinner. Later, when I asked how our son-in-law had found his roast pork dinner, he answered by saying, "Oh, I just moved a sprout and there it was!" Say no more!

At this point in time our hosts had a piano in the lounge (more about the piano later). Our youngest daughter, loved to mess about plonking on the keys and had managed to play by ear, Auld Lang Syne. After listening to her rendition numerous times our son-in-law, with his wicked sense of humour, asked her if she could play the song about weighing a pie? He laughed at our perplexed expressions and said, "You know, the one that goes, somewhere over the rainbow, to weigh a pie!" This had us all laughing out loud apart from Norman who didn't get the joke, probably silently seething at the thought of the hundreds of pounds he had spent on buying the piano.

The small portions Norman served up were considered more than adequate, yet over the years I noticed on many occasions if someone else was footing the bill for food he could happily wolf down whatever was on offer. Weddings, funerals and any family occasion where a buffet or a hot meal was served and he was in there, often taking home a doggy bag. That told me he could enjoy good food and a varied diet but not if he was paying. 0n a few occasions after Margaret died, we took Norman out to lunch at a local fish restaurant. He had no problem scoffing a fish, chips, peas, bread 'n butter and a cup of tea. All he left on his plate was the glaze! Not a bad effort for someone who couldn't eat much. And of course, he was never forthcoming with any contribution towards the cost, choosing to walk out of the restaurant first, leaving muggins (me) to pay.

Now, getting back to our huge festive blowouts, someone had to do the washing up. Norman took control of that exercise with his usual frugal quirkiness. Washing up liquid could never be squirted freely into the bowl of hot water, which was boiled in a kettle. A sewing thimble was kept by the kitchen sink for the sole purpose of measuring out the thick soapy liquid. One full thimble he thought adequate, never a drop more. And the choice of washing up liquid was most certainly the cheapest on the market.

I doubt that Norman realised that sometimes his obsession with buying the smallest amounts of food was often not the most economic choice. Buying the smallest tin of baked beans may have appeared to be the sensible choice but he could have had the family size tin for less money! And over the years, Margaret became well known in the local Co-op store for her frugal shopping habits. Not many queued up at the local Co-op's cooked meats counter and asked for one slice of corned beef. Yes, just the one slice for Norman's sandwich, never two. That would be frivolous. Two ounces of cheese was another regular order. Just enough to put in a mousetrap some of us would say but more than sufficient for Norman's butty. There was no such thing as buying more than what was necessary. With no fridge to store fresh foods Margaret stuck strictly to buying only what she needed each day. A classic example of ration and restrict.

Now, imagine waking up every morning and knowing exactly what you are going to eat that day. Norman nearly always took responsibility for the cooking even when they were both at home. Why? Well, he could make sure the food portions were strictly adhered to, making specific meals on specific days. Before she retired Margaret sometimes ate her main meal at work if she was working late as a nurse. That left Norman just fending for himself and he often considered a boiled onion with a slice of bread and butter a sufficient meal. Cups of tea or coffee were rationed to being made at the same time each day, accompanied by a ginger biscuit. Yes, it really was only ever one biscuit with no excessive dunking permitted!

I kept a secret from both Margaret and Norman for years. It would have given Norman a heart attack had he ever discovered my secret about ginger biscuits and sherbet lemons. On one occasion while having tea at Miser Mansion one of our daughters happened to mention they liked the ginger biscuits that Margaret gave them. These biscuits were bought from a baker's stall in a local market and were above average quality. Margaret had also taken to splashing out on a bag of sherbet lemon sweets, also bought in the market because the toffee rolls had been ditched at this time. And someone must have mentioned that Chris also liked these hard-boiled sweets because one day Margaret turned up with a bag of ginger biscuits and a bag of sherbet lemons for Chris and the girls to enjoy. Did Norman know about his wife's rash actions? Anyway, this became a weekly treat from Margaret and the first few weeks we as a family munched and chomped on the free goodies. But it wasn't long before we no longer wanted the biscuits or sweets but never dare tell Margaret. So, for years, week in, week out, we accepted her gifts, then as she left our home I threw them in a cupboard.

Not wanting to be deliberately wasteful, I took a bag of the ginger biscuits to work one morning and offered them to anyone and everyone who wanted one with their tea or coffee. They were devoured by all and sundry. So, this became a weekly routine for me. Margaret handed over the biscuits and I took them to work. As for the sherbet lemons, well there were only so many Chris could suck before he was fed up with them. This resulted in bag after bag piling up in a cupboard. I took a few along to work but they were slow to go. And then I had a brilliant idea. That year on Halloween, I happily dished out bags of sweets to anyone who knocked on our door for trick or treat. Sorted! I can't remember how or why Margaret stopped bringing her weekly goodies, but I once worked out the weekly cost and how much a year she had frittered away. As this went on for years it will have come to a tidy sum. Can you imagine how Norman would have reacted to that? I can!

Margaret had slowly become as bad as Norman with her penny pinching and on one occasion she told her younger sister, Mary, that she would like to spend a week living in her home to show her how to save money! She obviously thought her sister needed a lesson in how to live like a pauper, oblivious to the fact that normal folk liked their home comforts and a well-stocked food cupboard.

After Margaret's death in 2017, Norman's rationing of food became even worse. Having never being one for going into shops he started to give us a weekly grocery shopping list, not wanting to shop for himself. I remember Margaret telling me once that

Norman hated going into shops and if he ever went with her to any shop he would wait outside. Why?

An example of his odd behaviour was on one occasion when Margaret was in hospital, and he had run out of bread. Did he brace himself to go into a shop and buy a loaf? No! He'd got washed and changed to walk the short distance to our home and asked me to get him a loaf. What was odd about that? He had to walk right past the local convenience store to get to our house! What stopped him from calling in the shop and getting his own bread? Basically, Norman had set rules and routines that he wouldn't or couldn't break. A form of autistic behaviour perhaps?

So, for over sixty years he had left Margaret to shop for food, gaining herself a reputation for only buying the smallest amounts she could, while he cooked his small portions. This then became a pain for us when we started shopping for him as he only wanted two bananas, two tomatoes and two sausages. As most of the food we shopped for came pre-packed or pre-weighed out, it meant having to give him two bananas from our bunch of five, leaving just three for Chris and me. Norman would eat only half of a banana and leave the other half for the following day! This later changed to chopping a banana into three pieces, so it lasted a day longer. What the sticky over ripened banana looked like after being left for three days I dread to think.

Another delicacy that Norman rationed for himself was boil in the bag kippers. Now most folk would consider a couple of small boneless kippers a snack or a starter but not our Norman. Kippers were chopped into four equal amounts with one small portion to be eaten that day and the rest to be re-heated on following days. Now once the melted butter has been poured from the plastic bag the remaining portions of kippers would surely dry out after a few hours. Norman reheated his dried-up kipper portions by putting them on a plate, on top of a pan that covered a small amount of water. How this was supposed to re-heat anything is beyond me. And I wouldn't mind betting that the pan of water that he used to warm the kippers was used to make him a cup of tea. Waste not want not every time!

When he had a tin of mandarin orange segments the contents were shared out equally into five small dishes. One dish a day for each weekday. God forbid if the total number of segments didn't divide by five! What day would Norman have the extra segment? Decisions, decisions, decisions.

And not to waste anything, Norman even resorted to making a sandwich with just the last couple of leaves from a Little Gem lettuce he had us buying weekly for him. He added a sprinkling of salt to the soggy leaves making it yet another delicious lunch for him. He was nothing short of inventive. We had to increase the quantities we bought for ourselves to accommodate Norman's wishes. We bought blocks of cheese and then had to cut a small chunk off for Norman. Packs of sausages had to be split so he could have two sausages, never three! The amount of tin foil we were using doubled.

Eventually, Norman did manage to venture into the local Co-op store when we were on holiday or not able to go shopping for him on occasions. He quickly learned the true price of items and chose not to buy them. Then, for a weekly treat he started to allow himself a fishcake from his local chippy. One fishcake made him two meals, never to be consumed in one sitting! Why he wouldn't eat a full banana or fishcake baffled me, especially as he could push plenty of grub down his miserable throat when he wasn't paying for it! But he will have worked out just how many pennies he was saving by cutting items into two or three and every penny counted.

As time passed, Norman was still finding new ways to save a few more pence when it came to cooking. Whenever he had the oven on to cook his lamb chop or sausages, he began putting a metal pan with a small amount of water in the oven alongside the meat. Then, when his two sausages or miniscule lamb chop was ready, he used the warm water from the pan to make a cup of tea. The remaining water then used to wash up with! It mattered not that he brewed tea with warm and not boiling water because the teabag had already been used and drained of its flavour earlier in the day. But that mattered not a jot because he had saved a couple of pence by not switching on the kettle. I can only conclude that as Norman whiled away the hours, sat in silent darkness, he was constantly thinking of ways to cut back and cut down on anything and everything. That was all that mattered to him.

And as if making cups of tea with lukewarm water wasn't bad enough, Norman found another way of saving a penny. He drank from a tiny cup and decided that if he filled the cup with water and then poured it into a saucepan it was cheaper to warm the exact amount of water on the electric hob than boiling water in a kettle. After all, the element in a kettle must be covered, which was more water than Norman needed for his cup of tea. Again, I wonder what he would have been like with a smart meter in his home. He would have sat watching the meter every second of the day in a state of sheer panic.

Chapter 9

Cleanliness is next to Godliness!

Personal hygiene was not top of the agenda in Norman's world I quickly discovered. The norm for our Norm was to allow only one bath per week per person. The hot water tank was heated on Saturdays and one tank full of water had to stretch to four baths. That equated to not much more than a couple of inches of bath water each. I struggled with having to boil a kettle of water every morning then carrying it to the bathroom to have a wash or having to wash my hair in the kitchen sink with just a kettle full of water to wash and rinse. Being a nurse, I would have thought that Margaret would have insisted on a constant supply of hot water for her own personal hygiene if nothing else. With hindsight I feel that she went along with Norman's ridiculous behaviour just for a peaceful life. Having seen for myself just how obsessed with saving money he was getting, year by year, I suspect any opposition to his miserly ways would have resulted in an unpleasant atmosphere in their home. It will have been easier for her to shut up and put up.

Anyway, when it was time for their weekly bath, only a bar of soap was needed. There was never a sign of shower gel, bubble bath or fancy shampoos. I never saw any signs of deodorant or skin creams either. Norman used a bar of soap and an old re-sharpened razor along with an old mug filled with water from the kettle to shave. Prisoners in jail probably had a better selection of toiletries to hand. Again, I question why Margaret went along with it all. And I did try over the years to introduce the couple to nice smelling toiletries by buying them gift sets at Christmas. But the smellies never appeared in the bathroom afterwards.

Sadly, in later years, after Margaret had died, Norman stopped having baths or showers. He never had the water heater turned on in his flat and continued to half fill a kettle for his personal hygiene. But knowing this, I was still horrified to discover the state of his bathroom when I once had to spend a penny while waiting for a First Responder to come and check out Norman. He'd claimed he could not breath properly or walk and was adamant he was ill, so I had to ring 111 and get advice. It turned out to be nothing serious after a First Responder had done an ECG on him and checked him over.

However, on a later occasion Norman was admitted to hospital with Covid symptoms. On examination, nurses asked why he had holes in his underwear. Yes, he had good vests and pants but never wore them always saving them for later. I can imagine him wandering round the hospital ward in his tatty grey vest and baggy Y fronts with loose elastic, telling everyone how wealthy he was and everyone sniggering behind his back. What stopped him from disposing of his old worn clothing and wearing some that were not falling apart at the seams? You tell me!

While he was in hospital with Covid, Chris and I went down to Norman's flat to check on any food that may be going off and I was curious as to what state the other rooms of his home were in. It was immediately obvious that the flat was dirty with tons of dust and crumbs on the floor. That was nothing new, but what I saw in the bathroom that day had my stomach heaving. The bath and wash basin were an inch deep in scum. The windowsill was equally as scummy. And then I saw the toilet bowl! Apart from it being covered in pink scum, the inside of the bowl had never seen a drop of bleach for a long time, years probably. I dare not be too graphic with my description but believe me when I say the word "revolting" is not even a strong enough word to describe his bathroom.

I'd often wondered where he got his toilet paper from as by this time, we were doing all his shopping and he never put it on his list. Well, looking at what I saw settled in the toilet bowl I suspect Norman was using newspaper for his ablutions. Not that he ever bought a newspaper, but I knew his neighbour used to pass on a daily paper for him to read. Well, why waste money on two ply toilet tissue when you can have the Daily Express free of charge! I am sure I saw the evidence of this when I noticed a wooden spoon resting on the side of the bath, next to the toilet. What was he using the wooden spoon for? Well, what was stuck to that spoon looked suspiciously like human excrement. Had Norman been using the spoon to force his bowel movements and the newspaper up into the toilet pipe to flush it away? The Daily Express certainly wouldn't have flushed away with ease and probably needed a helping hand on its way! I can't think of any other feasible explanation. This was stooping to another level to save money. Yet on a later visit to the flat I saw what items were being stored in Norman's utility room. What did he have in there? A pack of six toilet rolls, bottles of bleach and numerous cleaning products, all unopened and certainly not bought by him. I suspect these were all provided during the Covid lockdown when emergency supply packs were distributed to the elderly residents by some charitable group. So, why wasn't Norman using these to keep his bathroom, and especially the toilet, clean and hygienic?

And if restricting hot water to the absolute limit wasn't enough, after Margaret died Norman even found another way to cut his electricity bill by not boiling a kettle of water to do his washing up. When he had boiled a pan of potatoes or any other vegetable the boiling water wasn't drained away down the kitchen sink. Such waste was not acceptable and the murky, starchy water was kept for the washing up! I cannot imagine the state of the plates or cutlery afterwards but if it saved Norman a few more pence that was all that mattered.

Another mystery was why did Margaret and Norman buy a brand-new automatic washing machine and then not use it? They had bought the washing machine while still living in Miser Mansion and tucked away in the utility room of the flat was the same silver washing machine. Yet Margaret continued to trek to the local launderette until her health started to deteriorate. My suspicions were that Norman didn't realise how automatic washing machines worked and that they all have pre-programmed wash cycles. When he bought it, did he think Margaret would be able to load it up and simply let the load swish about for a couple of minutes before rinsing? Did Norman think new machines worked like the old twin tubs where the user decided how long the wash would take and how hot the water was? And as it was a hot water filling washing machine then where was the hot water to come from if the boiler was never turned on? Had it had been a cold-water fill, then it would have used electricity warming up the water to the required temperature. Norman wouldn't want to use thirty to forty-five minutes of electricity just to wash his undies or heat a full tank of water that may not all get used. What other reason could it have been? So, Norman had bought a white elephant on that occasion. And again, I wonder why Margaret put up with it. Imagine having a washing machine to hand but still having to carry a huge bag of bedding through the town just because your husband refused to use any electricity. It makes no sense to me, but she obviously never put up any resistance and continued to let Norman have his own way.

And seven years after Margaret died there was still a denture with false teeth kept in pride of place on the kitchen window. Now the gnashers may have belonged to Norman who also had teeth missing. But why did he feel the need to keep them on display? I can only hope he didn't use them to crimp a plate meat pie or an apple pie! Nothing would have surprised me.

Chapter 10

Make do and mend!

Now, what does a normal person do with all the remains of pulled Christmas crackers and used serviettes after Christmas dinner? Throw them in the bin along with the turkey bones and left-over Brussel sprouts? Yes, I do realise that those who like to do their bit for the environment will separate them into different wheelie bins. But are these people truly recycling? Not in Norman and Margaret's opinion. True recycling is to use pinking scissors and crimp the torn edges of the ripped crackers then keep them until the following year when they would be placed once more on the dinner table. They were totally useless of course but they were brought out year after year. Yet some years when we dined there, I would send a box of crackers round to them days before Christmas. They rarely appeared on the table.

As for the used paper serviettes? These were carefully examined and folded neatly. Any that had traces of food had the two layers of paper carefully separated with the clean layer folded and put away for use the following Christmas. I kid you not! And it wasn't just the serviettes that had been put out on Christmas Day that were recycled! If Margaret ever dined out at a family celebration, she would sift through the serviettes that were left at the end of the evening and take home any that she thought could be re-used.

Margaret was a dab hand with the pinking scissors. Instead of buying her husband a birthday or Christmas card each year she would look through her box of old cards that other family members had sent over the years and find one she liked. With the top and bottom of the card crimped, removing the handwritten greetings, she would present her husband with the bodged card, complete with her own personal message. What do they say? "It's the thought that counts!" A lot of thought had gone into the recycling process. Margaret was getting as bad as her husband for penny pinching.

There were another couple of Norman's re-cycling tips we could all take note of. Breakfast cereal boxes and the bags that keep the cereal fresh can all be re-used to put rubbish in. And a sheet of old newspaper can be used instead of a tray cloth.

Now, what do you usually do when a hole appears in the soles of a pair of slippers? Buy a new pair of course! Or wait until Christmas or your birthday and hope someone buys you a pair as a gift. Not our Norman. He gave the term 'carpet slippers' a whole new meaning. I once had reason to go to my in-laws and couldn't help but notice what Norman was wearing on his feet. He had taken a pair of battered old slippers and a piece of old carpet that he had probably kept for decades and made a template of the sole. Then with some glue and makeshift stitching with string, he'd cobbled the slippers! His toes were still poking through the tops, but they were as good as new in his book. It mattered not that we had bought him a new pair of slippers as a Christmas present weeks earlier. He was keeping those in case he ever had to go into hospital. And on more than one occasion I know he cobbled old shoes that had loose, flapping soles by putting bolts through the insoles to hold the loose sole in place. Add to that a touch of superglue and Norman could get many more miles out of a pair of shoes. Norman was certainly nothing less than inventive.

Dead batteries were often put in the oven to warm, which meant Norman could get a little more life out of them. I believe this was a common act many years ago but in Norman's case he could afford to buy new ones which were only £1 for a multipack. That was the problem though. Norman didn't like to buy anything that wasn't necessary. He'd always begged for batteries from his workplace in later years he expected us to supply his batteries for clocks. Had we taken him a full pack costing a pound he would have been most upset.

Over the years, one by one the knobs on their old electric cooker crumbled and fell off but this was not a good enough reason to buy a new model. Why fork out for a new cooker when there was a quick fix at hand that was simple and free? Norman used a pair of pliers to turn the knobs on and off. Job sorted and not a penny spent! Then years later when the grill no longer worked and only two of the hotplates functioned, he still refused to get a new cooker. We often used to wonder if Norman had been cooking with gas would he have turned the gas off on the grill while he turned his bacon over? Probably! But joking apart, if he had ever thought he could save a penny by doing so he would have. I've often wondered if the first thing Norman did when he woke up, was look under his bed to see if he had lost any sleep!

As I said earlier, Norman wasn't prepared to splash out on new clothes, happy to wear other folk's cast offs. So, when Chris and I were getting married, unlike most parents who would want to dress up for a special occasion, what did Norman choose to wear? Well, he certainly wasn't prepared to splash out on a new suit for the occasion. He chose to wear a suit he had bought well over a decade earlier, priding himself that it still fitted him after all those years. Well on the small portions of food he ate it was hardly surprising. And that suit was given another airing almost thirty years later for the wedding of our eldest daughter! Would it have broken the bank to have splashed out on a new suit on both occasions? No, but it would have broken Norman's heart to spend cash on something he was only going to wear very occasionally.

Chapter 11

Short arms and deep pockets!

A year I will never forget is 1979. The last couple of months of 1978 and early 1979 are known for being the winter of discontent and rightly so. The country had been brought to its knees with trade union strikes and unusually bad winter weather. My nightmare started in January when I had our one-year-old daughter and a lorry driving husband who had been forced out on strike against his wishes. He had no grievance with his employer who paid him well. But with pickets knocking on our door, he'd been outnumbered and like so many more he felt forced into standing on a picket line. Along with the pressure we were under I had just discovered we had a second baby on the way.

When I gave birth to our first child, Joanne, in December 1977, we had a tidy sum in our savings account. I'd always been a saver from the day I was responsible for budgeting my first salary, aged sixteen. We had been married over five years before we started a family and were both earning good wages, so it was easy to save a little each month. Later, living on just Chris's wage wasn't a problem until the strikes started. Then our income came to an abrupt halt and no strike pay was ever forthcoming during those awful months.

The savings we had in the bank were slowly dwindling, week by week. The weather was constantly freezing outside with regular heavy snow falls that meant the pavements were never clear of snow and dangerous underfoot. Being so cold meant we had to have our gas fire on almost twenty-four seven to stop our home feeling like the inside of a fridge and to keep our young daughter comfortably warm. Apart from a small heater in our daughter's bedroom, the gas fire was the only form of heating we had. There seemed to be no end in sight for the strikes ending or the weather taking a turn for the better. It was a very unhappy time for most of the country as life descended into chaos. Well, you certainly find out who your friends are when the chips are down, and we certainly did.

Now, my mother had struggled financially all her married life. My father had suffered with depression all his adult life and had spent far too much time off work over the years for them to ever be able to save much, if anything at all. They were also being affected by the strikes as my father was only in his early fifties and my mother wasn't working. All heavy goods transport had stopped which affected other industries. Anyway, unexpectedly my mum called to see me one miserable snowy day, breaking her return journey from a shopping trip. She claimed she had been to Leeds market and bought far too much food for her and my dad to eat, claiming it had all been at knocked down prices. Rather than waste any of her bargain food she thought I might take some. Well, that was her feeble excuse for visiting me, but I knew the real reason.

That day Chris had been standing on a picket line for hours even though he was against the strikes. A bunch of angry militant lorry drivers had knocked on our door early that morning and practically forced him to join them. Anyone who refused to strike or showed any resistance to it were called "scabs" and threatened with losing their jobs when the strike ended. That turned out to be a load of rubbish but looked a real possibility at the time. That evening when he arrived back home from a picket line, frozen and hungry, I was able to make him a delicious warm meal with the compliments of my mother. We had pork chops for tea. She had also left us other meats and vegetables along with a few necessary items that were handed over to me as she repeated her excuse of buying too much and didn't want anything going to waste. And a few sweet treats were also included for her young granddaughter. I knew the bags of food had been bought especially for me and my family. As a mother she wanted to help her daughter and family in a time of need. This from a woman who had little but was always willing to share the little she had with her loved ones. She was a normal, loving mother and grandma who knew what it felt like to fall upon hard times.

A couple of days later, Margaret called round at our house, pretending she had called to see her young granddaughter, but I knew the real reason. Margaret was a secret smoker or at least she tried to keep it a secret from Norman. Possibly, smoking an odd cigarette eased the tension of living under such strict house rules but Norman must have known about her habit. A non-smoker can always detect cigarette smoke on a person. So, we'd exchanged words about the state of the country and there being no sign of the strikes ending or Chris being able to go back to work. Then, as she was leaving, Margaret made a comment that I have never forgotten. "Well, if Chris needs to borrow any money, just let us know!"

So, her son could "borrow" some money. That meant going cap in hand to Norman with his begging bowl. Chris would have robbed a bank to put food in our bellies before asking to borrow money. And had he stooped to the level of borrowing money we probably couldn't have paid it back. Nor would I ever have allowed him to go begging. But if Margaret had really wanted to help, she could have done it without making her son ask for cash. Did she think he had no pride? I've often wondered how much she thought we had in the bank. Probably tens of thousands but if so, how were we supposed to have saved so much while paying our bills and raising a family? Was she so blinkered from reality after living with Norman for so long? Perhaps. So, Margaret and Norman did nothing to help their only son in his time of need.

When I eventually rang the benefits office to see what we could claim during the strike, I was told we had to use our savings plus any strike pay the trade union forked out to its members. No strike pay was ever forthcoming. A few days later I received a bank giro cheque for the enormous sum of £2.50 from the benefits office. This was supposed to be used to feed our young daughter. In disgust I ripped up the giro. We weren't that desperate!

Norman was known for being backward at coming forward when it came to parting with his cash by all of Margaret's extended family. Over the years, numerous family gatherings were held in a local public house, usually on a Saturday night. Though never, ever did I attend any family get together of Norman's kith and kin, apart from an odd funeral. Anyway, it had become a bit of a standing joke between everyone (except Margaret and Norman) that on such gatherings, Norman would deliberately hang back from buying a round of drinks, allowing everyone and anyone else to do the honours all evening. Everyone reckoned that his plan was always to wait until the family had had enough to drink before offering to get his hand in his pocket when last orders were called. Well, it may have worked in his favour for a while but that was to stop. When I joined the family gatherings they were on his case and quick to put me in the picture about him being tight-fisted.

So, on one such occasion, the pub landlord rang his bell indicating it was time to order our last drinks of the evening. This was Norman's cue to make his half-hearted gesture. But, instead of everyone politely passing on his offer to get a round of drinks in, as what usually happened, it was time to see Norman squirm! As well as all the men accepting his offer of a pint each, the women in our gathering asked for a spirit and mixer drink instead of their usual half of lager or best bitter! What could Norman say or do except walk with a heavy heart to the bar and fumble in his deep pocket with his short arm for the single monetary note he reluctantly carried on him. Meanwhile, behind him he must have heard the tittering going on as he struggled to let go of his precious cash.

I was informed that in later years, after far too many occasions of allowing Norman to avoid buying a round of drinks, Margaret's three siblings and spouses secretly agreed to stick to buying their own drinks. That in turn led Norman to having to put his hand in his very deep pocket and cough up for his and Margaret's beverages. That resulted in a lot of swishing the dregs of his pint for far too long before he felt obliged to buy another one.

Now, fast forward to the year 1999 when Margaret and Norman had their golden wedding anniversary looming in November. How were they going to celebrate the momentous occasion? Would Norman feel he needed to push the boat out and break the habit of a lifetime? Not bloody likely! But Margaret seemed to want to mark the occasion, so what did she have planned?

Well, she told close family members that they were planning on having a family celebratory meal at a popular hotel restaurant that was about three miles away from their home. The couple had been to the hotel for a family christening a year or so earlier, so they knew what the set up was. So why on hearing these plans was I so sceptical about their promises and intentions? Because I knew them too well!

True to form, after guests had been verbally invited and accepted their kind invitation to dine out together, Norman had second thoughts about it all. What that meant was, he'd realised how much it would cost if he were expected to treat about twenty guests to a decent meal or even just to a celebratory round of drinks. The formal booking hadn't yet been made so plans were swiftly changed to having a party in Miser Mansion instead and it would only be a fraction of the cost. A party? That would have been a first! But a date was set for the closest Saturday afternoon to their big day for a family gathering. Sorted! Or not as it turned out.

Norman then had second thoughts about the family gathering and decided that if all the invited guests were in their small bungalow at the same time it would be too crowded. The solution? To have half the guests one Saturday and the other half on the following Saturday. What sort of a party is that? Which guests were going on which days? Who took priority and would be their guests on the first occasion? I suspected this change of events was nothing to do with Margaret, but she was going to appease Norman anyway. So, Margaret decided to invite her brother and two sisters along with their spouses for the Saturday closest to the big day. That meant their son, me and their three granddaughters were on the list for the second week with Margaret's old aunt and a couple more family members. Obviously, I was not considered important enough to be on the VIP list and to me this made it plain enough that her own son was not considered an important guest either. That was fine by me, I already knew my place in the family but how could they think their only son didn't deserve to be there? Then Margaret changed her plans yet again and I am certain that this change of plan was Margaret's and not Norman's.

As I've previously stated, our youngest girl, Melanie, was involved with a local amateur dramatic society and had started appearing in shows that were put on at the local town hall. Margaret liked to brag about her granddaughter's singing talent. Well, most grandparents would do the same, but Margaret wanted to show off Melanie's talent to her brother and sisters. So, she thought it was a good idea for Melanie to be put on the VIP list for the first party and leave her other two granddaughters out of it. Over my dead body was that going to happen! To say I was not happy at the obvious show of favouritism is an understatement.

Did Margaret ever stop and consider what her only son must have felt knowing he wasn't wanted at the VIP gathering. Or was it just me and my other two daughters, Joanne and Lyndsay, that were not wanted? But finally, after my refusal to split up my girls and far too many changes of plans, they must have realised everyone was either confused or annoyed about the party arrangements. So, Margaret and Norman finally succumbed to having just one party if you can call it a party. Eating a few butties and a sausage roll while sat on a hard chair does not equate to a party in my book!

When the big day arrived, we all congregated at Miser Mansion, but it was certainly not a party we were attending. I'm sure most of us there could feel Norman's reluctance at having to open his home to us and spend a few quid to feed us. And he had felt obliged to put the heating on to warm up the bungalow. The buffet was very basic to say the least and as for the booze flowing, a few cans of cheap lager and a bottle of sherry does not constitute a party celebration. I was driving later that evening and asked for a lager shandy. I took one sip of the contents of a glass Norman handed me and asked him if he could kindly show my glass the can of lager as there appeared to be no lager at all in my drink, just cheap sugary sweet lemonade. Wine was hardly flowing in abundance either. Norman had to control and ration everything. He just couldn't help himself from counting the cost of every little thing. Was it a celebration in the end? Was it hell and it wasn't worth the bother!

Fast forward a few years and considering that close and extended family were aware of Norman's reluctance to spend money, one of Margaret's nieces decided to chance her arm and ask him for a loan. A loan indeed! Whatever she was thinking at the time is beyond me. But she gave it a go.

So, imagine the scene when one weekend, without warning, Margaret's niece and her husband turned up at their door with a begging bowl in the form of paperwork for a loan. Apparently, after being separated for a few years, the couple had re-united and were not able to borrow the full amount needed for a new mortgage. Someone had come up with the brilliant idea of asking Uncle Ebenezer aka Norman to provide their shortfall in the form of a loan. Paperwork was presented for a gobsmacked Norman to read and hopefully act upon. Asking for a mere £100,000, the couple may have thought that they were asking a self-confessed millionaire for peanuts. Oh, how I wish I'd been there to see everyone's faces when they almost gave Norman a heart attack! He was still talking about that fateful day over a decade later. Needless to say, the couple went home empty handed with Norman probably needing a cup of hot sweet tea for the shock. Well, that should have been a lesson learned. Norman was more than happy to brag about how much money he had stashed away and that he had made his first million. So, when relatives turned up with a begging bowl, he only had himself to blame.

It wasn't long after this that we had to go to Margaret's brother's funeral. After the full Catholic service and a second service at the crematorium, we headed to a social club for the wake. Chris and I were ready for a much-needed drink, but when Chris got to the bar, he realised he had left his wallet at home! So, he turned to me to get out my purse. Well, whenever we went out together, I only took my small purse with just a few pounds emergency cash. That day I had slipped a £10 note into my purse which was fortunate given the absence of Chris's wallet. But that of course meant we were restricted to what we could afford to drink that afternoon.

Now standing directly behind us at the bar was Norman, Margaret had got herself seated, awaiting a drink. Naturally, Chris turned to his father thinking he could borrow a few pounds and as I was driving and giving them a lift, he would have been repaid as soon as we arrived home. Norman's response? He hadn't brought any money with him! Margaret had brought a token gesture to put into the collection as we left the church, so she had no cash on her. What was Norman going to buy their drinks with? Positioning himself behind Chris at the bar, he probably expected him to buy a full round of drinks and then Norman would swish his pint for the rest of the afternoon. Thankfully, the price of drinks was reasonable, and my tenner did buy a round for the four of us. But who knowingly goes to a wake in a pub or club and takes no money with them? Norman!!!!

Now as a parent and grandparent it is second nature for me to spontaneously treat my loved ones. Giving our grandchildren money to buy sweets or whatever they want when they are going home or pushing a tenner into my girls' hands and telling them to get a drink when they go out is normal. And if I've gone shopping for clothes with any or all my girls, I've often treated them to something they have been eyeing up. And if any one of my girls isn't with us then she gets the equivalent in cash later. What I give to one I always give to the others. It's not about how much it costs to treat someone; it's the pleasure of seeing a grandchild's face light up when they are given a few coins to spend. Priceless! I can remember how thrilled I used to get when my own grandad would put a threepenny bit into my hand as I was leaving him after a visit. Sadly, I can honestly say that never, ever have Margaret or Norman spontaneously given their grandchildren or their son anything.

On one occasion when our grandson was about two years old and very mobile, we had a ride out to North Yorkshire. Along with our daughter and grandson we had Norman in tow. He was by now a widower, so we thought it would be a nice day out and a chance for him to get to know his great grandson. Well, I can't say I noticed any normal interaction from Norman when we were in a park, watching our grandson playing or enjoying being on a swing. There was nothing in Norman's behaviour that showed he was enjoying any time with his great grandson. And when it came to buying the child an ice cream, he certainly wasn't forthcoming with any money. He probably didn't have any money on him! It was down to me to do the honours and buy everyone a cone and naturally, the free ice cream was devoured by Norman.

Any acts of giving were all for show or under duress and they could never say it was because they couldn't afford to! And what would it have cost to wrap a small gift up for each of their granddaughters at Christmas? Even a chocolate selection box would have been warmly welcomed on Christmas morning. It was never about the price but the thought behind it.

Chapter 12

Blood is thicker than water!

Blood is thicker than water. Well, that's what the old saying reckons. But is it? It certainly seemed true when it came to me joining Norman's family. From our very first meeting with Margaret, we crossed swords. I'd never had any problems previously when meeting any of my old boyfriends' parents or families. I remember the first occasion that Chris took me back to his home, thinking his parents would be in bed. We'd been out for a drink (or two) and arrived at their bungalow just after 9.00pm to find Margaret just about to go to bed. The obligatory introductions took place, then Margaret said something that really made me break into hysterical laughter. She referred to Norman as Chris's "Daddy"! Only small children or upper-class nerds usually made references to their father as "Daddy" and it seemed silly referring to Norman in such a manner. So, it was an unusual and very frosty start to our relationship. With hindsight I've often thought she became jealous that I was taking her only son from her though he had already left home at seventeen to join the army.

Margaret and Norman had a shotgun wedding, as they were commonly referred to back then and never got engaged. So, for over twenty years she had happily lived with just her wedding ring on her third finger, left hand, until I came on the scene. Chris and I had only been going out together for a few weeks when he proposed to me in October 1971 with plans for us to marry in the summer of 1972. Well, I say he proposed to me, and he did, in a fashion. What he said one night, while we were at Bradford Mecca, was that if he ever got married, he'd give his wage packet to his wife every week for her to deal with all the money. He didn't want anything to do with paying bills. Then after a pregnant pause, he casually asked me if I fancied looking after his wage packet. Well, after a few seconds of awkward silence, off I trotted to the Ladies room to relieve my bladder and think about what I assumed was a proposal of marriage. Well, how could I refuse such a romantic offer? After a couple of minutes of pondering the question and with an empty bladder, I'd made my decision and rejoined Chris.

"Ok, I'll look after your wage!" was my equally romantic response as I lifted my glass of lager and took a huge gulp. That was it, we were engaged!

We had little savings between us even though we were both working, but off we trotted the following Saturday in search of engagement rings. I eventually found the ring I wanted. Thankfully, the jeweller's shop was more than happy for us to place a deposit on it and keep it for me until Christmas. Then by the time Christmas was upon us we would have been able to pay off the remaining balance and collect my ring. We were able to do the same with a ring for Chris. And of course, when we returned home from our shopping trip, I told my parents what our plans were while Chris told his parents all about our intention to get engaged and the rings we had chosen. As it happened, we decided we wouldn't wait until Christmas and scraped together enough cash to retrieve our rings on the 6th November.

Now form your own opinions, but I found it very odd that suddenly after over two decades of not wearing an engagement ring, Margaret suddenly decided she wanted one. She knew how much my ring was costing and what gemstones I had chosen. I had opted for a small diamond surrounded by ten small rubies. So, just a few weeks later, why did Margaret decide to go to a more prestigious local jewellers and splash out on a diamond solitaire ring that cost three times the price of mine and was eager to show it off to me? Was she jealous of me or just wishing to show me that they had money in the bank? After all, they were now living in a very nice bungalow while I was living with my parents on one of the local council estates. So, was her timing for buying her ring coincidental or a deliberate act to outdo me? My money is on the latter. And an even bigger question is, just how did she manage to get Norman to cough up for her ring?

Well, in later years Norman did splash out on a couple more rings for Margaret, believing they would grow in value and were a good investment which turned out to be incorrect. And of course, whenever the couple did socialise, Margaret could flash her rings, showing off their wealth to all and sundry. But what Norman never knew was that after Margaret died and her rings were passed on, they were very hard to get rid of. None of my girls wanted to wear any of them, apart from just one ring that our eldest daughter still wears. Trying to sell them back to several jewellers was impossible. The rings were dated in style and not the precious stones we had been led to believe. Many jewellers just didn't want to buy second hand rings as they already had plenty in stock. In the end we sold them to a pawn shop for only a fraction of their supposed worth and split the cash between our three daughters.

So, Margaret and I crossed swords again before our marriage when she was told we would not be marrying in the local Catholic church. Chris hadn't voluntarily been in a Catholic church for years, having no interest in religion and though I wasn't very religious I had wanted to marry in my local C of E church ever since I had been a bridesmaid there when I was seven years old. That church felt special to me and was where I wanted to make my vows. I wasn't up for changing my plans which didn't go down well with Margaret. Yes, she may have attended her church almost every Sunday but if she'd been honest with herself, it was only to please her own mother, who was a staunch Catholic, and not through her personal choice. Questions were always asked if Margaret didn't attend at least one Mass on a Sunday. I agreed with Norman when he once said it was about what you do every day and not just on a Sunday that mattered. So, we weren't off to a good start in our relationship.

There were a couple of occasions in the early weeks of our marriage when Margaret made it obvious to me that I was not considered a part of her family. I wasn't a blood relative, just some young woman who had married her son and taken away her next of kin status. I truly was a cuckoo in the nest! And sadly, over fifty years later my status in the family had not changed and never would.

While we were having to live at Miser Mansion, one day I had to work an extra hour at work and arrived home after Chris (though it never was my home). What did I find when I walked into the lounge that evening? Margaret had cooked her son a full dinner of pork chop, potatoes and vegetables, served to him on a tray in their lounge. He was sitting in front of the fire with Margaret kneeling beside him, fussing over him like he was a child. How was I greeted by my new mother-in-law? Very off handed she said, "I didn't make you anything as I don't know what you like!" Charming! Nothing like making someone feel welcome was there? Was this a deliberate act to let me know I wasn't being welcomed into the family?

That same evening Norman arrived home after me to have his pork chop dinner also served on a tray while Margaret fussed over him. I had to settle for a sandwich made by my own fair hands. I really wasn't bothered about having a pork chop dinner, but Margaret had made it clear by her pre-planned actions that day that I was not family and nothing more than an unwelcome lodger in their home. And with hindsight, what was odd about that incident was the fact that Margaret and Norman usually ate small, bland meals and not a full dinner. Had she cooked pork chops specifically that day because she knew I was going to be late home? But that evening, I made my feelings clear to my new husband who admitted he had been put in a difficult position and had not been expecting his mother to have cooked a meal for him and he had thought there was food waiting for me when I arrived home.

Yet my parents always embraced Chris becoming a family member. My mother always treated him like her own son and in return he cared about her. He was happy to take my mother with us when we spent a few days in Blackpool with our kids and we had a couple of holidays with both my parents. This made it even more obvious that I wasn't and never would be considered family by my in-laws.

There was another occasion in those awful weeks of living with my in-laws where Margaret showed her true feelings about me being in their home. One day, on her way home from work, Margaret called at the local baker's shop to buy bread and splashed out on some individual trifles for tea. Now, I can't help but think this was a one off because normally the couple were restricted to a ginger biscuit with their evening cup of tea. But Margaret had splashed out on three small trifles. Take note, she bought only three trifles, not four. So, who wasn't meant to have one? Well, it was so bloody obvious that it was me who would be doing without the creamy dessert!

Now, I hate trifle and wouldn't have enjoyed one anyway, but Margaret didn't know that. As she handed out the trifles to her husband and son, leaving me out without saying a word was another blatant hint that I was a cuckoo in her nest. Chris took one look at my face and immediately rejected his trifle, insisting that he and I were going to have tinned fruit and cream. That didn't go down well. Wasting money on an extra trifle was bad enough but he was also making a point. I was Chris's wife, a fact she would have to accept.

My in-laws had a dark wood dining table and chairs that were only used when entertaining, which was very rare and under duress. While living there, in our first week of marriage, I once accidently dropped a coin from my purse onto the highly polished table. At lightning speed, both Margaret and Norman's heads spun round almost 360 degrees to give me disapproving looks followed by a close inspection of the table's surface. Living there was quite alien to the life I'd had with my parents. It was hard if not impossible to relax, having to watch my every move when my in-laws were present.

Norman was not amused when we said we were having a new double bed delivered. It was impossible for us both to get any sleep in Chris's single bed. But our comfort was less important than having to have Chris's single bed propped up in Norman's bedroom for a few weeks. It wasn't through choice we had our new bed delivered; it was sheer necessity. Norman made it obvious that he was not amused at my arrival causing disruption in his home. He seemed to think it was acceptable for us both to sleep in a single bed, which we did for a week or so. But it was very hard to sleep cramped together with one foot on the floor to stop us from falling off the bed.

About three miserable months after our marriage, we were finally able to move into our own new home. It was a Saturday in late November when we moved and not a day too soon for me. The sheer joy of having instant hot water and a warm fire to sit before was unimaginable. Not to mention being able to watch television as and when I wanted. No more having to watch every move I made about the house, afraid to touch anything. And no more feeling my presence at Miser Mansion was unwanted. If we'd had any choice in the matter, we would never have spent a single night under Norman's roof.

We'd had a dining table and chairs along with a three-piece suite delivered to our new home plus other essential items. But even as we were moving the few ornaments and bits and pieces we had collected, as well as our double bed, out of Miser Mansion I crossed swords with Margaret.

I felt it was our priority to get our bed put together as we obviously would be needing it a few hours later. Margaret was eager to start putting up the wall art we had bought. When I insisted on us getting the bed sorted, she made a sarcastic comment about knowing where she wasn't wanted and stormed out with Norman in tow. That was exactly how I had felt during the previous three months in her home!

One very memorable occasion when Margaret was exceptionally annoyed with me was the first Christmas in our new home. I can still smile thinking about it even after all these years. We had only been in the bungalow for about five weeks and though we had all the basic and necessary items for our home, we still had a long way to go before we had everything we needed in the kitchen. So, why my own mother suggested that I played host to our family members on Christmas day eludes me. But she did. Alcohol had been involved when I agreed. I was well and truly coerced into it while under the influence of drink. So, we were to feed and entertain six guests with me having no prior experience of preparing a traditional Christmas dinner. Our guests were to be my parents, my in-laws and my younger sister and her current boyfriend. Eight mouths to feed, what could possibly go wrong?

To ease my load, my mother offered to buy and cook a turkey which she would then bring to my home on Christmas Day while it was fresh from the oven. Having no idea of how to cook such a bird it was one less task for me to worry about. Margaret offered to loan me her pressure cooker to steam a Christmas pudding, though again, I hadn't a clue how to use one. All I had to do was prepare vegetables and arrange our dining table in a festive manner. Sorted!

After a small family gathering in the local pub on Christmas Eve I wasn't exactly in top form for cooking or hosting our guests. But not to be defeated the following morning I got stuck in to preparing the vegetables, set the table and waited for my family to arrive early with the turkey. What do they say about the best-laid plans of mice and men?

So, as arranged, at 1.00pm my in-laws arrived as I anxiously awaited my family to appear at any moment with the freshly cooked turkey. My family were late, and I sensed disaster looming. We waited and waited and waited. This was long before we had a telephone or the convenience of a mobile phone so I could do nothing but pace the floor and look out of our lounge window, hoping to see my mother walking up the road, clutching the warm turkey. By 2.00pm there was still neither sight nor sound of my family or the sodding turkey! At this point Margaret and Norman were getting very tetchy. They hadn't had much to eat that morning, expecting to be fed and watered by 2.00pm at the latest. What was I supposed to do without a turkey for dinner? Improvise!

Being our first Christmas as a married couple, Chris and I had been invited out to various family gatherings over the festive holiday and hadn't shopped for much in the line of food apart from the vegetables and pudding for Christmas dinner. What could I feed to my very irate in-laws to kill their hunger pains? I had little to offer other than a chunk of stand pie and tinned processed peas! What a delicacy and they were lucky to get that!

So, can you imagine the atmosphere around our dining table as we tucked into my Cordon Bleu offering? It was frosty to say the least. Margaret looked as if she was chewing a wasp as she ate, mumbling something about they would have been better off staying at home. What was I supposed to do when the turkey didn't arrive and why hadn't it arrived? Something had to have happened with my family to keep them from coming. And it had. Just as we were finishing our delicious pie and peas, my sister and her boyfriend arrived on our doorstep clutching the turkey in her arms!

After hearing the reason for the turkey being so late in arriving, off my in-laws trotted back home, with faces like a couple of slapped arses.

The fickle finger of fate had been so cruel that morning. My mother had cooked the turkey and was all geared up for their walk to my home when their chimney caught fire! This was 1972 and gas fires had not been fitted into their council house. It was common for folk to keep their coal fires burning day and night during the winter months which meant having their chimney swept regularly. Chimney fires were very common, but what a time for it to happen. The fire brigade was called out and swiftly sorted the problem.

My sister and boyfriend enjoyed a turkey dinner as did Chris, who had already troughed pie and peas. But my parents had decided not to come after the upset of the chimney fire. But we were all going to be meeting later that evening at another family gathering. Well, you can imagine what the topic of conversation was that evening and the grimacing expression on my in-laws' faces.

What I'm going to reveal next sums up the relationship I had with my in-laws but more importantly the poor relationship Chris had with his parents. In March 1977 I discovered I was pregnant for the first time. Naturally, once I had it confirmed by my doctor it was time to tell everyone. Our baby was due at the end of November though our baby didn't arrive until December. I told my parents who were thrilled at the thoughts of being grandparents. I rang Margaret's younger sister, Mary, who had become a good friend, and told her our news. And of course, we told other relatives and friends. What didn't either of us do? We didn't feel the need to tell my in-laws they were going to be grandparents. Why? I really don't know but it just didn't seem important. What does that tell you? I eventually told Margaret when by sheer coincidence one tea-time we were both coming home from work and had met while waiting for some traffic lights to change. We made polite conversation as we crossed the road and walked a short distance before we were about to part company. Then just as I was about to head off up the road, I casually threw into the conversation that I would be giving up work later in the year due to being pregnant. There, I'd said it and headed off home without giving Margaret a chance to respond.

On December 11th, I eventually gave birth to our first daughter, Joanne. Chris wasn't with me at the birth as he'd been with me through the day, and I'd told him to go home thinking I was going to be a long time in the early stages of labour with nothing much happening until the following day. I'd already spent two days in a drug induced labour with no success. We didn't have a telephone at our home, so he was going to come back to the maternity unit early the following morning. But he had no sooner left me when my labour became a cause for concern. It was suddenly action stations, and I was swiftly wheeled into a theatre to have a forceps delivery with our daughter arriving a few seconds before midnight.

My parents did have a phone, so my mother was making regular calls to the hospital wanting updates on my labour. Early the following morning after receiving the news that they had a grandchild they swiftly headed off to tell Chris the good news before he set off to the hospital.

Visiting times were quite different back then and after making a call from a public phone box to the hospital, Chris was told I was fine, but our baby was under observation in the special baby care unit and I was still recovering from an epidural injection, so it was suggested he visited me later in the day. By then I should have been reunited with our baby. Did Chris do what should have been the most obvious thing and go break the good news to his parents? No! I'm not sure how the news was relayed to Margaret and Norman, possibly by one of her sisters. I never asked when they eventually did come to visit me and their new granddaughter.

A close friend told me when she came to visit me in hospital that she had seen Margaret on a few occasions during the last few weeks before I gave birth. Margaret had been asking her if I had had my baby yet. Chris had not bothered to tell his parents when I had been admitted a week before I finally gave birth. That just about sums up the awkward relationship they had.

And another sign of the unnatural relationship we all had was how Margaret always referred to her grandchildren as "Baby". Until they could speak, she always referred to them as "Baby" and never used their names. She was always a midwife even when she was off duty. "How's baby doing?" she would ask me, as if she was doing her daily rounds in a maternity ward. It all seemed so impersonal.

Some months earlier as I was midway through my first pregnancy we were going on a week's holiday to Scarborough with four friends. I had planned for my mum to come and feed our two cats while we were away. Somehow, a couple of days before we set off on our jollies my mum and Margaret were at my home at the same time. The subject of our holiday came up and who was taking care of our beloved cats after an earlier nasty experience in cat boarding kennels. I was surprised when Margaret suggested she took on the cat feeding duties as she lived much closer to us so it would be no trouble. Well, my mum was happy to agree to it and I could see why she would think it made sense. Knowing Margaret was no cat lover, I left strict instructions about how much to feed our precious pets and how to clean their litter trays. But I still had serious doubts in my mind that it was not a good idea. Neither Margaret nor Norman had any time for pets and had already asked us if we would be getting rid of our cats when the baby arrived. NO!!!!

Halfway through our holiday I rang my mum to see if she had been down to our home and checked on our cats that day. Had Margaret been feeding them properly? It wasn't the news I was hoping to hear from my mum. She warned me that Margaret had been doing some cleaning in our home and most of our work surfaces and furniture were covered in a white residue. My mum had no idea what had happened, but our cats were still being fed. As you can imagine I wasn't happy on hearing that.

When we arrived back home, the second I set foot over the threshold I knew at once someone had been messing about with our stuff. A tinted glass topped coffee table was coated in a white residue as was our dining table and just about every other surface in our home. Then I found the evidence. JIF cream cleaner had been used anywhere and everywhere and left to dry! But worse was to come. Not long after we arrived home our next-door neighbour came round to see me. She wanted me to know what had happened to our cats while we had been away. What I heard fired up my anger in seconds.

Our cats had been allowed out and left out all day and some nights. One of our cats was unable to walk properly due to a deformity and he couldn't jump, so we always kept a special lookout for him when he was allowed out. And I had given strict instructions that the cats were not to be let out during our absence. But there was worse news to come. Our lame cat had fallen over our garden wall and onto the pavement beside the main road. He was unable to jump like normal cats so couldn't get back into our garden. Then he was seen crossing the main road and narrowly missed being hit by traffic. It was my cat loving neighbour who had been to rescue him and take him back to our home. There she had found Margaret taking down both sets of bedroom curtains to take home and wash, yet she had no washing machine at that time! She had shown no interest in the cats who were like babies to us and not just animals so you can imagine the rage that was boiling inside me.

When I went to look at my bedroom curtains it was obvious that they had been tampered with. Both bedrooms had the same plain mauve curtains, but they had been put back wrongly. Our bedroom curtains had signs of fading by the sun that was different to the pair in the spare bedroom. Margaret obviously hadn't noticed this. But more importantly she had no right to interfere with our home. I quickly realised that was why she was so keen to feed our cats. Not to help my mum out but to gain access to our home and do as she chose in our absence. And what was even more infuriating was that I had held a conversation with Margaret about a week before we went on holiday, when I had said I only had a month to work before I went on maternity leave. It was my intention to get our home in order during the weeks before our baby arrived. You might call it late Spring cleaning or nest building. Knowing my intentions, Margaret had been deliberately deceitful when she had offered her cat feeding services. I could never forgive her for that. It was a long time before I could bring myself to speak to her again. Had she been trying to tell me that she could do as she wished in her son's home and that my feelings were irrelevant? It felt that way.

Birthday gifts were rarely forthcoming from my in-laws, though in the early years of our marriage Chris was on a couple of occasions given a £5 note to buy himself a new shirt. No thought was ever put into gifts which were usually cash sums given as an afterthought. Chris and I have our birthdays only five days apart in March, with my birthday being on the first of the month and his on the sixth. One year I wondered if he would get another fiver to spend on a shirt and what would I be getting? A fiver to spend on myself perhaps? No such luck. The gift I received really did leave me speechless.

Margaret called after work to see me on my birthday while I was alone in our bungalow. She came bearing a gift and what a generous gift it was! Thinking I may get a fiver to spend, I was overwhelmed when she handed me two hand towels! Yes, two hand towels, not wrapped in anything, just folded in her hands. And better still she had gone to the trouble of washing the towels before she gave me them! So basically, I got two used towels for my birthday present. Wasn't I the lucky one to receive such a lovely, thoughtful and personal gift? Or was it just another way of letting me know that I wasn't considered family? It certainly seemed so at the time. Chris got a fiver to spend on a shirt again. Enough said!

I've lost count how many times over the decades I heard Norman tell someone that all his money was going to Chris. My name was never mentioned but I knew why. What if Chris did inherit Norman's money? Being his spouse, I would have a claim on his inheritance. What if I was to take half of the money and divorce Chris? Would I fritter away Norman's money on another man? He never said as much but it was obvious from the start that Norman had pondered about such eventualities. And later when the couple made Wills, Norman made it clear why he hadn't put me down as an executor or a beneficiary, saying he wasn't allowed. That was total tosh! Anyone can be an executor as it doesn't mean that person is a beneficiary. The truth was . . . I wasn't blood and they would be leaving me nothing.

As I've mentioned earlier, March 1979 was a very cold winter with the whole country suffering from national strikes by transport workers and the miners' unions and more. This was a very trying time for us and many more who suddenly found they couldn't work and received no strike pay. Sadly, on St. Patrick's Day, March 17th, I miscarried our second baby under very distressing conditions. For a few days prior I had been bleeding and been seen by a doctor who suggested I rested. The situation changed quickly that Friday afternoon and I knew I was losing my baby. I had my young daughter with me when I started feeling dizzy and began haemorrhaging badly, frightened I may faint at any second. I managed to ring my GP's surgery who assured me that a doctor was on the way to see me. And within no time my regular GP was at my door after walking from the surgery in thick snow. He knew it would be difficult to drive the short distance to my home in such a bad snow fall.

Thankfully, Chris arrived home just in time to see my doctor calling an ambulance for me. But due to the national strikes, most ambulance crews were not working, so emergencies were being covered by military ambulances. I was lucky, it was a regular ambulance crew that came to my rescue that evening. But the heavy snow prevented the vehicle being able to get anywhere near our bungalow. In desperation, I had to be practically dragged by the two-man crew through snow drifts into the safety of an ambulance. Then the ambulance got stuck in the snow on the journey to the hospital and the crew were concerned about the amount of blood I was losing. What happened to me that night was a frightening, physical experience and mentally distressing. And at the end of it all I had lost our baby. Any mother would have had empathy and sympathy for my loss and the trauma preceding it. I had an emergency operation to stop the bleeding and an overnight stay in hospital. I arrived back home the next day, still hurting physically and emotionally.

I'd only been home about an hour when Margaret called round unannounced. She didn't know I had even been in hospital. Chris hadn't bothered going to tell his parents that I had been rushed away or had lost our baby. Once I was taken in the ambulance Chris had carried our one-year-old daughter through the snow drifts to my parents' home for them to care for her so he could be free to visit me. It had never occurred to him to take her just the few hundred yards to his own parents. What does that tell you?

So, on hearing our sad news Margaret flippantly said, "It's for the best!" As a mother, nurse and a midwife, I would have expected a little more sympathy even if it was fake. Was it for the best? The best for who? Not for me! Not for Chris! And not for our baby! But it probably was for Norman. He had been spared having yet another person with a possible claim on his cash at some point in the future. But he was oh so wrong on that score. We still had plans to increase our family and did so the following year. And sadly, it wasn't the last time Margaret said something insensitive about my being pregnant.

One thing I did notice quite a lot over the years was how Margaret always referred to their wealth as Norman's money and never hers or theirs. He held the purse strings. She was in the dark as to where his cash was stashed. A classic example was on Christmas Eve 1981. After nine years, Chris and I had moved from our bungalow, but we were still living near my in-laws. It was only a move across the main road, but we had bought a much bigger house with a large garden. By this time, we had two young daughters, Lyndsay being fifteen months old and Joanne was just four years old. After spending five months renovating and decorating our new home we decided to have a party as a housewarming on Christmas Eve, inviting friends and family. All was going well when the clock struck midnight. Then I had a special announcement to make. I was pregnant with our third child! My parents were delighted! It was an extra Christmas present in their eyes. One or two others were shocked that we were expanding our family once again but still pleased for us. But Norman's face literally drained of colour on hearing our good news. As I left the room to join friends in the kitchen, I heard Margaret say, "Oh Norman, your poor money!" Those few words summed up the situation perfectly. Money was far more important than having more grandchildren to love. Though I never saw any evidence of there being any real love for their grandchildren.

And I've often wondered if Norman was disappointed that Chris and I had not presented him with a grandson. He was desperate for his money to be kept in the family name and girls usually change their names when marrying. He won't have seen that he had been blessed with grandchildren that others would have loved to be blessed with. The future of his money was far more important.

There was another example of Norman not welcoming a family member into his home. Again, it showed Norman's true colours. Margaret's mother, who had allowed Norman to live in her home when he had married her daughter, who had also been an unpaid childminder for years, was not repaid with the respect she deserved in my opinion. The poor woman who was now widowed and frail had just spent time in hospital. She lived alone in sheltered accommodation, only a spit away from Margaret's elder sister, who for months, every morning and night, as a dutiful, loving daughter had called on her mother to make sure she was fine, like any caring daughter would, before going to work for the day. So, when Margaret's mother had recovered sufficiently from her illness, she needed short term care and support in place before she could be discharged from hospital. Now, which of her four children lived in a bungalow and was a nurse? Margaret of course! She was the obvious choice to open her home up for a few weeks while her mother fully recovered. Margaret and Norman lived in a bungalow, had a spare bedroom with a single bed so it shouldn't have been a problem. As you can imagine, Norman wasn't thrilled at having a house guest but was backed into a corner. Under duress he agreed to let the old woman, who had helped him so much when he had married Margaret, go live in his home. I had the greatest sympathy for the old girl having to bend to Norman's weird regime.

But once his unwanted house guest had recovered sufficiently and was able to move back into her own little bedsit she was swiftly shipped out of Miser Mansion. And it didn't take Norman long before he got rid of their spare bed. He made it perfectly clear that his mother-in-law wouldn't be welcome to stay again! And when she did become ill again and needed home care it fell to her other two daughters to provide it. Margaret, the professional nurse was an obvious choice to look after her ailing mother, but it was never going to happen. Norman had made that perfectly clear!

In the early 70's I worked at the same company as Norman's sister-in-law who was married to his youngest brother. I got the impression from our regular conversations that Norman wasn't close to his siblings. I recall her telling me that one Sunday she and Norman's brother had paid an unexpected visit to Miser Mansion, taking with them a couple of their grandchildren. Not a wise move. From the visitors setting foot over the threshold, Norman was on guard watching every move the children made. When I spoke to Norman's sister-in-law the following week, she was quick to tell me how unwelcome and ill at ease they had felt. I knew that feeling all too well. No plans to re-visit Miser Mansion were ever made. On this occasion blood certainly wasn't thicker than water! From what I experienced on meeting them and what Norman often said about his siblings, they were all very sociable, enjoyed a drink, a smoke and a social life. In Norman's opinion they were all frivolously wasting their money.

Chapter 13

Promises, Promises!

As Norman's bank accounts were steadily increasing, he wanted anyone and everyone to know he was worth a bob or two. At times he told out and out lies about how generous he was with his family. Yes, over the years there were promises made to us of financial help and offers to buy things we needed. And it wasn't just his immediate family that were subject to his broken promises. Though on most occasions it was Margaret who made the many promises to us that never materialised. Did she go back to Norman and tell him what she had done when she'd made some promise without thinking it through? How did he react to her frivolous actions? I'd like to have been a fly on the wall if she ever had told him.

Going right back to 1971 when I got engaged to Chris, Margaret made her first promise that would be broken and never mentioned again. Our parents arranged to meet up in a local public house to discuss our forthcoming wedding arrangements. All went well and it had been taken for granted that following tradition, my parents would foot the bill for the wedding reception. But Margaret kindly offered to chip in and pay for the glasses of port and sherry to be offered to guests to raise a toast to us, the soon to be happy couple. But no way was Norman going to break with tradition and chuck a few quid in the pot to ease the financial burden we had put on my parents. Well, our wedding came and went, as did the passing weeks after my parents had footed the entire bill for our wedding reception and no money was never forthcoming to cover the cost of the drinks. The subject was never mentioned again by Margaret or Norman. My parents hadn't asked for any help towards the cost, Margaret had volunteered to pay.

But what will have upset Norman on our wedding day was Margaret's impromptu invitation to all the family who had congregated in the local pub after our wedding reception. This was long before wedding receptions lasted an entire day and night. She had downed a few glasses of sherry (probably paid for by anyone but Norman) and thrown caution to the wind. Their bungalow was only a couple of hundred yards away from the local pub, so was the obvious place to continue celebrations when the landlord called last orders. Well, according to my mother, food that had been left over from our wedding buffet was taken back to the pub and the food that what was still left over was carefully carried to the bungalow. It was there my mother discovered first hand just how strict Norman was about wasting electricity when a tray of mushroom vol-au-vents had been placed in the oven to re-heat. This was of course before we were all afraid to reheat food and health and hygiene took over. When my mother and Margaret's elder sister went to check on the contents of the oven, they were surprised to find it still cold. Why? Norman had turned the power off to the cooker by the main red switch, like he always did after using it. Did he not tell them the cooker was turned off on purpose or genuinely forget to mention it? Not that it mattered in the end because the red switch was flicked on by Margaret's sister and the vol au vents were satisfactorily heated up. Not even on his son's wedding day could Norman forget about saving a few pence.

There were many more promises from Margaret in the run up to our wedding. We were told that as a wedding present, Norman would pay the deposit on our new home. We had already paid the £135 deposit from an insurance claim paid out on Chris's Lambretta scooter, after it had burst into flames one morning. But the thought of another £135 coming our way that we could then use towards furnishing our new home was welcomed. But of course, the cash never materialised. It was about four months after our wedding when, we had finally moved into our bungalow, that Margaret finally coughed up a lesser amount of cash which we used towards paying our solicitor's fees.

Another example was when I once said how much I liked a reading lamp that was in the lounge of Miser Mansion. Immediately Margaret said we could have the lamp when we married and foolishly, I believed her. Why wouldn't I? Well, the lamp remained in Margaret's possession until her dying day and was never mentioned again!

Over the years there were numerous occasions I was made to sound like a liar because of grossly exaggerated tales and lies told by my in-laws. One such occasion was about three years after we had married. We were guests at a family wedding, along with Margaret's extended family. Her brother, Austin, and his wife, Mary, the couple who had bought us the lovely pan set for a wedding gift, were also at the wedding. So, over a drink at the wedding reception, I brought up the subject of why I had never thanked the couple for the pans and how Margaret had put them on display in her own kitchen without telling me. Then while we were chatting, I mentioned that I wanted to move from our little bungalow and into a bigger house but would have to wait a while until our finances were better. Mary looked at me in genuine bewilderment and then said, "Why on earth would you want to move and take on a mortgage when you have a new bungalow that was bought outright as a gift. You don't know how lucky you are!"

I asked Mary to explain her comment but already had an inkling as to why she had said it, and I was right. Margaret and Norman had led their families to believe that the bungalow had been a wedding present from them to us and the full cost of our bungalow had been covered by Norman! As if! When I went on to explain that we had taken on a twenty-five-year mortgage with the Northern Rock Building Society, the couple were genuinely shocked and not amused at been led up the garden path about Norman's generosity and nor was I! They were not amused about the pans being put on display either.

Over the years there were many occasions when I was told how lucky we were to have all our new cars paid for by Norman. Lucky? Really? To which I always answered with a question. If that was the case, then why had we got bank loans to buy cars and had successfully reclaimed the PPI that had been added on to the loans? More deception and lies from my in-laws. And in more recent years when we have paid cash for our cars, I doubt Norman had a clue how much a new car cost. And if he had then there was no way he would have coughed up the cash!

When our eldest daughter was about three years old Margaret once asked me which school I would be sending her to. Well, we had two decent infant and nursery schools only a stone's throw away from where we lived so that wasn't a problem. As for a choice of secondary school, the local grammar school, which I had attended had closed and pupils had been moved to a new all girls high school, again just up the road from our home. We had years before we needed to make any serious choices about a secondary school, but Margaret jumped straight in with another promise. She was determined that she and Norman would pay for their granddaughter to go to a very prestigious school which I wasn't too familiar with. I'd heard of the school and knew it was quite a travelling distance away, but we had a few years to mull it over. Well, that was the first and last I heard on the subject. It was all pie in the sky as always.

Fast forward fifteen or more years and a similar promise was made about paying for our youngest girl, Melanie, to go to the very prestigious RADA (Royal Academy of Performing Arts) in London. Melanie was going to be taking her A levels in Dramatic Arts and Business Studies and was heavily involved in a couple of local amateur dramatic groups. Yes, she was considering having a go at making a career in the world of entertainment, but RADA was not one of her choices for further education or training in the entertainment business. She was in fact thinking of being a Butlins Redcoat after we had spent holidays there, where she could gain her Equity card. Back then, to work in the theatre or on television a budding actor/entertainer had to be a member of the Equity trade union. But Margaret continued to push our daughter towards going to London and seeking fame and fortune, insisting she would cover all the costs. But as usual, as it got closer to the day when applications were to be submitted to RADA, Margaret went silent on the subject. She never spoke about RADA ever again and no further offer of financial help ever materialised. Surprise, surprise! Neither I nor Melanie had been enthusiastic about RADA but what if the offer of all the expense being covered had swayed our thoughts? Then what would have happened? How cruel was that to make such a big promise to her own grandchild? But what also angered me was the blatant show of favouritism Margaret showed towards

Melanie, simply because she was able to brag about her appearing on the stage. This was an example of how our other two girls were often sidelined.

Going back to the 1980's, one of the best tales I heard about Norman's generosity that had circulated in the area was about the financial allowance Chris was getting each month. After work one afternoon I'd gone to the local shop for something to make sandwiches with for packed lunches. While the usual woman who worked behind the cooked meat section was serving me, she came out with a cracking statement that rendered me speechless. "I don't know why you bother working in school dinners when you get all that allowance every week from your father-in-law!" What????

I'd recently taken a temporary job working in the kitchen at the local grammar school. I hadn't gone looking for a job. After a conversation at a bus stop with a woman who lived nearby, I was unexpectedly asked if I fancied a couple of hours a day, working in the school kitchen up to Christmas. Washing up and cooking were and never will be something I enjoy but the twenty pounds a week wages were tempting. This was in 1988 and an extra few pounds each week for three months would help towards the cost of my children's presents. I hadn't worked for eleven years but we were managing nicely on one wage though a bit extra was not to be sniffed at. So, as you can imagine I had to ask the woman serving me in the shop, "What allowance are you referring to?"

"They give you a hundred and twenty pounds a week!"

"Really? And exactly how and when do we get this money?"

"Oh, I don't know, it was my next-door neighbour who was telling me. They were chatting to your in-laws when they were out walking. They said how much they help you with your finances."

Unbelievable! It was all total fabrication, and I made sure in no uncertain terms that the woman clearly understood that the claptrap my in-laws were spouting was an out and out lie. Because it was. Would I have spent two hours a day wearing rubber gloves and washing up after hundreds of school kids for a meagre twenty quid a week if we really had been getting such a big weekly allowance? Never! But I did quiz my husband later about where he was banking the allowance from his parents. He hadn't got a clue what I was rambling on about as I suspected because we had joint bank accounts and what was his was mine etc. Just why did my in-laws feel the need to tell such lies? Was it just an excuse to tell everyone who would listen about their wealth? What other reason could it have been? Anyone who knew Norman well knew that he would think twice about giving you the steam off his shit! Sorry for being so crude but it was true.

And with hindsight, I'm pleased that we never did get an allowance because after Christmas that year I was offered a permanent job in the kitchen at another local grammar school. I worked there for five years as a school dinner lady and loved it! I made friends for life and had many brilliant nights out with my workmates and still have wonderful memories of that era.

One of the regular promises that were made to Chris never materialised. For years after we got married Norman would say on occasions that when he and Margaret died their bungalow would be passed to Chris. Presumably at that point neither Norman or Margaret had any thoughts about moving out of their home and why would they? They had a suitable bungalow in a nice quiet area that would be suitable for them right up to their deaths. And of course, assuming they lived to a ripe old age, Chris and I would by then be senior citizens, and a bungalow would be ideal for us to live in. Please note that the emphasis was always on the bungalow would be going to Chris and not to us as a couple. Well, that was all forgotten when Norman sold his home just to get the extra cash that would help him reach his million pounds target. But what if we had taken him seriously? As it happened, there was no way I would ever have moved into that bungalow. It would have cost us far too much money to update it and the thought of Norman's ghost roaming around every time I left a light on was enough to put me right off.

One thing I have never knowingly done to my own children or grandchildren is make a promise I didn't intend to keep. Sadly, that was not the case with Margaret and Norman. Their promises always involved dipping into their bank accounts which obviously went against all that Norman believed in.

One of Margaret's first impulsive promises she made was about five years after we had moved into our first home, a newly built bungalow. But sadly, it really was the house that Jack built, full of shoddy workmanship and inferior fittings. The bungalow only had a side entrance door which may have looked good when we first saw it, but we quickly realised that it was poor quality and not fit for purpose. In winter the cheap wooden door would swell when it snowed or rained heavy and on more than one occasion it was impossible to get it to close properly. There were many times in winter that I had to go to work leaving the door unlocked, unable to turn the key because the door wasn't lined up correctly. To rectify this, we had to shave off the bottom of the door so it would close and lock. But of course, when the warm weather came the wood contracted again and was too small to fit the frame correctly. Eventually it didn't fit securely whatever the weather. It was neither use nor ornament and we desperately needed a new door. But by then I was pregnant with our first child, so we needed all our cash to buy baby items.

After our baby was born in December 1977, one evening Margaret came visiting and commented about the difficulty she had trying to open and close our exterior door. On impulse she said, "You need a new aluminium door, we'll buy you one!" Aluminium doors were the new style doors that folk were replacing old wooden doors with. I would have loved a new door of any kind, but an aluminium one would have been the answer to my prayers. What did we get? Nothing! Zilch! Bugger all! The subject was never mentioned again by Margaret and the ill-fitting door was still hanging on its hinges when we sold the bungalow in 1981.

So, in January 1981, Margaret was making and breaking promises yet again. Four months prior I had given birth to our second daughter, Lyndsay, so it was time to think about moving from our small two bedroomed bungalow into a bigger house. We'd had our mortgage for almost ten years and the market value of our bungalow had quintupled. But of course, that meant all properties had increased in value. Anyway, we'd decided to put our home on the market and began to look in the local newspaper for suitable houses for sale.

One semi-detached house, just across the main road from where we lived, had been up for sale for months and it was no mystery as to why. The house was home to a very scruffy family with unruly children. The exterior windows and doors were an awful shade of green and were peeling badly. The front and back garden had been neglected and become a mini wilderness. It was obvious why there had been no offers made on the property. However, the adjoining house looked quite different. That property had been lovingly cared for, and it showed. But as much as the location of the scruffy house was perfect, I chose to look at other properties in the area. Many were fine and would have been quite suitable, but none felt just right. It was only after speaking to the wife of our local shopkeeper about my house hunting that I began to look at the scruffy house in a different light. "Look at the potential of the house and not the peeling paint and scruffy gardens," she advised. And I did.

So, I booked a viewing of the scruffy house which probably shocked the vendors. Off I went with my three-year-old and my baby in her pram. On arriving at the side door, I was welcomed with open arms and invited into the kitchen from hell. Nicotine and grease sticking to walls is not a welcoming sight for prospective buyers but worse was to come. Basically, the whole house was filthy from floor to ceiling. The stench was enough to make me gag but I didn't shy away. It was obvious their children had caused damage to the inner doors, scrawling over them with felt tip pen or had smashed holes in them. But look at the potential of the house, I kept reminding myself.

Yes, it really was disgusting and far worse than I ever imagined it could be. But it was also perfect for what we wanted and regardless of the filth, it felt like I'd found our next home. Our three-year-old daughter even commented that she liked the house as we looked around. That evening, Chris went to view the house after I'd forewarned him about the state of it. Look at the potential, I'd reminded him. And he did.

The price was right. I knew I could get a bit knocked off if we put in an offer and we would have money left over to strip the house of everything, start from scratch and make it our own. Yes, we were both in agreement that we should buy the property. Job done. And luckily within a couple of days we had sold our bungalow to first time buyers for the full market value. It was just a matter of waiting for solicitors to do their jobs. We were all sorted and satisfied with our choice of a new home.

A couple of days later, when she called round (her excuse to have a crafty smoke on the way), we told Margaret that we were moving and where to. She said little about our proposed move, but I suspected she was taking everything on face value and not seeing the possibilities the scruffy house offered. Then, around 8.00pm that same evening who was banging on our door? Margaret! It was unusually late for her to call. Why? Well, according to Margaret, her and Norman didn't want us to buy the house we had put an offer in for and wanted us to look for something better! And . . . wait for it . . . they would pay the difference on the price of a better house! No actual figure was mentioned but she assured us they would pay the extra cost. Really? Once bitten and all that, naturally I was sceptical from the beginning, but Chris thought we should at least have a look at properties that had been out of our price range. So, we did and found a brand-new pair of semi-detached houses that had just gone on the market.

That weekend we trotted off to see the new builds, keeping an open mind on the price. Yes, the semi we viewed was ready to move straight into, no work needed on our part and only three thousand pounds more than the scruffy house we were supposedly buying. Common sense was telling me this may be the better buy, but something just wasn't right. The property didn't have the right feel about it. It didn't feel homely, unlike the scruffy one. Anyway, we walked back to my in-laws (they were childminding while we had our viewing) ready to tell them what we had seen.

The second Norman thought we may be serious about buying the more expensive house his body language changed. Looking uncomfortable as he spoke, he rambled on about not making any hasty decisions and other claptrap until he finally spit it out. His money was all tied up in bonds and long-term investments meaning he couldn't lay his hands on the three thousand pounds or more that we would need. He had to give three months' notice to withdraw cash, or he would have to pay a penalty! Basically, any money we might need was not going to be forthcoming and if he was pushed, it would take ages to get our hands on it. At that moment Chris and I were obviously thinking alike and made our excuses to leave. We would stick to our original plan and buy the scruffy house under our own steam as originally planned. So why did Margaret make such a big issue about helping us financially when she must have known Norman was not on board with her plans?

Our new home was in dire need of a complete refurbishment, needing new kitchen units fitting before we could live there. Maybe Margaret felt guilty at Norman's reluctance to cough up on her last promise when she suggested we visited a new kitchen supplier that had recently opened in the village. And yet again she hinted that she would pay for the new units. Well, we did visit the kitchen supplier and chose some units that were to be fitted the day after we got the keys to our new home. We had also ordered a new cooker, so it was all systems go. Did Margaret cough up for the kitchen units? Of course not! But I think she had a guilty conscience on that occasion and eventually Norman parted with the cash to cover the cost of our new cooker. In comparison it was only a small fraction of the price of the kitchen units. And we didn't get the cash until a few weeks after moving in and not before, when it would have been more beneficial to us. Margaret was messing with our lives with her false promises. And she didn't learn from that lesson either, but we certainly did.

Once bitten, twice shy! Well, around the mid 1990's history repeated itself. We'd been living in our home since May 1981 and very happy with our choice, once we had replaced all traces of the previous scruffy owners. Our mortgage was small in comparison to what many other couples were paying, and the position of our home proved to be a bonus over the years. Living close to a convenience shop that lived up to its name, especially in bad weather, it had never been an issue for us.

So, totally unexpected, Margaret came knocking on our door one evening, around 8.00pm. Can you see a pattern forming with her visits? Anyway, I suspected she wanted to either use our telephone or she was bringing us bad news. What other reason could it be at that time of the night? Wrong! She'd been to visit her elder sister that day and seen a house across the road that was up for sale. And? Well, Margaret and Norman wanted us to buy it! Just like that! Had we expressed any interest in moving or made any negative comments about our home? No! So, what was so special about the house she had seen for sale? It was away from a main road and close to Margaret's elder sister's house!

Margaret had no idea how much the house was on the market for or what condition it was in. All she knew was that it had been owned by two old spinsters and in her opinion was a better house than ours. When I pointed out that the property would probably need updating throughout and we had no desire to move again or have a bigger mortgage, she rambled on about giving us financial help towards the cost of moving. Really? Hadn't I heard this once before? Chris was working away that week so had no idea what was going on. I had zero enthusiasm, but Margaret was adamant we should move away from the shop and the main road. Why? Had we ever expressed a desire to move? No!

I went to work the following day and out of curiosity rang the estate agent responsible for selling the house Margaret was so adamant we bought. As I had suspected, the house had not been updated in decades by the two spinster sisters, and it needed gutting internally. Well, at least the estate agent was honest with me. And the house wasn't as big as our home and only had a small garden. It was just as I had expected. But, out of devilment I wanted to see Norman's reactions to Margaret's promise of financial help and that evening went to see them.

Norman's face said it all yet again. I estimated how much it would cost to bring the house up to date and how much property prices had increased since we had last moved. When I mentioned a figure of what we would need to make it our home Norman immediately responded by saying he knew it would need "doing up" and we were better off where we were! What he meant was he didn't want to cough up. So yet again Margaret had been making promises that would never happen and had sent me on another wild goose chase. But what if we really had liked the thought of moving and got our hopes raised? Then what?

Then there was another statement from Margaret that never materialised. This must have been around 1991. Chris was walking through the village to go for a Saturday lunchtime pint after working that morning. En-route to the pub he came face to face with his mother who had been doing some shopping. In their brief exchange of words Margaret told Chris that she and Norman were going to start helping us financially, now that our girls were growing up and the cost of everything was rising. This was a totally unprompted statement but must have appeared a genuine promise as Chris was quick to tell me about it when he got back home. Again, it was the first and last we heard of it.

But for me the meanest and most cruel promise that my in-laws ever made was in March 1993. Both Chris and I have birthdays in the first week of March, so when Norman proudly presented Chris with a photocopy of a formal piece of paper for his 43rd birthday (no mention of it being for my birthday as well) we were naturally confused. The document was some kind of trust fund, naming Chris as the sole beneficiary even though more than one person could have been named. Along with the photocopied document was a piece of paper with a handwritten text quoting £131,643 would be tax free after seven years. The policy was connected to the trust fund and would also have a bonus added on to the initial amount invested. This scrap of paper was, on further examination, the back of an old seed packet (nothing was thrown away that could be re-used) but it was in Norman's poor handwriting.

He went on to explain that come the year 2000, just as Chris would be reaching his fiftieth birthday, the policy Norman had taken out and put in a trust fund would come to fruition. Chris would receive over £150,000 when a bonus was added! The money would enable him to reduce his long working hours and spend more time at home. Well, what can you say to such a generous gift? I said nothing but my mind was working overtime. What was the catch? Sceptical? Yes, I most certainly was. If Norman struggled to cough up small amounts, would he really be able to part with such a large amount of cash and remember this was 1993, when it really was a large amount.

No way was I going to live the next seven years, thinking we would become financially secure at the end of it, only to be disappointed. So, I made an appointment at the local building society with their financial advisor. I already knew that this was where the trust fund and policy had been set up. Off I trotted, clutching the copies of the paperwork, expecting to come away disappointed. And I did!

The financial advisor looked at the papers I'd handed him and naturally explained that he could not discuss the matter as it wasn't my policy. I was already prepared for that and explained how Norman had led us to believe we would be drawing the money on Chris's fiftieth birthday. Then I began to ask hypothetical questions about such policies and trust funds After a short silent pause, I got the hypothetical answers I was expecting. So, such a policy could be cashed in and given to Chris after seven years without any tax owing on it. The key word was "could". The policy was on both Norman and Margaret's life with the option to cash it in. As Norman controlled almost all their finances that meant it was up to him what and when anything happened to the policy. Just as I had expected, Norman hadn't given his son anything other than another vague promise.

So, when March 2000 finally came around and it was the moment of truth, what grand gesture did Margaret and Norman make their only son on his fiftieth birthday? Well, it was obvious when nothing more had ever been said about the policy over the passing seven years and the big day got ever closer that no cash was going to be forthcoming. And it wasn't. Then, our eldest daughter threw a spanner in the works on the eve of Chris's birthday by announcing she was getting married, so my thoughts had turned away from the possibility of coming into money and replaced by making wedding plans.

The following day was a Sunday and Margaret paid us a visit, clutching her son's birthday card. What gift had she come bearing? Had she got the original policy for Chris to cash in? She came with nothing! She asked me a question instead. "Would you like some new fitted wardrobes for Chris's birthday?" It didn't have the same ring to it as "Here is the £150,000 we promised you!" I dismissed her by saying I had more important things to concentrate on now we had a wedding to plan and left it at that. I always had it at the back of my mind that no money would ever be forthcoming, but Chris always thought it might. What kind of parents make such huge promises and then just dismiss them with no explanation? They were continuing to mess with our lives and my anger was slowly festering. And just for the record, Chris received nothing for his fiftieth birthday apart from a card.

Another promise that fell by the wayside was about premium bonds. During his time in the army, while posted in Germany, Chris sent money home on a regular basis to be deposited in his bank account and to buy him a few premium bonds each month. However, the premium bonds were bought in Margaret's name and not Chris's. I had no prior knowledge of this when we married. The subject only came to light when in the late 1980's I won a competition for Trust House Forte gift vouchers, totalling £250. To use the vouchers, I invited both sets of parents and few close friends to dine out at a large hotel. We wined, dined and tried different cocktails during a very enjoyable evening, costing us not a penny. Norman found his appetite that evening when he knew he was eating for nothing. The couple always claimed they didn't have big appetites hence the meagre portions Norman dished up. This was obviously not true and on other occasions when food was in abundance, provided by someone else, he always found he had a healthy appetite.

Now, in conversation that evening, Margaret mentioned that Chris had some premium bonds which she was keeping, being in her name, and should they ever win a prize she would give the money to him. A likely story! Now, I do know that there were a few wins after that evening because Norman couldn't wait to tell Chris about Margaret's good fortune whenever she had won a prize yet never did a penny of it come to us. And when Margaret died, the bonds were included in her estate. The total was just under two thousand pounds. There were times early on in our marriage when that money would have come in very useful, and had I known those bonds existed I may well have suggested that Chris cashed them in. This was an example of Margaret being equally as tight fisted as her husband or she was afraid to part with any cash. I'll never know why.

It was bad enough when Margaret made her false promises to me and Chris, but she made promises to our eldest girl, Joanne when she was in her teens. The first instance was when she promised to pay for her a pair of new trainers that she had seen and wanted. I knew nothing about this until my daughter asked me to order the trainers from a catalogue I used to buy from.

Apparently, Margaret had promised her that she would pay the weekly instalments. Well, true to form, the trainers arrived and the first couple of instalments were paid by Margaret, as promised. From then on, the trainers were never mentioned and no further payments forthcoming. Guess who paid the rest of the instalments?

A few years later, Joanne was training as a hairstylist and Margaret encouraged her to have driving lessons. Again, Margaret said she would be paying for them. And once again the first couple of lessons were duly paid for by Margaret but then never mentioned, nor was any more cash forthcoming. Our girl did continue to have lessons but with no thanks to Margaret.

Fast forward a few years and Joanne had got a mortgage and bought her own home. She had all the necessities and furniture she needed when she moved in and then a couple of weeks later Margaret paid her a visit. This time when Margaret told her to buy new window blinds and she would pay, our girl wasn't fooled into believing her. Which is just as well because the subject was never mentioned again.

Norman's money was like a carrot on a stick dangled before a hungry donkey. It was always just beyond reach and when anyone got within touching distance, the carrot moved further away. The one good thing that could be said about Norman was that he never really promised us anything while he was alive, which in a way was better than the many broken promises his wife made. All Norman ever talked and worried about was what would happen to his money after he died.

Chapter 14

All for show!

A classic example of "all for show!" was obvious to me during the few weeks I had to live at Miser Mansion. Norman came home from work one evening just after I had arrived. Margaret was working late at the maternity unit and Chris wasn't going to be home that evening so that left just me and Norman spending the evening together. But from the second he entered the bungalow he was a man on a mission flying about with a can of furniture polish and a duster. What had brought about this sudden desire to spruce up the home? A fellow workmate was coming to see Norman's home! Why? I never knew why but sat in awe as he whizzed around with the duster, placing ornaments in precise positions. Then, out came a rolled-up rug that had been stored away in a wardrobe. I had never seen the rug before, so it obviously didn't get many airings. The rug was meticulously displayed in front of the fire, putting the finishing touches to Norman's cleaning spree.

Miser Mansion was an attractive looking bungalow with the exterior being clad in Yorkshire stone. Norman had put time and effort into their home and built a feature stone fireplace that ran the length of the lounge. He'd fitted some ceiling beams with a metal chandelier taking pride of place in the centre. Their dark wood furniture completed the ye olde worlde look Norman had created. The décor wasn't my cup of tea but to many it may have been. Norman was proud of his home, proof that he had gone up in the world and wanted to show his handiwork to his workmate. However, Miser Mansion was just a well-furnished property and nothing more. For a property to be a home it must be filled with love and happiness and I never felt that when I was there.

A chap did call later that evening and was shown around the bungalow, mumbling his approval to Norman. Was this visit to quash any rumours that Norman perhaps wasn't the wealthy man he claimed to be? After all he was known for begging free stuff from the company stores and for his reluctance to spend money on anything. Why would anyone think he had a nice home? Anyway, it was job done and before the visitor had closed the door behind him the rug was back in the wardrobe. It really was all for show because I don't recall ever seeing that rug ever again until 2025 after Norman had died and we cleared out his flat! It's just a pity the visitor hadn't called unexpectedly and found the usual pile of Rileys toffee roll wrappers thrown on the floor, next to the fire. Or better still, Margaret's girdle thrown over a chair arm, which she often did when she was settling down on the sofa for the night.

Now, going back to 1961, Chris was attending the local Catholic junior school and like all the other pupils in his year, he sat his eleven plus exam. He failed! Well, at that time there were usually only a handful of pupils from each school that did pass the exam and go on to a grammar school education. And of course, not every child is destined or wants to have an academic career, with many going on to have successful careers in manual work. But this wasn't good enough for Margaret and Norman. Chris was told by his mother that he was going to sit an entrance exam for a more prestigious Catholic college.

When the big day came, off went Margaret with her son in tow to sit the entrance exam. But what Margaret wasn't aware of was the simple fact that her son did not want to sit the exam or go to the college. He was happy enough to go to the Catholic secondary school with his mates. So, what did Chris do? He deliberately messed up the exam papers, putting down wrong answers. He didn't want to trek miles every morning when he could catch the local bus provided to take pupils to the secondary school. He wanted to go with his mates and had no desire to have an academic or clerical career. So, the idea was all down to his parents, who I am certain would have loved to have thrown into future conversations that their son attended a prestigious college.

And I can remember Margaret saying to me when I first started dating her son that Chris was very intelligent, but he didn't try hard enough at school. This was in response to her discovering that I had been to a grammar school and was working in a bank at the time. But I was quite capable of forming my own opinion about the young man I was destined to marry.

I've often wondered if the couple were somewhat disappointed that their only child had not been more academically minded and pursued a more upmarket career rather than eventually choosing to settle into a life as a lorry driver. It doesn't have the same ring to it as being a solicitor or a doctor, but their son had also served his country in the armed forces so they should have been proud of him for that. It mattered not a jot to me that I married a manual worker.

My thoughts about Margaret and Norman's disappointment about Chris choosing to be a lorry driver first occurred to me many years later after a short conversation with their next-door neighbour. She was a lovely elderly lady who often spent time working in a dress shop in the village which belonged to her daughter. One day I went into the shop looking for a new dress from the collection on display. Whilst doing so I was chatting away to their neighbour who had asked about my three young children. Then she said something rather odd. She commented on how hard it must be for me to have three young children and a husband who worked away during the week. Then she added that she knew it was worth it because Chris had a fantastic wage!!!!

I already knew the answer before I asked how she knew about my husband's fantastic wage. And I was right in thinking it was Margaret and Norman who had told her. To which I swiftly but politely put the lady straight on a few matters. First and foremost, my in-laws didn't know how much Chris's weekly wage was. And secondly, he wasn't on a fantastic wage as no lorry drivers at that time were ever paid fantastic wages. He earned enough to feed and clothe us all and pay our mortgage. At no time had he or I ever disclosed to anyone else just how much he received in his wage packet. My in-laws were lying and in my mind were trying to impress their neighbour. By the time I had chosen a new dress and was leaving the shop, their neighbour had been well and truly put in the picture about Margaret and Norman's assumptions. Once again, their lies were all for show.

Now, on the rare occasions that Norman did get his hand in his pocket, and it was rare, he and Margaret had to make sure everyone knew about it. Many people over the years have been confused as to what was the truth and what were just misleading tales the couple were spinning. Even Norman's younger brother had been under the impression that all our holidays and every car we had ever bought had been paid for by his generous and wealthy brother. He even dared to contradict our eldest daughter when she tried to put him straight on the subject. The truth was that Norman did cough up for the cost of our two-week cruise around the Mediterranean to celebrate our silver wedding anniversary. This was one impromptu promise Margaret made in Norman's presence, but he wasn't a happy chappie when he found himself backed into a corner by his wife's spontaneous promise.

It all started when we were having our slap-up Christmas dinner at my in-laws in 1996. At some time during the meal Margaret began telling us about her elder sister's recent trip to the USA to celebrate her golden wedding anniversary. The trip did sound brilliant, to which I expressed my wish to see certain parts of the world and that I'd always wanted to go on a cruise. On impulse, Margaret suddenly announced that they would pay for Chris and me to go cruising for our forthcoming silver wedding anniversary the following August. Just like that! And she continued asking where we fancied going on our travels and to get the cruise booked after the Christmas holidays. All this was promised without any consulting with Norman who remained silent, probably hoping it was another of her flash in the pan ideas and we would all forget about it.

Now, me being sceptical about Margaret's promises I took her offer with the proverbial pinch of salt, until she came to our home a few days after the Christmas holidays. Had we booked our cruise and how much was it going to cost? This time she was adamant that we got it sorted and would have the money ready as soon as we knew the cost. Again, I was still very wary, but Chris was convinced she meant it and as a last resort we could always pay for the cruise ourselves. So, I started to look at brochures, still not convinced we would ever see the cash. Once I'd found what seemed a suitable itinerary round the Mediterranean, I trotted off to the nearest branch of Thomas Cook, still a little wary about any cash being forthcoming from

Margaret. After all, she would have to get Norman to withdraw money and that was a huge challenge.

A while later we all attended a family get together in aid of Margaret's brother's birthday. Well, it wasn't long before Margaret began telling everyone about the cruise we had booked and made sure she slipped it into the conversation that they were footing the bill. The emphasis was on their generosity of course. Except at that stage, we hadn't received a penny from her. It was still all promises and possibly pie in the sky once again. However, on this occasion the cash did materialise but not until it was time to pay the bulk of the cost, many months later. I'll never know how she managed to get Norman to part with the money, but she did. But what if we hadn't had sufficient cash in the bank to pay for the cruise when it came to it and Margaret had broken another of her promises? What if Norman had kicked up a fuss when it came to paying up? Did Margaret ever think about that? And I ask, why didn't the couple spend some of their money on a cruise for themselves?

And just to prove how out of touch with reality Norman was, he offered to loan us their large suitcase to take on our cruise. Well, I was intrigued as to just how big this suitcase would be and dutifully paid a visit to Miser Mansion to find out. The suitcase was no bigger than a vanity case. I would have struggled to get our toiletries in it, yet Norman thought we could both get enough clothes in to last us a fortnight! And it looked like something servicemen were issued with when being de-mobbed after the war! I politely refused his kind offer!

March 1992 was another occasion when Margaret made a huge fuss of presenting me with a cheque for my fortieth birthday. But what she didn't tell my friends and family was that I hadn't spoken to her for almost a year, after an incident where she had been venting her anger at me and my girls about something trivial.

Our girls had been to have tea with Margaret and Norman one Tuesday. It had become a regular occurrence, but for me it was getting harder and harder to get the girls to go. Basically, they just didn't want to. I often had to use bribery to get them there. Our daughter, Lyndsay, was very hard to persuade which I always suspected was due to her feeling the odd one out.

Margaret had made a fuss of her first grandchild, Joanne, who inherited Chris's genes with dark brown hair and dark brown eyes. She'd been eager to make a promise about sending her to a private school (though that never happened). Our youngest, Melanie was involved in amateur dramatics with friends and neighbours making regular comments to Margaret about seeing her in shows. Hence the numerous gifts she was showered with. More about that later.

But our middle daughter, Lyndsay, was nothing like her sisters. She inherited a lot of my personality and physical features. I suspected she often felt second best in Margaret's eyes and probably did show her resentment towards her grandmother. Margaret once asked me when Lyndsay was approaching school leaving age what I thought she may do when she left school. I got the impression that she didn't have high hopes for my daughter to which I replied in no uncertain terms that Lyndsay had been blessed with common sense! And she would be successful in whatever career she chose. She had already been an ambassador for her school when she had visited Gaza in a foreign exchange trip to the Middle East and had featured in a book and a Channel 4 tv documentary about it. And Lyndsay went on to have a career in the police force before starting her own online business which was very successful.

So, on one occasion after having tea, Margaret marched my girls back home and the second she set foot through my door she began her venomous tongue lashing. My children had no respect, were unruly and blasphemous! Blasphemous? Well according to Margaret, they were. Lyndsay had used the word "God" when showing her annoyance at Margaret that day. Now, if you don't believe in God, Jesus and such then it is just a word. I often used the word when annoyed and I had held a conversation with Lyndsay about religion years before. She had said one day that she didn't think all the tales about Jesus were true. She was at junior school and had listened to all the lessons especially the bits about the meaning of Christmas and had formed her own opinion about it all. I respected my daughter's opinion as there are no facts about any religion, only tales passed down for centuries which we are expected to believe. It was no big deal to me but coming from a Catholic family it was to Margaret. Each to their own.

Now on this occasion my mother was at our home when Margaret stormed into our lounge. She was shocked and confused as to what was happening as Margaret spat her venom at me and my girls. My poor mother was speechless as she watched on and listened to the abuse being hurled at me and my girls. She couldn't believe how angry and nasty Margaret had been about something so trivial.

Anyway, our brief and insulting exchange of words ended with Margaret storming out of my house hurling a final insult at me. She implied that my eldest girl was going to end up in a council flat, unmarried with a baby by the time she was sixteen!!!! All due to my bad parenting of course. Well, it wasn't me who had got pregnant out of wedlock was it? I had been married over five years before I had my first child. And as it turned out my eldest girl doesn't have any children, and my other two girls were in their thirties before they each had one child.

But after her vicious tantrum I refused to speak to Margaret and ignored her if we passed in the street and my girls didn't go round for tea anymore. That will have pleased Norman though because I've heard through a trusted source that he used to moan at work about the amount of food my girls ate on their visits. They had to buy an extra loaf of bread each week to feed the girls and that didn't go down well with Norman and his strict budget.

I had never gone looking to stir up trouble, but Margaret seemed to be picking an argument with whoever didn't live by her rules or had a differing opinion. So, it was only because most of Chris's family were invited to my fortieth birthday party that I softened and agreed that Margaret and Norman could attend. I didn't ask them personally and left that to Chris. Margaret would never have refused an invitation from her son but may have refused one from me. I didn't care if they came or not.

At my birthday party, which I held in a local pub function room, Margaret waited until I had a few guests milling around me before pushing herself forward. Then, waving a cheque in her hand for all to see she said loudly, "Treat yourself to something nice!" The cheque was for one hundred pounds. Why couldn't she have handed over the cheque without making a show of it to everyone or slipped it into a card? But no, parting with money was a big issue and she wanted everyone to know how generous they were being. Margaret hadn't made a big issue of presenting me with two well washed towels on a previous birthday! What would her family have thought of that big gesture? Now, nobody else knew what they had given their only son for his fortieth birthday, two years earlier. Their generosity was overwhelming! All they had given their son was a tenner pushed in a card to buy himself a birthday drink! Where was his cheque for a hundred pounds so he could treat himself? In his dreams. Mine was simply all for show.

A couple of days after my party it was Chris's birthday. What would he be getting for a present? I saw his face as he opened a cheap birthday card from his parents only to find nothing else with it. Not even a fiver or a tenner for a birthday drink! Though Chris said nothing I could see the disappointed expression on his face. So, just as I thought, my cheque really had been all for show. I was tempted to tear up the cheque in disgust at how she had treated Chris. But then I had a better idea. What did I treat myself to with my hundred pounds? Nothing! I paid it into our joint bank account and used it to pay some bills. How could she not want to give her son a small gift and even more so after her big public gesture when giving me a cheque? Her mentality was getting as bad as Norman's.

I specifically hated the way Margaret blatantly favoured one granddaughter over the other two. Somehow, on occasions she managed to have some spare cash to fritter on our youngest, Melanie, that I assume Norman knew nothing about. Her first blatant show of favouritism was in the early 1980's when our girls were very young. Margaret had asked what we were getting the girls for Christmas. Well, I mentioned that amongst many other gifts I was planning on buying them a wicker chair each as it was getting to be a bit cramped if we all wanted to sit on the sofa to watch television and the kids were eager to have their own chairs. I'd already seen what I wanted and had plans to buy them. The chairs were twelve pounds each, but Margaret insisted that she buy the chairs instead. I was dubious as I knew how she had made so many promises and broken them. But she was determined to buy three chairs. I reluctantly agreed thinking I may end up buying the chairs in the January sales if they never materialised on Christmas morning.

Well, Margaret did keep that promise, well almost. On Christmas Eve three chairs did arrive for our girls but only two were wicker chairs. The third chair was an upholstered chair made of dark wood. Yes, it was a child's chair but more a piece of furniture than the casual wicker ones. I hated that chair on first sight! It didn't fit in with our furniture and it wasn't wicker! Margaret made it clear the expensive chair was for Melanie. This was the start of her showing favouritism. Being Christmas Eve, it was too late to send the rotten chair back, so on Christmas morning I had to lie to my girls about why the youngest, Melanie, had a different chair. Later I discovered the rotten chair cost over fifty pounds, which was over four times the cost of a wicker one. And I hold my hand up to encouraging my girls to abuse the chair. If anything was spilt or stuck to the upholstered seat, I made no attempt to clean it off. If it got knocked or scratched, I said nothing. But if they were to disrespect the wicker chairs, I was straight on their case!

When all my girls were in their teens, I can only describe them as being like chalk, cheese and chewing gum! So, on another display of favouritism, our youngest was going to be in a show at the town hall that evening and later at an after-show party. Being a Saturday none of us were early risers. So, when I eventually got up and ventured downstairs I found an envelope on the mat behind the front door. The sealed envelope had not arrived via Royal Mail but been pushed through the letter box early that morning. The envelope had just one name on it: Melanie. Intrigued at what it could be I took the envelope upstairs for my daughter to open. What was inside? A solid gold chain! With it was a note from Margaret telling her to wear the chain that evening at the after-show party!

My first thought... where were the gold chains for my other two girls? My second thought was how ugly the chain was because it was not ladylike or feminine in any way. It was more befitting of hanging around a dog's neck! The chunky chain was more suitable for a man and certainly not something most women would choose to wear. So, why had Margaret bought it? As usual it was all for show and she wanted her favourite granddaughter to be the belle of the ball, showing off her expensive chain. It may have been all for show, but it never happened! The chain was never worn and eventually traded in for cash. But what annoyed me the most was seeing the looks on my other two girls' faces when they were both reminded that they were not Margaret's favourite granddaughter.

On at least two more occasions Margaret showed her obvious favouritism by taking Melanie out shopping during the school holidays, while I and the other two girls were at work. Our eldest girl had left home by this time so didn't get to see what greeted me and Lyndsay on arriving back home one evening. It was Margaret's latest display of favouritism. A large selection of clothes had been bought at a Readmans outlet store for her favourite granddaughter, but not a single item for her sisters. Again, I saw the look on Lyndsay's face when she was reminded that she didn't hold the same status with Margaret. On another occasion Melanie arrived home with an expensive pair of leather knee length boots from a very popular store. Again, the boots were to be worn at some am-dram function. Yet again, this was all for show and an expression of her favouritism. And on yet another occasion, a cheque for a hundred pounds was pushed through our letterbox with just one name on it. Yes, once again it was for Melanie. I saw the look on my other girl's face when she realised there was nothing for her or her older sister.

Did Margaret realise the hurt she caused my other two girls? Did she care? Her actions were so obviously for the purpose of having folk think her family were well off and to try and make her favourite granddaughter stand out in a crowd. For me, I would rather she had followed Norman's tight-fisted attitude and not shown her favouritism. I was the one who had to pick up the pieces of her pathetic attempts to show her wealth and favouritism.

Another occasion when Margaret didn't seem to know that her actions were hurtful was one Christmas. I was never sure why, but she bought me a bottle of Estee Lauder Youth Dew perfume, which wasn't cheap. Yes, I'd worn that perfume many years before like many more women had, but it was no longer my perfume of choice. Maybe we had had another big disagreement because usually I got nothing. But on Christmas Day when Chris opened his gift from his parents all he got was a five pack of Hamlet cigars, which at the time wouldn't have cost much more than a couple of pounds, if that. Couldn't she have bought him a bottle of aftershave or just not bothered buying for either of us? How her mind worked was a mystery.

And there was one very sad occasion that didn't rest easy with me. When Melanie had turned fourteen, she had managed to get a leading role in an amateur production of Sweet Charity. This was a big achievement for someone so young and new to the society and Margaret was making sure everyone knew this. But on the day of the dress rehearsal, we had a tragic death in our family. My twelve-year-old niece had died of brain injuries caused by a car running a red light and the hit 'n run driver ploughing her down on her way home from school. For four days she had been unconscious in an intensive care unit, fighting for her life, until the decision was taken to turn off life support.

That evening Melanie didn't want to go to the dress rehearsal. She had just lost her cousin. So, I went round to tell Margaret the sickening news and that her favourite granddaughter wouldn't be rehearsing. Her response? She must go as the show probably wouldn't be able to go ahead! Margaret was a friend of my niece's paternal grandmother, who was naturally heartbroken. My mother had lost her youngest granddaughter and was distraught. But Margaret was adamant the show must go on. I decided the decision was up to my daughter, who feeling under pressure, succumbed to Margaret's wish. Make of it what you will, but as a grandmother herself, where was Margaret's sympathy or compassion? As she was dining out on her granddaughter's newfound fame in the local community, two other grandmothers were nursing broken hearts.

As for Norman, he wanted to be a wealthy man but not for any pleasure his wealth could give him. Apart from being a millionaire he wanted anyone and everyone to know that he was one. Margaret had become almost as bad as her miserly husband by bragging about their wealth but never coming good on her endless promises. It was all for show. Years ago, our local newspaper would print the details of folk who had died and left a sizeable estate in their Will. I would often read how much someone I may have known had left to relatives or to a charity. When he died, Norman wanted the details of his estate to be in the local paper, proving to everyone who had known him that he really was a wealthy man. Was he aware that most folk couldn't have cared less about what he was worth? And can you blame folk when he lived and looked more like a pauper? Alas, this tradition fizzled out decades before his death.

Chapter 15

Travelling light!

As you can imagine, knowing Norman's frugal lifestyle, he didn't fritter away his cash on lavish foreign holidays. So, after a year of hard graft what better way to relax than a few days in Blackpool. Not a full week of course, just Monday to Friday. Though they did have two trips away most years. Remember, the illuminations cost nothing to see and walking the length and breadth of the Golden Mile each day is also a free activity. Now, I do know that Margaret loved to watch others feeding the fruit machines in the amusement arcades. Did Norman ever have a flutter and spend a few pence or let his wife have a gamble? Not on your nellie! With so much free entertainment to hand what more could one want from a holiday? Well, how about starting with some fun.

Their holiday started by getting a coach to the seaside. Then on arrival, Norman would carry their little suitcase (only big enough to hold my toiletries for a week) that held a couple of changes of clothing, to a small boarding house in a quiet backstreet. Margaret trotted along beside him carrying her shopping bag which held their trusty thermos flask and a packet of ginger biscuits.

If their little room was cheap enough with two meals a day included, plus tea making facilities, that was all they required. I don't know if they ever had the luxury of an en-suite bathroom, but it will not have been a priority when booking. The price will have been the most important detail. After breakfast, each morning Margaret would fill the Thermos flask and off they trotted to spend the day walking the length and breadth of Blackpool watching others spend their money, having fun. They walked for hours, mile after mile, stopping for a rest in a seafront shelter for a cup of tea and a ginger biscuit, carefully carried in

Margaret's shopping bag. It was the same routine, day after day, unless it rained when they were forced to go window shopping to kill time.

The landlady of their regular Blackpool boarding house often took pity on her poor downtrodden guests and would offer Norman a pair of free cinema tickets or complimentary tickets for a show on a pier that she didn't want. Little did she know Margaret and Norman weren't on their uppers but chose to wear second hand clothing and dress like tramps. Then before they left to go home, Norman would scour their room, looking under edges of carpets and in all nooks and crannies for any money any previous guests may have lost or left behind. And on occasions he did find an odd coin or two. Result! He could arrive back home with more in his pocket than he started with. Life didn't get any better than that for him.

And then one year the couple decided to really splash out and have a change of location for their holiday. Bored with Blackpool, knowing every crack in the resort's pavements, off they trotted to Skegness on a National Travel coach. Being so well travelled, the couple thought one seaside resort was very much like another and hadn't pre-booked any accommodation. With no telephone to ring around the hotels beforehand they had been convinced it would be easy to find a cheap backstreet boarding house. But unlike Blackpool, Skegness doesn't have anything like as many small guest houses and what there are get fully booked well in advance. So, it came as a bit of a surprise when the couple arrived at mid-day and began searching for cheap n' cheerful accommodation displaying a "Vacancies" sign.

After walking around the resort for hours, Margaret and Norman were just in time to catch the coach back home! They were lucky that there were a couple of seats to be had on the return journey as they were booked to travel back later in the week. We were told there were no vacancies to be had in the Skegness hotels, but I suspect the truth is that Norman wasn't prepared to pay a bit more for superior accommodation. Skegness has a Butlins holiday camp just a short bus ride away, but no way would Norman have given that any consideration. Whatever it was that had them returning home the same day, money will have come into the equation. And again, Margaret went along with his miserly ways and stubbornness. I'd have told him to get off home while I stayed behind and enjoyed the change of scenery and sod the expense!

Yet once, just once, Norman was persuaded to go abroad for a holiday. Pressure was put on the couple to visit Margaret's elder sister's timeshare holiday home in Portugal. Neither Norman or Margaret wanted to fly (and probably Norman didn't really want to go) but arrangements were made for the two sisters and their respective spouses to travel by car and ferry to Portugal. Having no passports Norman and Margaret were able to buy one-year passports that were available in post offices in the 1980's. I should imagine Norman had some regrets as the cost of merely travelling to Portugal was racking up. Then they would have to fork out for the cost of food as they were self-catering and maybe a few meals out. That would have given Norman's wallet a real beating. Afterwards, I was told that they never got into the holiday spirit and wouldn't even shell out for an ice cream cone when walking about in the hot sunshine. Anyway, the outcome was that foreign holidays were not to Norman or Margaret's liking, so they never ventured out of the country again. And, true to form, Norman took along his trusty thimble on his foreign travels to ration the washing up liquid!

When it was time to pack up and travel back to Blighty, Norman was horrified that his sister-in-law insisted on leaving any unused washing up liquid, toilet rolls and bathroom toiletries in the villa. Heaven forbid that they should leave a few sheets of toilet roll. After all, half a roll would last Margaret and Norman a week! And even a squirt of washing up liquid left behind would have really upset Norman. I bet he lost sleep over it, just thinking about the few pence they had wasted.

Once in a conversation with her younger sister, Mary, Margaret said that if Norman died first that she would like to go on a world cruise! Really? When asked what was stopping Margaret and Norman going on a cruise together, Margaret simply smiled and gave no answer. That tells me that Margaret would have liked to travel and not be stuck trudging the streets of Blackpool every year. So why didn't she insist on proper holidays? I think we can guess the answer.

Now just when we thought Norman couldn't get any worse with his penny-pinching holidays, he did. One year the couple made a big announcement to Chris. They had decided that they were not going to go to the illuminations in Blackpool that year because the couple had decided to do something completely different. What exactly was this going to be? Were they going to go on a Mediterranean cruise or a nice coach trip down south? No! Wait for it . . . instead of having a holiday in Blackpool, they were going to (drumroll please) . . . have a joint of beef for their Christmas dinner! Now is it me? What does a joint of beef cost, especially a very small one, in comparison to a trip to Blackpool? Was Margaret involved in making that decision or had Norman told her what they were going to do? We will never know the truth, but they had stooped to an even higher level of thriftiness. It was a no-brainer for Norman choosing between a few days away or a joint of beef for Christmas. Unbelievable!

Chapter 16

Frustration, Feuds and Fury!

It wasn't through choice that when I married Margaret and Norman's only son, that we had to live with his parents for a few weeks. These were frustrating and very miserable weeks and not the perfect start to our marriage. But they were certainly eye opening. I had never been in anyone's home who lived like my new in-laws. Margaret lived for over sixty years under her husband's strict regime so in some respects she deserved a medal! But in another way, she deserved a good slap for allowing her husband to dictate every aspect of her life.

By the time Margaret was approaching retirement age she had risen through the nursing ranks and was not only teaching midwifery but was on a board of examiners. This position was high profile, came with a lot of responsibility and a generous salary with an excellent pension. Yet Margaret never had a landline phone to receive or make important phone calls for work or personal issues. Norman was adamant a phone was not a necessary item. But one morning I received a call at home from Margaret's elder sister who was the bearer of bad news. Their mother had died. She had tried to contact Margaret at work but had been told the worrying news that she had not arrived at work that morning. Nobody seemed to know where Margaret was.

As I lived close, I was asked if I would walk to Miser Mansion and see if Margaret was at home and if so, I was to tell her the sad news about her mother. Off I trotted to Miser Mansion and knocked on the bungalow door. I waited for any sign of life. I knocked a little louder and waited yet again. Still no reply. So, I had one last go, knocking as loud as possible before I turned to leave. Then I saw a moving shadow through the glass door panels. When the door finally opened a few inches, I was shocked at what I saw. It was Margaret peering round the door but could easily have been Morticia from The Addams family that I was looking at.

Margaret's hair was bedraggled, hanging over her shoulders, her face pale and drawn. She looked dreadful and was still in her nightie even though it was almost noon. When I explained I was calling because her sister had been trying to contact her at work, she knew immediately what bad news I had come to deliver. She broke down in tears, a frail and obviously ill woman. When she pulled herself together, Margaret told me why she hadn't been at work and asked that I contacted the hospital and explained her absence. Margaret had been having many bouts of acid reflux which we knew about, but that morning her symptoms had become so severe she had been vomiting violently, was in a lot of discomfort and didn't have the strength to get herself ready for work.

Apart from not being able to contact work and explain her absence, Margaret had no way of ringing for help or calling a doctor. Why did she not insist on having a phone installed? A telephone wasn't considered a luxury anymore and was often a necessity. I wonder what Margaret's work colleagues thought about her not having a phone. They would have known she was on a very good salary and had a husband working as well. How, as a woman who held a high-ranking job, did she explain the absence of a phone in her home without revealing the details of her frugal lifestyle with Norman?

Virtually overnight Margaret's life was turned upside down when she was diagnosed with stomach cancer. Margaret had been suffering with indigestion and acid reflux for months and had been originally told she may have an inflamed gall bladder. It wasn't long before Margaret had another sudden and violent vomiting attack one evening that left Norman flapping. He ran to our house and asked me to ring an emergency doctor. Margaret was seriously ill. Any normal person would have realised how important it was to have a phone for such occasions, but not Norman.

It was only a couple of weeks after her diagnosis when she was able to have her life saving operation. This was due to being put to the front of the queue for surgery, because of her being in the nursing profession and her prior professional association with the surgeon. He performed her operation just days before Christmas. It was this consultant who a couple of years later was put on a sabbatical and Margaret supported him on television in her Marks & Spencer outfit which was returned to the store the following day. So, she survived her operation but her road to recovery was going to be slow and she knew that she wasn't going to be able to return to work for a long time, if at all.

After her operation, by the time Margaret was going to be fit enough to return to her heavy work load she would have reached retirement age. The decision was made that she should retire early which made perfect sense. With Margaret's career officially ended Norman then decided he would also retire early. Margaret's NHS pension was way over and above the amount needed for the couple to live comfortably until their official retirement dates and their state pensions could be drawn. After a battle with cancer most normal couples would have envied their financial position and relished the chance to relax, see more of the world, having holidays abroad. But that is what normal couples would do and not Margaret and Norman.

I have always wondered how a woman who held such a high-ranking position and was a force to be reckoned with in the nursing world could ever allow herself to stoop so low when it came to some of Norman's money saving rules. Margaret had become used to having authority in her career, giving orders and being respected in the higher circles of the nursing profession. Having to give up her career so suddenly must have been devastating. My mother first met Margaret in August 1971 when she was in hospital recovering from her hysterectomy. Chris had told his mother about her being in hospital which was where Margaret was working as a midwife at the time.

According to my mother, one afternoon while she was in her hospital bed, the ward doors were suddenly flung open and in walked a nurse who marched down the ward, eyes scanning every bed until she found my mother's. It was Margaret. I gather from what she later told me that Margaret was a formidable figure even though she was small in stature and the young nurses on the ward were immediately aware of her superior presence.

Margaret's name was well known in the nursing world, and this was made obvious to me in 1977 when having our first child.

I was admitted to the local maternity unit to be induced. This was where Margaret had worked before moving to a higher post in another hospital. I was feeling very tearful one day, which due to hormonal overload was quite normal. But I had been left for five days, anxiously waiting for labour to start after a few false alarms. Then on a routine ward inspection a high-ranking nurse was doing her rounds and came to my bed to see how I was feeling. I just happened to ask if this nurse knew my mother-in-law. Did she! I saw the nurse's face change when she made the connection between me and Margaret. Talk about action stations! She had no sooner left my bedside than I was visited by a consultant who was very concerned about my low mood. I'd been given Prostaglandin every day during that week to induce me. But though I had spent hours in labour each day the drug didn't have the desired effect and hadn't put me into the second stages. The result was that I was told to go home for the evening and relax. Then I was to return on the Saturday afternoon, to be prepped and ready to be physically induced the following morning. Just the very mention of Margaret's name and I received the VIP treatment for the rest of my confinement.

So, after her life saving operation and her battle with cancer, which sapped every ounce of strength from her for months, Margaret had lost her career and health in one fell swoop and found herself suddenly stuck in her home, day in and day out with Norman calling all the shots. It was this, I'm sure, when Margaret's frustration turned to anger. She was suddenly powerless in making any decisions in any aspect of her life. Norman was now controlling her, calling the shots all day and every day. I ask why, when it was initially her private pension that enabled Norman to retire early, didn't she make her feelings known and insist on having a say in her home and in her lifestyle?

She had once, very early on in our marriage, mentioned an incident when Norman was a young man and had been the butt of a joke. A young chap he worked with had made a sarcastic comment about Norman not pulling his weight on a job they were doing. This flippant comment resulted in Norman showing his fiery temper and rage by lifting very heavy paving stones onto a truck. Normally it took two men to lift the stones but in a fit of anger Norman did it single-handed until the job was done.

And I once asked Margaret why the feature fireplace that Norman had built in the bungalow suddenly had a hole in it. I was shocked by her answer. A few nights earlier Norman's next-door neighbours were being noisy (it was about 9.30pm but that was late in his book). Norman couldn't sleep for the noise or what he called noise. He always had the volume on his television turned down low. Perhaps he thought it used more electricity to turn up the volume. Who knows. But he had a family of four for neighbours who probably didn't feel the need to creep around their home in the dark like silent shadows! Anyway, that night, in anger, Norman banged on the dividing lounge wall hoping to stop the noisy neighbours in their tracks. When that didn't stop the noise, he vented his anger by taking a hammer to the room length feature fireplace he was so proud of and smashed a hole in it. After seeing her husband's temper at work, perhaps that was why Margaret opted for an easy life and kept her mouth shut.

Anyway, after slowly recovering from stomach cancer and probably realising that she was a very lucky woman to have survived her ordeal, Margaret was adamant that she wanted a piano in her home. Finally, she was putting her foot down with Norman. She couldn't play a note but had always longed for a piano and wanted to have lessons. There's nothing wrong with that. Maybe just for once in her married life she felt she was entitled to treat herself after surviving cancer. And at some point, Margaret must have asserted her authority, making a decision that was very unpopular with her husband. Or it may have been that Norman was so grateful for still having his wife beside him with her very generous pension that he relented and allowed her to have a piano. I will never know how she managed it, but she got her wish, and a piano took pride of place in their lounge. And I'm certain that Norman will have been adding up the expense, probably seething, but on that one occasion he appeared to be showing some compassion for his long-suffering wife.

Margaret had searched newspaper adverts for pianos for sale and eventually found one at a fair price. Then, she had the added expense of using a specialist removal company to transport it to her home safely. The piano had to be carefully manoeuvred through the small entrance porch and then through the narrow hall and into the lounge. Once it was safely in her home, as pleased as she was, in truth it cluttered up their lounge. But Margaret had achieved her lifelong desire with or without Norman's approval.

Though she never had any lessons, our daughter, Melanie, loved to tickle the ivories when she went for tea, playing Margaret and Norman her version of Chopsticks and more. Margaret also loved to play around on her treasured piano but never sought to have lessons which I thought was odd. She had the time, the piano and the money to pay for them so what stopped her? Though she never admitted it, I was told that Norman was constantly on at her about the extravagant, unwanted piano. Well, it was unwanted by him, but Margaret obviously loved it.

But it was only a few months later that the removal company was back at Miser Mansion and taking the piano to a new home. I know that Norman will have slowly chipped away at his wife for spending money on something she couldn't and would never be able to play. No encouragement will have been given for her to at least try to learn. What Margaret wanted was irrelevant unless it was financially beneficial to Norman. The cost of the delivery and removal plus the purchase price of the piano will have constantly preyed on Norman's mind. Just how much interest had he lost on the money that had been frittered away? Though she never said anything I suspect Margaret's anger and frustration was quickly mounting due to the complete lack of any control over her life.

Now, imagine going out for a leisurely stroll every day and being expected to use the dirty, smelly public toilets on the way home, just so a few pence could be saved by not having to flush the toilet at home! Really? Yes really. Most folk would only enter a public toilet in sheer desperation. But to feel pressured into going to spend a penny for the sake of saving tuppence beggars belief. However, it is sadly true that Margaret went along with it. Why? Any normal wife would have given that idea short, sharp shrift. And having been a nurse Margaret would have known just how unhygienic public loos were. Was she afraid to say "no" to her husband? Norman was one very happy chap when he had a water meter installed. He could keep a careful eye on his meter readings which was far more important than having his wife suffering the stench from the germ riddled public toilets. And I have no doubt he will have seriously rationed the amount of water used each day, cutting back as far as possible.

In winter, having a daily stroll meant not having to have the gas fire on for an hour or so. But returning to a chilly home meant nothing compared to the savings he made. It was a win win situation for Norman, but it was Margaret's pensions that were paying all the household bills at that point! And still she kept quiet, going along with his penny-pinching ideas that were getting more and more extreme.

Once she was back to near normal health Margaret gained a bit of a reputation in our small village for being very outspoken, often airing her views where they were not wanted or needed. She could no longer assert her authority at work or in her home, so the local shop assistants, librarians and teachers were all subjected to a verbal tongue lashing at some time or other. It was usually trivial things that Margaret kicked off about. One instance was while she was reading the free daily newspaper in the library when a teacher from the local junior school brought her class to choose new books. The young children were chattering as they searched the shelves for suitable reading material. The poor teacher didn't know what had hit her as Margaret stormed up behind her, barking personal insults and questioning the woman's teaching abilities for all to hear. And what had upset Margaret so badly? The children were not observing the rule of silence! Well, the fact was that the children's section never had a "Silence" rule to follow. How did I find out about her upsetting outburst? One of my daughters was among those children in the library!

That afternoon I went to pick up my girls from school and Lyndsay told me what her grandmother had said and done that day to upset her class teacher. I felt compelled to speak to the teacher and apologise for Margaret's behaviour. The teacher really was upset, but after telling her she was not alone and hadn't been the only person to be singled out for some unnecessary verbal abuse, she was a little calmer. There were no excuses for Margaret's behaviour, but I had a bloody good idea what the real cause was. In a word: Norman.

It seemed Margaret wasn't keeping her nasty verbal outbursts to just me and the poor folk in our village. As I've stated in a previous chapter, Margaret made a weekly trip to a market where she bought ginger biscuits and sherbet lemons. Well, when she first started buying these I was working as a catering assistant at a grammar school (better known as a school dinner lady). My job was to make sandwiches and then work the cash register, taking payment off the kids for their meals. But we had a couple of women who came in for just two hours a day to do the washing up, which there was an abundance of. It was hot, hard work scrubbing a huge number of dirty plates, pans and dishes within a specific time frame.

Now, one of these ladies was called Denise and she was a physically large lady, not fat but tall and perhaps a little manly in stature. With her wearing spectacles I often though she looked a little like Dame Edna Everage, but she was a nice enough woman. So, one day we were all having our lunch sat around a table, catching up with any gossip, like women do. It was a Wednesday and Denise had been shopping to the market before coming to work. But she had suffered a rather nasty encounter with a woman while shopping and was still furious and upset at the verbal insults she had received from a stranger, while looking over a pile of second-hand clothing on a market stall. What was the cause for this? While sorting through the items strewn across the stall, she had picked up an item that another woman was also eyeing up. Denise was accused of snatching it from the hands of this other woman though Denise was adamant that she hadn't. The female stranger launched a verbal attack on her saying she knew what Denise and her *ilk* were like and much more. The description of the word *ilk* means a type of person one generally dislikes. What did this stranger know about Denise? Nothing, because they had never met before. So, who was this woman who disliked Denise and her *ilk*?

The description Denise gave of the woman with a venomous tongue matched that of my mother-in-law! But there was one important detail that confirmed to me I was right in my suspicions. The verbal abuser had a very prominent black mole on her chin. Coupled with the woman having hair in a tight bun, thick rimmed glasses and a beige raincoat like Margaret wore I was in no doubt who Denise had been confronted by. And the word *ilk* was exactly the sort of description Margaret would and had previously used. So, I ask, just who did Margaret think she was to dish out such an insult to a woman who was living on a tight budget and simply looking for a bargain item?

Another of Margaret's viscous tongue lashings was targeted on her own younger sister. It was brought about after we'd had a family gathering in a local restaurant to celebrate Margaret's brother's birthday. This was the celebration where Margaret had told everyone about how they were paying for our forthcoming cruise. Someone had suggested that we guests paid for our own meals and chipped in a couple of pounds each to cover the cost of the birthday boy's meal and that of his wife. Margaret's sister had passed on the suggestion to all concerned and happily, we all chipped in. After all it wasn't a lot to give but it was a nice gesture for a lovely couple.

A few days later, when Margaret's younger sister left her place of work, someone was anxiously waiting outside to talk to her. Who was waiting outside? Yes, it was Margaret with all guns blazing, determined to give her sibling a right ear bashing. Now having been on the receiving end of Margaret's acidic tongue far too many times, I can imagine how vicious her comments will have been. Basically, Norman and Margaret were not happy at being put in a compromising position of having to pay towards her brother's birthday meal! Spending a penny more than they needed had obviously upset them. Or was it Norman that was the smoking gun and he had sent his wife to fire the bullets? Either way, Margaret reduced her younger sister to tears and all for a few pounds. And bearing in mind that it was Margaret's brother who had paid for their wedding taxis when Norman was a penniless bridegroom makes it a despicable act in my opinion.

I was too often on the receiving end of Margaret's angry outbursts, be it my choice of clothing or my choice of haircuts for my three daughters. It didn't matter because if she didn't like what she saw, then she was quick to air her disapproval in a nasty way. On one memorable occasion Margaret had called to look at the television listings in our daily newspaper, just as I was serving my girls with their tea. Chris wasn't coming home that evening, so it was just me and our three girls sat at our dining table with dinner plates full of eggs, homemade chips and beans. It was early January and on our dining table I had placed various jars of pickles that were left over from Christmas, along with the usual condiments and a bottle of HP sauce. Margaret took one look at the table and started mumbling about something being bloody ridiculous to which I assumed she didn't approve of the abundance of pickle jars. Or maybe it was what I had cooked for my girls. What had I done wrong? The pickles needed eating, the girls wanted to eat them and were happy with what I had dished up for tea, so I could only assume she disapproved of us having so much choice. And it wasn't as if she was being asked to pay for anything. But she would never show that side of her behaviour in her son's presence. It was always aimed at me.

One year, ski trousers were back in fashion. So, I bought each of my girls a pair of black ski pants and brightly coloured bat wing jumpers to wear with them. Margaret turned up one day as my girls were wearing their new outfits. She went straight into a rant about me dressing my girls as bait for paedophiles!!! These were ski pants and jumpers that covered most of their bodies. You would have thought I'd got them dressed in erotic underwear the way she kicked off. Totally uncalled for and way over the top. I wasn't a fit mother it seemed. Well, that went down well with me as you can imagine.

I was also a bad mother for allowing our eldest girl to have her hair cut into a short 'n spiky hairstyle that was very fashionable at the time. Margaret had lectured our daughter about her new hairstyle looking ridiculous whilst having tea at Miser Mansion one day. What Margaret didn't know was that I also had had my hair cut into the spiky style. She kept quiet when she saw me and my new hairstyle that day, but my daughter was quick to tell me all that had been said when Margaret was told about my new spiky haircut.

And another very trivial thing that had Margaret spitting venom was a pair of white ankle socks. Yes, a pair of socks! And what was so bad about an innocent pair of socks? Well, because our eldest girl, who was at high school at that time, had asked me to buy her a pair of thick white ankle socks to wear for school, I did. That was my crime. It was on one of Margaret's flying visits to ours, to read my Daily Express television listings, that she spotted our girl wearing the socks. “Bloody disgusting!” was the comment she made as she stormed out of my home. What was so awful about a girl wearing white ankle socks? Yes, they were thicker than most because they were probably classed as boy’s socks, but was that so awful? Something so trivial was enough to light the blue touch paper and ignite Margaret’s temper and frustration.

Another example of Margaret’s unnecessary shows of anger was way back in the early 80’s when it was my eldest daughter’s birthday. We were having a small party for her at home with a few school friends, nothing more. It was a Saturday morning in December and my mother had called down to see her eldest grandchild on her birthday, as you do. She hadn’t been specifically invited because she was welcome to come to my home at any time. But then we had another unexpected visitor. Margaret’s elder sister called in to give my daughter a birthday card, nothing more, nothing pre-arranged. And then there was another knock on my door. It was Margaret who was not expecting to see my two adult guests who were by that time mucking in with preparing the buffet for the kids. Within a second of setting foot in the kitchen Margaret was snarling and hissing at me about it being obvious why she wasn’t invited to the party and that she knew her place. Then she stormed out, almost taking the kitchen door of its hinges before any of us had a chance to explain. It wasn’t long after that Chris arrived home from work oblivious to the upset and I wasn’t going to enlighten him.

Later that day after the party ended, I marched round to Miser Mansion all guns blazing ready to give Margaret a dose of her own medicine. When I got there Norman let me in and I marched straight past him to confront his wife. Boy did I let rip! I put her firmly in the picture about the party and then told her I knew they didn’t think I was a good wife or mother and that I also knew they didn’t think I was good enough for their son. They were gobsmacked! The worm had turned. Between them they waffled some apologies saying they didn’t think I was a bad mother, but I wasn’t listening. I’d already started to walk away. But Margaret then asked if Chris knew about the day’s events or know the reason for me coming to see Margaret? No! I made it clear that it was me and me alone behind my visit. That seemed to be the answer Margaret wanted. She never, ever, criticised me when her son was present and never showed him her nasty side.

Now, whatever I said in anger that evening must have hit a raw nerve. A couple of weeks later, the day before Christmas Eve, Margaret called at our house. She was very sheepish when I opened the door and let her in. She wanted to know if they could buy our girls new bicycles for Christmas! I shrugged as if not bothered either way and carried on with my cleaning, flicking a duster over our polished surfaces. I had already sorted out my daughters Christmas presents and wasn't desperate for them to have bikes.

Anyway, on Christmas Eve two bikes were brought round to ours and some cash to buy our youngest child a new pushchair. She was growing out of her pram and though I had a suitable pushchair that had been used for our second daughter I was planning on buying a new one. I said nothing as she made her peace offering knowing it wouldn't be the last time I crossed swords with Margaret.

Now, there was one occasion when I was practically accused of stealing by Margaret. For whatever ridiculous reason our three girls had, they all decided to spin Margaret and Norman a lie about me shoplifting! They had been to tea at Miser Mansion one day and on their return home I was confronted by Margaret the second they all got over our threshold. Was it right that I had been caught shoplifting and was going to appear in court for it? Err . . . No! Why did she think that? Well, my darling daughters had told my in-laws that I had indeed stolen a few items from a supermarket that had little value though I can't now remember exactly what those items were. Why? Because they thought it would be a laugh to wind up my in-laws or something like that. Unbelievable. But what I did notice was the anger on Margaret's face as she asked me about my imaginary crime. She thought I was guilty before getting the facts from the horse's mouth. Did she want to believe I'd become a thief? What if I had, would she have tried to understand why I may have committed the crime? I suspect it was the threat of my name being printed in the local newspaper, bringing their name into disrepute. And though I made it clear that the girls had been playing a prank, albeit a stupid one, I strongly suspect that Margaret will have scanned the local newspaper's court reports every week for the next few months, just in case I had lied. As you can imagine when Margaret had stormed off home, I had words with my girls about how their silly lie had caused a lot of upset.

Another occasion when Margaret came calling, full of fury, was when our eldest girl was about thirteen. One night she had been out with her mates, hanging out together like young teenagers did back then. She arrived home at the time we had agreed and made a confession to me. She had been having a crafty cigarette with her friends and been seen by Margaret's elder sister. My daughter knew that it was a sure thing that her being caught having a crafty smoke would get back to Margaret and me, so she had come clean before any wagging tongues could get to me first.

As a lifelong non-smoker who married a smoker, this didn't alarm me. At school most of my friends had tried smoking while underage though I found it repulsive. It was what young folk did and as much as I wasn't happy that my daughter had succumbed to having a crafty cigarette it didn't have me recoiling in horror. In the scheme of things, it was far better than her trying out drugs. I wasn't going to lose any sleep about it and was thankful that my girl had chosen to confess to me.

Well, true to form, just a couple of days later I had a visit from a very angry mother-in -law. Did I know my unruly daughter was smoking? Yes, I did! What was I going to do about it? Nothing! Well, that really had Margaret fired up which I thought was very hypocritical as she was a smoker! Margaret often used the excuse of coming to our house so she could have a cigarette away from a disapproving Norman. Kettle calling pan or what? I was an irresponsible mother in Margaret's opinion. No surprise there. My girls would never amount to much in her opinion. And I knew that she was hoping one of our girls would want to take up a career in nursing, just like she had, but that was never going to happen.

As it will have become obvious, I was an easy target for Margaret to vent her anger at. I strongly suspect that all her anger was caused by her miserable life with Norman. She had lost a job she loved and been highly respected in her profession. Suddenly she had no say over what happened in her life. It often felt that I could do no right for doing wrong in Margaret's eyes.

And it became obvious to me over the years that she had a very awkward relationship with her only son. She knew little about his personality which I assume was due to him spending so much time as a child with his grandparents while she and Norman were at work. She once told me that Chris hated cats and would never have one as a pet. This was early on in our relationship when Margaret learned that my family had two cats. Well, little did she know, but when we were engaged her son would often call at the local chippy on his way to my home and buy a fish as a treat for our two cats. He loved playing with our moggies, rewarding them with prime haddock. And when we married and finally moved into our new bungalow, Chris came home from work one day with a ginger kitten that he had brought from a litter at a mill he had been delivering to. Then he turned up about three weeks later with another kitten! This was the runt of a litter from another feral cat at the same mill, but the poor mite had deformed back legs. Chris had overheard someone suggesting that the lame kitten should be destroyed by driving a lorry over its frail body. He quickly moved the kitten into the safety of his cab until he had finished his multi crop deliveries. Both kittens lived long lives full of luxury and love with us. Does that sound like a man who hated cats? But I am sure Margaret always thought it was me who had brought those kittens into our lives and the many more cats that followed.

When I met Margaret for the first time, she wore her hair in a tight bun and did so for many years after. Then on one occasion in the 1980's she threw caution to the wind and had her long hair chopped down to just above shoulder length and Norman wasn't too happy about it. In my opinion it was an improvement from the stern unimaginative bun. But the new style didn't last long. After all, haircuts cost money while pulling her long locks into a bun cost nothing. I wonder who influenced her decision to grow her again and why?

Then, Margaret found another way to vent her anger by writing to the local newspapers to express her views about current affairs or local issues and she became well known locally for her strong opinions. I do think she was desperate to have her voice heard even if she couldn't have any say in her home life.

On one occasion Margaret had got on her high horse, desperate to be heard and booked the main room in the town hall to hold a public meeting about some changes being made to council rates that she disagreed with. And she had an acquaintance, who was a local councillor and was willing to go along and support Margaret. I went along to the well-attended meeting, and it was obvious when Margaret got up to speak that she was in her element. She had the respect of her audience which probably reminded her of what she had lost when she retired. Now if she ever told Norman that there was a fee for hiring the room I don't know but suspect not because at the end of the meeting Margaret asked if everyone could donate towards the cost!

On another occasion Margaret got on her high horse about the introduction of new rules about paying for care home fees and how some poor souls would have to sell their homes to foot the bill. Determined to make her feelings known she wanted to organise a protest march down Whitehall! When I heard about her plan, in Norman's presence, I offered to organise a coach to take supporters down to London. I added that we would need to get a taxi from the coach station or take the tube. Well, this was obviously worrying to Norman who mumbled something about it being costly. And sadly, this was the last I heard about it. I can only imagine that he had put his foot down about the financial strain on his bank account! Once again, he had quashed her plans.

Now through her letters in both our local and national newspapers, which were always very well written and had valid points to make, Margaret came to the attention of the local Conservative party. So, when she was approached about standing as a councillor in the forthcoming local elections she must have been elated. Finally, someone was interested in what Margaret had to say and respected her views. And she really would have been a force to be reckoned with in the council meetings. She would have made the late Maggie Thatcher look a pushover. But once again her hopes and ambitions ended before they had begun. Why?

If Margaret had stood in the election, I am certain she would have won a place on the council. Now, that would have meant regular trips to the council chambers. And as meetings were usually in the evening, finishing late, that would probably have meant her getting a train or a taxi home. Taxi? Taxi's cost money! And regular meetings would have meant her being away from home more, throwing Norman's strict regime into disarray. And there would have been the regular social events and maybe a mayor's ball to attend. And of course, Margaret would have wanted to dress accordingly and not attend in her charity shop wardrobe.

She had once managed to look the part when appearing on television and then returned her outfit to Marks and Spencer, but Margaret couldn't borrow decent clothes from the famous store on a regular basis. The bottom line was that if she was to stand for election it would be costly and time consuming. And the downtrodden wife may have got even more ideas above her station after mixing with other likeminded people. That may have suited Margaret but certainly not her husband so that was another wasted opportunity to be her own person. Norman was having none of it. If it had been me, knowing I had no money worries to hold me back, I would have told Norman to put up or shut up. The threat of divorce would have sent shivers down Norman's spine just thinking about having to split his money down the middle. But that is what I would have done and not what Margaret had the courage to do. So, it's not surprising that all her frustration, anger and resentment had to be released somehow and aimed at someone. Sadly, I was too often the one on the receiving end of it all.

Nobody was exempt from getting a tongue lashing from Margaret, not even her GP. She had been to the surgery one day to make an appointment, not having the benefit of having a telephone to ring for one. All the appointments were taken by the time she arrived on their doorstep which must have annoyed Margaret. After a face-to-face confrontation with a staff member and losing the argument when she demanded to be seen, Margaret's anger exploded. In no uncertain terms she told the staff and her regular doctor where they could shove their appointments and that she would be registering herself and

Norman at another practice. Her frustration was possibly because she was being reminded that her previous status in the world of nursing no longer counted for anything. She was just another patient with no special privileges.

Anything and everything seemed to anger Margaret. She once blew her top over an exceptionally silly matter. My mother treated Chris as family, often making more of an effort to please him than me! That was fine by me when she came bearing little gifts for him. Then one day she turned up with a pair of boxer shorts for Chris. But not just any old boxer shorts. These had Postman Pat on them! She'd seen them on display on a market stall and as they were cheap, she had bought Chris a pair as a bit of a joke. And he wore them! But on one occasion Margaret came calling as I was folding my washing into a neat pile. She spotted the shorts and asked what they were in a very snooty voice. On being told that my mum had bought them for Chris she sneered as she said, "Bloody disgusting!". Why were the boxer shorts disgusting? Was it jealousy that my mum had bought her son such a personal item or was she just angry and needed any excuse to vent her anger? You decide because I couldn't. Or was Margaret simply jealous of my mother having such a good relationship with Chris when she hadn't?

And even a blind man could see how there was such a huge difference in the relationships between our girls and their grandmothers. Margaret must have been aware of this and possibly jealous of my mother. But who's fault was that? You only get out of a relationship what you put into it. My girls witnessed so many of Margaret's temper tantrums when she vented her anger at me and as young as they were they may have held grudges for her doing so.

Whose fault was it that Margaret never gave her family any gifts without it being a special occasion or after a nasty argument. I don't even remember receiving a gift of any kind when any of my babies were born, not even a simple Babygro. Yet both of Margaret's sisters turned up with items of clothing for all my new editions to the family. And thinking about it, I don't remember her wanting to pick up and cuddle any of my babies on first meeting them. For a midwife who was used to handling babies you would think it would have been second nature. On the two occasions I saw each of my grandchildren for the first time it was natural to want to hold them close to me, bonding for the future. But that was me and not her.

Now, fast forward to December 1994 when I decided to invite my in-laws for Christmas dinner at ours. Why? Well, my father had died in November, so it was our first Christmas without him. Instead of anyone going to Miser Mansion for dinner, I suggested they came to us for a change. I'd asked my mother to come dine with us and as I was making a dinner anyway what difference did two more guests make? So, it was all arranged for us to dine at 3.00pm. Chris, my mother and our two eldest girls and I would go out for a pre-dinner drink, leaving our youngest girl watching the turkey cooking. Margaret and Norman were to arrive at ours for 3.00pm, choosing not to join us for a drink. Everyone was happy with the arrangements, or so I thought.

So, bearing in mind the disastrous pie and pea Christmas dinner we had when first married, I was determined to show my in-laws exactly what a Christmas dinner should be like. I bought a variety of fresh vegetables and not just the obligatory sprouts. I also chose a luxury Christmas pudding that would serve eight of us, a large turkey and much more. I was going to push the boat out and see just how much my in-laws could eat when it wasn't them paying for it. Come Christmas Eve I was all sorted with vegetables prepped and more. Unlike our disastrous dinner of 1972, I was feeling confident that our Christmas dinner would be a success. Then we had an unexpected visitor about 6.00pm.

Margaret had come to tell me that she and Norman wouldn't be dining with us after all! Why? Well, Norman wanted his dinner at noon she said and didn't want to wait until 3.00pm. I couldn't decide whether to be angry at being given such short notice or relieved at not having to entertain them! I strongly suspect it was Norman who was being awkward but as usual he sent his messenger to deliver the news. How would Norman have felt if he had spent money on extra food for guests and then they didn't turn up? Furious! He would have gone ballistic at the money wasted. But again, Margaret had let him call the shots. And as it happened none of the food went to waste.

If I am painting a picture of how angry Margaret had become, then it is only fair that I reveal what she was like when she was once let off the short choke chain Norman used to control her. One rare occasion was on a day out to Blackpool. I can't remember how it came about but a coach trip to the famous illuminations was planned for me, my mother, Margaret and her elder sister (who I considered a friend) and my three young girls. So, off we went for a day at the seaside.

I had cash in my purse to spend on my girls not giving a thought to what cash Margaret may have taken with her, if any. But she was to surprise us all that day. From hitting the Golden mile Margaret wanted to spend, spend, spend. She wanted to go in the famous Blackpool Tower including the circus and ballroom, ride in a landau along the promenade and walk round the Pleasure Beach. And she seemed happy to get her hand in her pocket to pay for these. After buying my girls novelty hats to wear she wanted to play on the slot machines, not caring that she would never come off winning. And to end a very busy day she insisted on buying the girls sticks of Blackpool rock and not just a small stick. No, she insisted that they had the more expensive striped walking sticks. Then once back on the coach, as we settled down for the journey home, she passed me a handful of cash saying, "I took it to spend so I'm not taking it home, give it to the girls!" It wasn't a lot of cash she passed to me but what did that tell me?

Margaret had behaved that day like an animal that had spent its life being caged up and had suddenly found freedom. Simple pleasures we take for granted she had been denied. How many times had she pounded Blackpool promenade with Norman, wanting to spend a few pence in the amusements, just having a little bit of fun on her holiday. How often had she wanted to ditch their trusty thermos flask and ginger biscuits and buy a hot dog on the sea front or savour a bag of chips? Was it too much to ask of Norman to spend a few pounds and allow his wife a little fun? After all it was Margaret's good salary and later her private pension that was helping Norman achieve his ambition. How Margaret had managed to syphon off some spare cash to spend that day I don't know. Did she ever tell Norman how frivolous she had been that day and how much she had enjoyed herself experiencing a few simple pleasures? Doubtful. But her behaviour that day said it all.

And I was reliably informed that Margaret never forgot that her brother had paid for the taxis to her wedding. Decades later, on hearing that her brother was travelling to America for a special wedding anniversary holiday, Margaret gave him some dollars and a note saying the cash was to repay the cost of the taxis, with interest. I doubt Norman knew about this. I can only surmise that she really did have a heart and a conscience but hid them well.

Most grandparents I know have a toy box in readiness for a visit from their young grandchildren. I certainly have and so do my friends. Many of the toys and games have been passed down or are from charity shops, costing little but worth a fortune if they entertain our little ones. And playing games with our young ones is also a way of bonding with them, laughing and having fun together, the age gap disappearing during those precious hours. This was something my girls never had at Miser Mansion. If they wanted to play, Norman would get out his collection of rubber bands, paper clips and those small wires that can be twisted and used to seal a bag. Playing silly games together was something else Margaret was either denied or chose not to do. Is it any wonder I had to bribe the girls to go for their tea each week? But she did on occasions show her creative side when any of our girls were needing fancy dress costumes. Margaret was very good at turning old clothes into exceptionally good outfits that were immediately recognisable.

Another instance of Margaret being mentally frustrated was when she decided to write a novel. I suspect the idea came to her when she discovered it was my ambition to write a best seller. At that time, I had taken up entering consumer competitions as a hobby and was being very successful at it. I'd found it very easy to write ten-word slogans and was entering numerous competitions every day and winning most of them! Then I progressed to writing small articles for magazines and was receiving financial rewards. I'd had an idea for a novel many years before I got around to writing one and had once mentioned this in conversation with Margaret. By this time, she had got used to seeing her letters being regularly published in numerous newspapers so possibly saw writing a novel as an extension of her newfound writing skills. It was only a few weeks later that she sent me the first three chapters of a story she had started writing. They were written in pencil on A4 paper which she wanted me to read and give my opinion. This went on for months until she had a completed novel in her hands.

Now, once her work was completed what was she going to do with it? Well, Margaret paid someone who she knew to type it out. Then what? The internet wasn't something most of us were familiar with or had access to back then, so Margaret's only option was to post her completed work to publishing companies. The weight of the paper would have made it very expensive to post and once the only copy of her work had been sent off to a publisher, she wouldn't have had another copy to keep or post to other publishers. To have her manuscript photocopied numerous times would have proved expensive. The cost of trying to get her book into print would have been far more than she ever expected or was prepared to pay. And had Norman discovered the cost of everything he would have not been happy. Unless she could have generated an income from her writing Norman would have seen it as a waste of time and money. So, her manuscript was put to one side, never to be read by anyone but Margaret and me.

Well, that was the case until Margaret was in her eighties and had started to be seriously ill. By that time, I had already had a few novels of my own published. I asked if I could have Margaret's novel to put onto a Word document, with a view to submitting it online to publishing companies. She agreed but had died before I'd finished converting it from paper to a Word document. I still have the novel stored on my laptop and the original paper copy. At some point, I would like to see the romantic novel Margaret wrote widely available as a paperback. I won't be claiming the credit for it either. I will use the pen name she had chosen, Mae Austin. Those were the Christian names of her parents.

Looking back, Margaret's outbursts of insults and criticism about me and my children could have caused problems in my marriage. In anger, had I told Chris about my many confrontations with his mother it may have caused us to argue. But the way I saw it was that he couldn't be held responsible for what Margaret said or did. She never showed any hint of anger in his presence. So, I kept schtum about her, never criticising her in his presence. There was no way I was going to let Margaret come between me and my husband or break up my family. And who knows, maybe she was jealous of me and what I had. I had a husband who didn't want to hold me back but encouraged me in any new pursuits or hobbies I took up. And over the years I have had many! I had a natural mother/daughter relationship with all my girls. My social life was good, and I had close friends to enhance that. I may not have always had a healthy bank balance, but I was more than happy with my lot. Margaret had none of these, just what Norman allowed her to have.

In an earlier chapter I commented about how Margaret had changed from glamourous to grinch. Now I may not have been around when Margaret was a young, carefree teenager but I did see a different side to her in the early years of my marriage.

Before we had our first child there was a period when my parents had started to join us at the local Liberal club on Saturday evenings. And when asked to join us on occasions, Margaret and Norman did so! Margaret seemed to enjoy herself even though it was obvious that Norman wasn't prepared to really let his hair down and have some fun. He was happy to sit swishing his pint while Margaret got a taste for a popular drink called a Pony. This was sherry with a kick, it claimed, and both my mother and Margaret seemed to think it lived up to expectations.

I honestly believe that for that short period Margaret enjoyed having a social life, escaping the miserable conditions she lived with at home. As for Norman. . . he will have been thinking of just how much money was being thrown away on drink. So, when we had our first child it was the excuse Norman needed to not fritter away his hard-earned cash on alcohol. Instead, he and Margaret offered to babysit on Saturday nights. My parents had already made it clear they were happy to care for their much-loved granddaughter which had prompted my in-laws to offer their services. So, on alternate Saturday nights we left our children with Margaret and Norman. There was one big difference though. My parents always enjoyed looking after our daughter and the two other girls we eventually had. But it quickly became more of a nuisance to Norman who didn't like disruption to his daily routines. He liked to work on Sundays for the extra money so needed to go to bed early. He wasn't amused when we arrived home after the pubs shut! The love he had for money always ranked much higher than the love he had for his grandchildren.

Chapter 17

Moving on up, moving on out!

Now, as people get older it is often the case that they move out of houses and into bungalows or maybe a ground floor flat. It makes perfect sense that living on one level is easier than having to climb stairs as we age. So, what possessed Margaret and Norman to move out of a lovely bungalow they were proud of, which was within spitting distance from us, that had flat gardens and a convenience store quite close to it? Why did they choose to go live in a council flat? And it wasn't a ground floor flat they moved into but a top flat in a block of four. So, they had moved out of Miser Mansion and into Cell Block H! Well, that was my first impression of the property they had moved to.

How they were able to be allocated a council property when they were living in very suitable accommodation remains a mystery. They certainly hadn't been on any housing list and had they been would have had little or no points. My suspicions were that Margaret just happened to know a local Conservative councillor, who had then become the mayor. So, I suspect a few strings were pulled in the council's housing department.

The stairs leading up to their new council flat were communal, made of concrete and quite steep. Yes, the flat was close to the village centre and the shops, but no closer than the local convenience shop they were near before. Nor did the flat have a balcony to sit out on, just a communal outdoor area. Another factor that had me pondering was the fact that there would be rent to be paid on the flat. So, again, why move from a mortgage free bungalow in your advancing years into a first-floor council flat and start paying rent?

The answer was given to me by Margaret's elder sister: Money, money, money! The market value of their bungalow was

£152,000 at the time they sold up. Banking the cash from the sale of their home took Norman within touching distance of having a million pounds to his name. That fact was more important than the negative aspects of moving into a top flat and paying rent. Again, it appears Margaret, who had always loved her bungalow, just went along with her husband's plans regardless of what she may have wanted.

One excuse Margaret gave for wanting to move out of the bungalow she loved was her failing eyesight. Yes, she did have poor eyesight, but she was using the excuse that she feared for her safety when crossing the main road, especially the very busy crossroads that she had to use to get to the local shops. It was a valid point, as anyone who has had to cross at any busy traffic lights will know. Far too many motorists take little or no notice of the traffic lights, chancing going through at red, with pedestrians taking their life in their hands to cross the road. But she could have walked the alternative route and used the pelican crossing a few yards down the road.

But then Norman told me the reason for their move was because Margaret feared for *his* safety when crossing the main road. Both just excuses to justify their odd behaviour. I didn't believe their excuses for a second because before and after Margaret died, Norman used to walk miles almost every day, crossing numerous main roads on his travels.

Before they moved, when Margaret's younger sister suggested getting a taxi once a week to take her shopping to a large supermarket to avoid the dreaded crossroads, Margaret's response was. . . "Taxis cost money!" She obviously didn't want to splash out once a week on a taxi for shopping or was she afraid to suggest it to Norman? I know what I think. And of course, without a telephone to hand how could Margaret ring for a taxi?

So, the couple moved into their new abode, but it needed improvements to make it homely. I didn't visit the flat for a long time after they moved in so never saw the original state it was in. From what Chris has told me Norman found some ex-display kitchen units going very cheap at a local DIY shop. The price must have been good, or he wouldn't have bought them. And he certainly wasn't going to pay for the delivery of them either so what did Norman do? I was told that he carried each unit home on the bus, one unit at a time. I have no reason to think this is a lie. Norman had made and fitted kitchen units for their bungalow years earlier so he had some skills that would help him re-fit the flat's small kitchen. Did he request permission from the council to fit kitchen units? Doubtful.

Norman built a small fireplace in the lounge of their new home though the room wasn't designed for one. But they never had any type of fire installed, choosing a large flower display to fill the gap where a fire might go. And once again the tiled back of their newly built fireplace held Norman's famous trademark. When I first saw it, I noticed the five lines of beige tiles were all nicely lined up but my eye caught sight of the bottom line. He'd only gone and put a line of tiles that were out of sync and used two bits of tiles instead of a full one again. To me it was so obvious I couldn't believe it. My eyes were drawn to the bodged area every time I visited. It was a reminder of the bodged tiling job he'd previously done for us. Why did he spoil what was a half decent job by trying to save the cost of one ceramic tile? Why didn't Margaret say something because she couldn't possibly have missed seeing the fault?

Norman was totally obsessed with saving money even when it was someone else who was footing the bill. Years earlier, he'd been far too eager to help decorate our eldest girl's first home, a ground floor flat, when she moved in with her soon to be husband. Why he thought his services were even needed was a mystery. Our daughter's fiancé was a painter and decorator, so they didn't have a problem with getting their flat painted. But Norman was adamant that he had holiday to take and would be able to do the painting while the couple were at work. Reluctantly, Norman was let loose with a tin of emulsion, a paint brush and four bare walls. How can I describe his handywork? Slapdash? Yes! And it was obvious Norman had been very economical with the paint. The walls were covered with streaks of paint that had either been watered down to make it go further or he'd stretched each brushful of paint to the max. Another false economy. The damage was put right by the couple later by giving the walls two decent coats of paint, but they had to buy extra paint to cover up Norman's slapdash effort. A few months later when they moved out of the rented flat and into a house. Norman's decorating services were not sought!

I'm not sure if it was when my in-laws were allocated the flat or just after moving into their new home that the council wanted to update the old heating system. Instead of electric overnight storage heaters which were years old, a new boiler and radiators were to be installed by the council, at no extra cost. But it was a great big "NO!" from Norman. He reckoned that the heat from the flat below would warm their home, as would the heat from the flat at the other side of the main lounge wall. Well, some would beg to differ, but it was a theory that to his dying day he stuck to, only turning on the electric storage heater in the lounge when the weather outside was exceptionally cold. The rest of the time it was back to wearing an extra layer of clothing, usually an old dressing gown. Even when his wife was suffering from Parkinson's disease in her late eighties it wasn't a good enough reason to be frivolous with the heating!

It wasn't long after their move into the flat that Norman reached his life's goal and had a million pounds invested in ISAs and insurance policies. To celebrate his achievement, Margaret's siblings and respective spouses were invited out for a meal in a local pub. Unfortunately, one sister and her husband had a holiday booked and couldn't accept Norman's very generous offer. I'm told that when our Norm was told he had two less guests to pay for he couldn't help but smile at knowing he would be forking out less cash to mark the occasion. But Margaret must have had her conscience pricked and sneaked an envelope with cash inside to treat the absent couple to a meal whilst on their holiday. Please take note that Norman's only son and his family were not invited to this celebratory meal. In fact, it was years later that I found out about this celebration. Again, it was obvious that close family didn't come first in Norman's book. And as a mother, why didn't Margaret want her son taking part in the celebrations? Was the meal all for show, so Norman could finally show Margaret's family that he was successful and had amounted to something after all? Probably.

So, his decision to sell their bungalow had helped him achieve his target but there were lot of negative issues to that decision. When Margaret's health started to deteriorate, before becoming seriously ill, she slowly lost her mobility and was housebound in a top flat. Had they been living on the ground floor she could have been helped to shuffle outside to spend some time in the fresh air and sunshine and able to meet others from the neighbouring flats. Instead, she was stuck inside month after month. She even wrote begging letters to the council asking to be re-housed in a bottom flat or a council bungalow. Margaret couldn't get out to post the letters herself and Norman must have refused to do so or lied about posting them, because I discovered a few of Margaret's letters in her personal belongings after she died, letters that were never posted because Norman wouldn't have wanted the expense of moving again and all it would entail. And what did Margaret's needs matter if he was worth the magic million that he had strived for?

And what was going through Norman's head when he came up with one suggestion is beyond me. They had been in the flat for over a decade and Margaret's ill health was starting to take its toll. So, what does Norman want to do? He wanted to buy the flat from the council! He had received a letter to say he could buy the flat for £40,000 and had seen one of the flats in another block go up for sale at almost double that price. Was he thinking of buying and then selling it off quickly? What he hadn't realised was that once he had bought the flat, he was responsible for the maintenance and repairs. In his ignorance he thought if the council did any improvements to others in the block, they would include his. Wrong! I quickly put him in the picture about how he would get a bill for a percentage of the cost. And he hadn't realised that if he had wanted to sell the flat, the council would insist on the flat being sold back to them for little or no profit, if it was within a specific number of years from buying the property. Norman was shocked on learning that but then suggested that he went ahead with buying the flat and when he and Margaret had passed away then Chris and I could move into it! No! No! No! First and foremost, I didn't like the flat which I always referred to as "Cell Block H". And why as we were getting older would we want to move into a top floor flat of any kind? But he'd seen ££££ signs flashing before his eyes when the council sent him that letter!

Numerous times I raised the touchy subject of having a telephone installed. It was always the same response: We don't need one! But to be fair to Margaret, she did eventually buy a very cheap and basic mobile phone on a pay as you go tariff. I suspect this must have been when she started having health issues and wanted to be able to contact help if needed. Norman was not amused when he realised the phone had to be put on charge every few days which would cost him a few pence every week.

True to form, he rationed the charging time and once she was housebound, he often didn't top up her phone card. When she became very frail and confused on a couple of occasions Margaret somehow managed to ring our landline but what she said didn't make sense. She was concerned about Norman needing a brain scan and insisted that his doctor would be taking Norman personally to Leeds for a scan. I think this was brought about by Norman having blackouts and Margaret being unable to get off the sofa to help him. We know he did have a few funny turns after she died and would wake up on the floor, yet he never told his doctor. And years later in the summer of 2022 Norman went on a coach trip to Oswaldtwistle Mills along with many of his neighbours from the surrounding flats. As everyone got settled, ready to tuck into the three-course lunch that was included in the price, Norman blacked out at the table, his nose in his bowl of soup! That must have been worrying for the poor folk who had organised the trip. But Norman regained consciousness and continued to eat his lunch. Well, if he'd paid for it, he certainly wasn't going to leave it. Now did he ever tell his GP about his blackouts? Doubtful.

On two other occasions Margaret rang us when Norman was out and insisted that we had a complete makeover of our home! She was insistent that we had a conservatory built, all new furnishings and more. What was going through her mind at that time? Regrets perhaps that she had not helped her family and made so many broken promises to us?

Norman lived the best part of a decade longer than his wife, still adamant that no telephone was needed. The old mobile that Margaret had used had been thrown in a drawer never to be used again. But not to be defeated, we gave him a second hand, big buttoned mobile, complete with sim card, to use in emergencies. And yet again the damn thing was either turned off or not charged.

It never occurred to him that it could be a lifeline for him in times of need. Or was it more important to save a few pence by not charging it? I know it was the latter.

Living alone with no telephone meant we couldn't check on Norman on a regular basis even if we had wanted to. He seemed content with that, but I had concerns when he began telling Chris about things and people he was seeing in his flat! On two occasions he told Chris he had seen a very tall Christmas tree in the corner of the room. The tree was beautifully decorated and on one occasion it fell over, landing in the middle of the lounge floor.

Then on another occasion he was adamant that his deceased wife had spent the night beside him in bed. And on a later occasion he had just got into bed when a young man crept out from behind the bedroom curtains, jumped over the bed and out of the door! Obviously my first thought was... dementia! What else could it be? However, after more internet searching, I discovered that there is a condition called Charles Bonnet Syndrome. It's caused by degenerative eyesight, usually in the elderly. Well, Norman had his cataracts removed decades earlier but never had a pair of prescription glasses. He'd managed with a magnifying glass or some old non-prescription reading glasses that had been passed on to him. If he could see the numbers in his passbooks that was all he needed from spectacles. No way would he invest in expensive prescription glasses.

And Norman had not been amused when I once arranged for Margaret to have a home visit from an optician. As much as she had never accepted me as a real family member I couldn't just stand back and see a sick old woman struggling to see. Years earlier she had needed jam jar bottom lenses, but modern lenses were much improved but still costly. So, when she became seriously ill and her eyesight deteriorated badly, she couldn't see their new television even though it had a large screen. But no sooner had she got her very expensive new glasses when her health rapidly went downhill. Norman probably saw the glasses that had cost him a few hundred pounds as a total waste of money if he couldn't then use them for himself. Margaret's welfare was always measured in cost and not her needs. So very sad and so very selfish.

Chapter 18

A swinging brick for a heart!

Margaret and Norman were married for over sixty years. Anyone who saw them on their walks around the area probably thought they were a truly devoted couple. Well, things were not quite like that.

Early in 2017 Margaret was eighty-seven years old and failing fast with Parkinson's disease. But she was trapped in a first floor flat, unable to get outside at any time other than by being physically carried out. But the steps up to their flat were quite steep and Norman who was then aged eighty-eight and wasn't strong or agile enough to carry her. So, while he went to sit outside with neighbours on sunny days his poor wife sat alone in her home that had become her prison.

Sadly, Margaret had to be admitted to hospital on a few occasions before her body gave in to her illness. But what I found so disgusting and upsetting was Norman's attitude towards her failing health. There were occasions when Margaret begged her husband to go to their neighbour's flat and ring for a doctor or an ambulance. On more than one occasion he refused, not wanting the fuss and secretly I suspect he knew that if she was assessed by doctors, they would say that Margaret needed carers coming into the home. Or she would need to be taken into residential care and either way it would be costly.

On one occasion he refused to ring for Margaret some medical help and set off on his daily walk. Margaret somehow managed to drag her frail body out of the flat and onto the landing to shout for help. A neighbour heard her distressed cries and rang for an ambulance. Norman had returned home before the paramedics arrived but made no effort to go with his distressed wife. He even commented to me that he'd watched the ambulance parked in the nearby carpark for nearly an hour before taking Margaret away. The crew were obviously caring for her while waiting for a slot to deliver her into A & E. So why didn't he sit with his wife in the ambulance until it was time to take her away?

Another occasion when Margaret felt desperate for help, she had to resort to slipping a note into Chris's jacket pocket when he had been sitting beside her on one of his Sunday morning visits. Unaware of the note, it was over five hours later when Chris was getting changed that he found it in his pocket. We'd been out for a lunchtime drink totally unaware of Margaret's cry for help. She was begging her son to ring for her an ambulance as Norman had repeatedly refused to do so. On a hunch I checked our landline for any messages only to find we had a message from the local hospital. Margaret had been admitted. So, off we dashed in a taxi to A & E, not sure what had happened to make Norman finally call an ambulance. Margaret was weak and on seeing her I doubted that she would ever be going home again. But she did. And again, Norman didn't feel the need to accompany his sick and confused wife in her hour of need.

Then there was another occasion when she had to be admitted in a confused state of mind. She was refusing to take off her clothes for the nursing staff. It was obvious Margaret was losing the plot and getting very anxious and agitated. On that occasion she came out with a classic speech that summed things up for me. "Do they know how much you are worth Norman? Do they know who they are talking to?" There she was, her days numbered, but still in her confused mind she was thinking about Norman's money. Please note that she referred to the money as Norman's and not hers or theirs! And sadly, no amount of money could have saved her.

On Margaret's final admission into hospital, we were visiting with Norman in tow when she begged a doctor to be taken into residential nursing care. She no longer wanted to live in the flat, afraid of being ill with no access to any help. She knew her days were numbered and wanted to be cared for properly. At that point I was unaware that Norman was having to carry Margaret from their bed to their sofa and to the toilet because she had no strength in her legs. But Norman was adamant that he could take care of her at home and would not acknowledge her plea. And of course, he had to mention the cost of such a stay in a care home, claiming he didn't have sufficient funds readily available. Where had I heard that comment before?

Now because of Margaret's failing health and Norman's reluctance to be shown how to use a cash dispenser, she had asked me to take her debit card and draw out cash for them when needed. It was the current account that all their pensions were paid into. I also took charge of dealing with fuel companies and council payments as well as their shopping. So, whenever I drew out cash for them, I got a receipt that showed the account balance. I knew exactly how much they had in their account. Norman was not amused when I said there was sufficient funds in that account to cover her fees for six months. That would have given him time to free up some of his ISAs and replenish the current account. He wasn't happy at my suggestion, but Margaret seemed relieved and was adamant she wanted to go into care.

The doctors assessed Margaret and had no qualms about her fragile state, agreeing that she should be in a nursing home. Meanwhile, Norman was still insisting that he could care for all Margaret's needs, but his claims were ignored by all. Hence, Margaret was moved to a care home about a couple of miles away from her home. It was me and Chris that went to the home to look around and not Norman. He was still sulking about how much it was going to cost him. But she only lived three weeks after arriving at the care home which proved that she knew she was dying and wanted proper 24/7 care. And Norman didn't have to withdraw any cash from his precious ISAs!

But I will never forget how callous Norman was during his wife's last few days on this earth. After three weeks of her health deteriorating daily, Margaret eventually slipped into a coma. Whenever he wanted to visit, Chris and I had taken it in turns to ferry Norman to the home, stay with Margaret for a while, then return later to bring Norman back home later in the day. On Good Friday, the day before she gasped her last breath, Chris had taken Norman to the care home at lunchtime and left him sitting beside his wife. I then went back at 4.00pm to see how Margaret was. She was unconscious, obviously in her last hours, so I asked if Norman wanted to stay the night with her. Did he want to be with her in her last hours? The nursing staff would have made sure he had food and drinks when needed. No! In the time I was there, all he spoke about was how much Margaret could pass on in her Will without paying inheritance tax! He laboured the point over and over, worried that some of his money would be leaving him and would be going to his son. But his wife hadn't yet died and if hearing is the last of our senses that we lose, then she may well have heard him prattling on about money. There wasn't a hint of emotion in him. I truly believe that Norman was more upset at the thoughts of losing some cash to his son and Margaret's excellent NHS pension than losing his wife. And he probably felt relief that the care home fees would not be mounting up even though at that time I was personally fighting for them to be free of charge. Before she was ill, Margaret had helped others to get free 24/7 care. My final words to Margaret, as I left her room for the last time were "I'll carry on your fight!" and I did.

It was around 2.00am on Easter Sunday morning I got the call to say Margaret had passed away and to ask me which undertaker they needed to contact. Norman having no phone meant that nobody could contact him with the sad news, but after seeing how he had behaved towards Margaret hours earlier I decided the news could wait until later that morning. And when we did go see him to tell him his wife of over sixty years had died, he showed no emotion of any kind.

I remember very clearly when the lovely lady from the undertakers visited us to plan funeral arrangements. She said she didn't want to upset Norman as she handed him a leaflet with the choice of coffins. "Oh, you won't upset me!" was his response. And she didn't! Now, even after all the years of confrontation I had with Margaret I found looking at the choice of coffins emotional, but not our Norman. Was he simply keeping a stiff upper lip? Doubtful!

Later, when the invoice for Margaret's care arrived, I continued to fight with Social Services about it. The home care fees should have been free due to her needing 24/7 nursing care. After many phone calls and sheer determination, I got the cost of her three weeks stay cancelled. I didn't do it for Norman but as a dutiful daughter-in-law for Margaret, who had campaigned for years and helped get free care home accommodation for others.

But all that happened over Margaret's last couple of days re-enforced my belief that money came first and foremost for Norman. And the cost of the funeral, catering at the wake, death certificates and probate fees were all taken out of Margaret's estate or paid from our current account. Not once did Norman ever ask how much anything cost or offer to get his hand in his pocket to pay for anything. So basically, it was Chris and I who footed the bill for the funeral as it was deducted from what money Margaret left in her Will. And it surprised us both that after all her years of studying and working in the nursing profession, Margaret had very little money in her own name. It was peanuts compared to what accounts had Norman's name on. And rumours ran rife in our hometown about how much Chris had inherited, fuelled by Norman's lies. Even the undertaker knew that she was handling the arrangements of a wealthy woman because she told me so! Someone had spoken to her and asked if her company was arranging Margaret's funeral and if so, did she know that the deceased was a millionaire! Had Margaret also been bragging about Norman's money? Though Margaret's name had been on some ISA accounts Norman still considered it all his.

Now, what is the most precious possession anyone can have? What must surely be the answer for the majority of normal folk is. . . their children. But Norman wasn't normal, and he certainly proved it to me in his last years. The last months of 2021 and all of 2022 saw Chris, Norman's only son, suffer the most horrible effects of having pancreatic cancer. A tumour blocking his bile duct was diagnosed. This caused Chris extreme suffering as he went through procedure after horrible procedure to halt the cancer and keep him alive until he could have a Whipple operation and hopefully save his life.

Nine admissions into hospital, with some for over a month at a time, were a trying time for Chris and me. Then of course we had our daughters and grandchildren equally worried and sickened at seeing him looking and being so ill. We all endured the endless setbacks with his treatment which started with a blood clot after having a stent put in his bile duct. This delayed chemotherapy and then we all got Covid. Worse was to follow. He had a stent put in his blocked stomach after a couple of horrendous and frightening bouts of projectile vomiting. After that, for a few weeks Chris could only eat ice cream, jelly or soup, nothing solid. Three times he developed sepsis due to blocked stents in his bile duct, coupled with severe adverse reactions to his chemotherapy. At least three times he was in great danger of dying from infection. If anything could go wrong to set back his operation it did.

The stress of seeing my husband of fifty years suffering, along with the uncertainty of him ever making a full recovery certainly took its toll on me. Living under the strain, I became ill physically and mentally having anxiety attacks and a horrible attack of cellulitis that completely covered my face. I couldn't go out in public for a couple of weeks due to looking so horrendous. We were both experiencing a nightmare that seemed to be never ending.

During the whole of that very stressful period both Chris and I were showered with an abundance of kindness from friends and acquaintances, all sending their love and best wishes for Chris to have a full recovery. I was truly humbled by the support I received during the nightmare I was living through. My closest friends were incredibly supportive and for that I will be eternally grateful. Then I reached out for help with my anxiety attacks and a lovely lady came to my rescue. She helped me overcome the panic and fear that was making me ill and my life almost unbearable at times. I will never be able to thank her enough for her patience and help. And even the chap who owned the local fish and chip shop insisted on sending Chris free haddock for his tea one day after hearing how he was struggling with chemotherapy side effects and had little appetite. It was one small, kind gesture that meant so much to me and I confess to shedding a few tears as I was handed the parcel of fish with that kind man's best wishes.

And how did all this trauma that Chris and I were going through affect Norman? Not one bit! When Chris was first admitted to hospital and finally diagnosed as having cancer in his bile duct, I told Norman the upsetting facts and how Chris was on a waiting list to have an operation that hopefully should save his life. I casually threw into our one-sided conversation that Chris could have his operation quicker if he was to go as a private patient. No matter how much detail I went into when telling him about his son's illness and the latest painful procedure he'd had to endure, Norman was unphased by it all. As a parent, if I'd had a million pounds sitting in bank accounts, then I would have jumped at the chance to get my child treated privately and swiftly. Norman chose not to respond to my comments which was the response I had expected but thought it worth a try.

Even when Chris was in grave danger of dying from sepsis on three occasions, Norman had no reaction. This was his only child, next of kin, his flesh and blood. Was he hiding his feelings? No! It mattered not one bit that his son was so ill, or his family were living with the fear of losing him. Did Norman have a heart? No! He had a swinging brick in its place. So how did I finally come to that conclusion? Well, not once did Norman ever ask about visiting his son. He could have gone visiting many times with me had he wished. But then I discovered something else that confirmed that he was truly heartless.

Norman had been out one day on one of his daily walks around the block when he met one of our male friends. Their brief conversation turned to Chris's health. Our friend, knowing what Norman was like, tried to drill into him just how ill Chris was and exactly how he had suffered some awful procedures and symptoms, even life-threatening ones. He even mentioned that Chris had been warned by his consultant there was a good chance of him not surviving his Whipple operation, hoping the reality of the situation would sink into Norman's one-track mind. Well, that was a waste of time. What was Norman's response to hearing such awful news about his only child? "I hope our Chris doesn't die before I do because I'll have to make another Will!"

So, there we had it! The thought of having to make a new Will was more troubling to Norman than his son's life. With that one statement I was done with my father-in law. He could die alone, rot in hell for all I cared. He just wasn't human and certainly undeserving of my respect let alone any sense of duty to care for him.

Chris did eventually have his operation, and he survived it. That day I'd been alone from 6.00am until 3.00pm when the consultant rang me to say the operation had gone as expected and Chris was in recovery. I thanked him, then ended our call before

I broke down and sobbed my heart out. No words can convey the relief and emotion I finally let out as I ended that phone call. After a few minutes I pulled myself together and started to make the phone calls and texts about the good news that everyone was waiting for. But out of sheer spite, I refused to go tell Norman the good news about his son surviving his operation. As far as I was concerned, he could stew for a few days, wondering if he needed to make a new Will! Three days passed before I forced myself to go see Norman. When I did give him the news it was accepted with not a hint of emotion.

Chris then had a slow recovery ahead of him that had numerous complications. But he survived and that was what we had all we wanted and prayed for. He finally came out of hospital the week before Christmas 2022. At no time did Norman think to ask one of his neighbours if he could use their phone to ring his son. Yet on an earlier occasion he had been to his neighbour's flat when he wanted us to know he had come home from a stay in hospital after getting Covid. He could ask his neighbour to ring us when it suited him but not to see how his son was. I rest my case.

On Christmas Day 2022 Chris felt duty bound to visit Norman with a gift. I was reluctant to see the miserable old sod but as Chris was not able to drive, I had to chauffer him. How can I describe Chris's appearance when he was discharged from hospital? Without exaggerating in any way, his naked body resembled one of those poor souls who survived the concentration camps. He was a walking skeleton. For weeks after he came home, Chris wore jogging bottoms under his jeans to stop it being so obvious that his legs were like matchsticks. Multiple layers of shirts and jumpers bulked up his torso. Chris's posture was that of an old man and walking was difficult due to nerve damage in his legs. But did Norman show any concern about his son's physical appearance? Did he even notice? Do I really need to answer that question?

So, when it came to buying Norman a festive gift. . . if I had to spend any money on him it wasn't going to be much. A bar of Aldi's economy chocolate and a bag of their cheap humbugs was sufficient I thought. After all Scrooge often made references to a humbug.

A few months later in 2023 Chris was back on chemotherapy again which meant a weekly trip to the hospital for bloods taking and a return visit the following day for his chemo session. During this time Norman had seen that interest rates had gone up on certain ISA accounts and he had two ISAs that had just come to fruition. He was determined he was going to get the new rate. So, he managed to get his backside out of his chair and clutching his precious pass books he struggled to catch a bus and visited the building society he used. When it came to making a few more pounds he could get out and about but not once did he ever express any desire to visit his sick son whether he was in or out of hospital. Norman's actions always confirmed my suspicions.

Months later, when Chris caught Covid again due to his very low white blood cell count, he developed a chest infection. Anyone who has had chemotherapy or lived with someone who has undergone chemotherapy will know how serious this can be. Chris was in danger of developing neutropenic sepsis, a condition often caused by having a low blood count, hence unable to fight off infection. We didn't know for a week or so that he had Covid and presumed his initial lethargy was due to the heatwave we were having. But being the dutiful son, he still insisted we went to do Norman's shopping as usual, though Chris was flagging, hanging over the trolley as we walked around the supermarket. Within a couple of days, he was having coughing spasms that made me think he had a chest infection. It was only on a whim that I thought to test Chris for Covid. We were shocked at his positive result. Hence, we had to make an urgent trip to the hospital's Acute Oncology department. There he had antibiotics given by a drip and finally allowed home from hospital with suitable medication after threats of him having to stay in for twenty-four hours. Days later, Chris was still being a dutiful son and went to get Norman's shopping list. He'd tested negative by that time as he had been feeling ill for almost two weeks prior to me doing him a covid test.

On hearing about his son's bout of illness, Norman was only interested in a programme that was going to be on television that evening. What was it that had his interest? A programme about families having problems getting their inheritance! No surprise there then. And then Chris remembered that a few weeks prior,

Norman had been coughing his guts up when he had called to pick up his shopping list. Was it Norman who had passed the Covid virus on to his son? No hygiene practises would have been observed by Norman if he suspected that he may have had Covid. That would cost a few pence in cleaning products and boiling water.

I honestly believe that Norman chose to bury his head in the sand when it came to his son being ill. It didn't fit in with his plan to pass on his money. Norman was convinced his son would outlive him. But nobody knows how long anyone will live, be it due to accidents or illness. Nothing is ever certain in life. But this fact didn't fit in with Norman's plans to pass down his cherished cash. The thought of his savings going to his granddaughters, who had husbands, partners and children was one he did not want to accept. If passed down to them, his cash would be split numerous ways and none of his granddaughters had kept their maiden names after marriage. Norman would never think that should his family get a decent financial windfall after his death they would put it to good use. His money was for saving and investing, nothing more.

After Chris's Whipple operation it was months before I set foot in Norman's flat again. And as nasty as it sounds, I secretly hoped that my next visit would be to clean up the mess after Norman had snuffed it.

Chapter 19

Cursed cash?

Now, I have often wondered if any money Norman parted with was cursed or jinxed. Why? Well, back in the very early 1990's Norman must have had a sudden pang of guilt about not helping his son financially and Margaret making various promises that were always broken. Or it's more likely that he'd thought of another way to make a few more quid in interest by using his unsuspecting son. For whatever reason it was, one day when Chris had paid a dutiful visit to his parents, they gave him an official looking form to fill in and sign. He brought the form home for me to see and complete, under the impression that his parents were going to transfer some cash to us. As usual I was sceptical and when reading the form noticed that only Chris's name was on the form. I swiftly added my name to it! But it wasn't clear exactly what sort of transaction this would be or what type of bank account it may be. But we filled it in then Chris duly returned the form to Norman. Exactly what was he planning on giving us?

A week or so later, when Chris was on another of his dutiful visits, he was presented with a passbook for the local building society that had a cash amount recorded on it! Had Norman really parted with some cash? That's what it looked like on face value. Now, what Norman didn't know was that being a regular customer at the building society, I had become quite friendly with the staff. At that point in time Chris was paid weekly and in cash. So, every Monday morning I would walk our girls to school and then call into the local branch to deposit some cash. Some weeks it may have only been to pay in a few pounds if we'd had an expensive week. But I, being a saver by nature, always made sure we didn't live beyond our means and always put a little aside each week. The following Monday after Chris had been given the new passbook, I took it with me to the building society to ask a few questions.

Well, it came as no surprise to learn that though Norman had transferred cash from his account to the new one with our names on, the money was tied up for five years. The interest rate was good, but no withdrawals were allowed during that period. It was for a few thousand pounds but certainly wasn't life changing cash. So, though he had given us some money we couldn't spend it in any way! Wasn't that another way of keeping the money under Norman's control because that was how I saw it. He didn't want to help us out at all. Nor did he know how financially secure we were. He probably thought we lived like him and were banking bags of cash each week. This was annoying and I wasn't prepared to let Norman dictate what we could and couldn't spend. He should have just given us the cash and let us decide how we wished to use it or just not bothered.

So, I explained to the regular cashier, who I had got to know quite well, how we had not been properly consulted about the type of account that was going to be opened and emphasised it was no use to us having cash that could not be used in an emergency. She understood our dilemma and had a quiet word with her manager. Without any fuss the account was closed and the balance transferred to our joint Paid-Up Share account. We now had a small amount of Norman's cash in our possession!

What we didn't know at that time was how our lives were swiftly about to change. From the time we had Norman's cash in our names, anything that could go wrong did so! Household items broke down and needed replacing and more, but then our lives took a downward spiral. Chris had been on the waiting list for an operation on his hand. He had developed Dupuytren's Contracture which makes fingers pull into the palm of the hand and they can't be straightened without surgery.

Unfortunately, he had just given his notice to quit his job and start at a new company the following week, but that never happened. Chris had received a date for his long-awaited operation that coincided with him starting his new job. He knew his hand was getting worse by the day and couldn't go much longer without it being operated on. So, he couldn't start the new job and had effectively made himself unemployed.

The following few months after his operation were financially crippling for us and when he could go back to work, he had no choice than to work for a driving agency which gave him work on a week-to-week basis. Then after the Christmas period his agency work dried up. We only had my poor part time wages coming in while Chris searched for work. We used our savings to live on, not Norman's cash, until Chris was able to start work again. As far as the benefits office was concerned Chris had made himself unemployed and we had to use any savings we had. This went on for a few weeks because the Christmas rush for deliveries was over and it was the beginning of a new year, so nobody needed any new drivers.

The anger I felt at the predicament Norman's money could have put us in was off the scale. Knowing the money was never intended to be spent I felt it was cursed. It seemed that no matter what Chris did or where he went to seek work, he was hitting a brick wall. And then what seemed like a miracle happened.

I had finished work around 2.30pm one Tuesday and with time to spare before picking up the girls from school I had gone straight home to see if Chris had been lucky in his job hunting. It was a great big "No!". With my heart in my boots off I went to school feeling thoroughly sickened, wondering how we were going to manage in the future with little income and only our savings to keep us afloat. Determined that our girls didn't sense my low mood, I smiled as normal when they came out of school and headed off to get them some sweets. Then, as we all arrived home, just as I got one foot over our threshold, everything changed. Chris had got a job! In the few minutes I had been out, Chris had received a phone call from a tanker company he had visited the day before and they were offering him a job with an immediate start. Our prayers had been answered.

As soon as Chris was back behind the wheel of an articulated lorry, we were back on track. He was driving a tanker usually filled with hazardous chemicals all over Europe with good wages and excellent expenses, so our bank account was quickly replenished and looking healthy again. But it has always stuck in my mind that our run of bad fortune was due to Norman's money. He only wanted us to invest his cash and not spend any of it. He had no concept of the true cost of raising a family.

Was his money really cursed? I felt so and I took great pleasure when I went to see Norman a while later to tell him we had cashed in the five-year investment account and why we had been forced to do so. He said little but I knew he wasn't pleased. I cared not a jot! But at the back of my mind there has since been a nagging thought that at any time in the future, should Chris ever inherit his father's money, would it bring us good fortune or just a lot of problems again?

Chapter 20

Money, Money, Money!

A fact that Norman never considered was that by the time he was a worth a million pounds it wasn't a fortune anymore. Multi-millionaires were being created every week for those who were lucky on the lotteries or premium bonds. These really were winners who Lady Luck had looked down on. Norman had sacrificed so much that he was unbelievably poor in every other way.

Sadly, in 2017 when Margaret died, Norman was able to scrimp and save a little more. Common everyday cleaning products were never on his shopping list hence his bathroom became a real health hazard, especially the toilet! No trips to the launderette, just a bit of swilling out his dirty undies in the sink after boiling a kettle for hot water of course. He took to saving used tinfoil that still had dried blood from raw pork chops congealed on it, hoarding bread wrappers and much more. Basically, he let the state of his flat go to pot, and it wasn't because he was physically disabled in any way. Most days he would spend hours sat in his chair, alone and in total silence, constantly adding up the figures in his different passbooks, right to the last penny. Why and for what purpose?

Margaret and Norman had lived with a very strict menu at mealtimes. This continued after her death and with nobody else to please but himself he was able to cut a few more corners and save a few more pennies. We were doing the bulk of his shopping for him from the short pathetic list he gave Chris every Sunday. Each Monday Chris would drop his shopping off at the flat around lunchtime. But one Monday he arrived just as Norman was putting his dinner on a plate. "I'm having egg on toast today!" Norman proudly declared. However, when Chris looked at the humble plate of food it consisted of a fried egg on a slice of buttered bread. When he pointed out to Norman that his bread hadn't been toasted, his response was, "I don't put it in the toaster!" Now if the bread wasn't toasted it was an egg on bread or an open sandwich that Norman was having. But of course, by not toasting the slice of bread he was saving a couple of pence in electric!

Occasionally, someone would throw a spanner in the works leaving Norman in a quandary. One example was his regular Thursday lunch of a fishcake bought from the local chippy. Norman always claimed the fishcakes were way too big to eat in one sitting and only half was eaten on the day of purchase. The other half warmed up on a plate, over a pan of hot water, the following day (why didn't he use his microwave?) then the hot water was used to make a cup of tea! So, when our beloved Queen Elizabeth II upset his routine by celebrating her Platinum Jubilee, he was not amused. The chippy had closed that Thursday lunchtime but was opening at teatime. This was not an option for Norman. He simply could not change his set routine. So, even though he had lamb chops and sausages in his freezer, he made do with cheese sandwiches for two days! The meat in the freezer was earmarked for other specific days and nothing or nobody (including our late Queen) could change that.

As the years went by Norman never ceased to amaze me with his inventive penny-pinching ways. I've already stated that he had a strict menu that he adhered to, but he even found another couple of ways to save a few coppers. Each Monday we did his shopping, keeping to his list and each week Norman asked for two bananas, not a bunch, just two. As I've previously mentioned, we discovered that he was restricting himself to eating just a half of a banana, leaving the other half for the day after. Well as we all know, bananas quickly turn brown once peeled so what the left-over half was like is anyone's guess. Now if that wasn't bad enough, Norman then started dividing a single banana into three pieces, lasting him three days! Yuk! What the reasoning behind that stays a mystery. Why couldn't he have simply asked us to get him a bunch of bananas and eat a full one? Remember the potato in the eggcup! If that wasn't taking OCD to the limit what was?

Then he found another way of saving a penny. He was already making one teabag last for four cups a day. But then hit on the idea that if he didn't boil the kettle he could save on the electricity. Instead of using the kettle he carefully filled his small teacup (and it was small, resembling a teacup that you would find in a children's tea service) with water and poured it into a small saucepan. Heating up such a small quantity of water on the cooker was faster he reckoned. I've no doubt he will have measured out exactly how much water was needed to cover the element on the kettle and decided it was wasting fuel boiling water he didn't need. Whether he was right about saving fuel by doing this I don't know. Nor do I know of anyone else who would even think about doing such a thing. And why couldn't he just microwave a small cup of water? And milk was knocked off the menu once Margaret died so cups of tea and porridge made with just water tasted just as delicious without milk he claimed. I can only surmise that Norman spent many hours of every day thinking of new ways to cut costs. But for what?

For over fifty years I watched, listened and stood in awe of Norman's obsession with money. He was totally blinkered to anything and everything that he had sacrificed in his lifetime. But that was his choice, and I respected his right to find every possible way he could to save money. However, I didn't respect his right to force others to comply with his obsession.

Did Margaret have any inkling about his obsessive personality before she was pregnant and married to him? Was there a point reached where she realised penny pinching was how the couple were going to live their married life together? Was she onboard with Norman's chosen lifestyle or too afraid to speak up? I do know that she hated the thoughts of living alone and on a couple of occasions when Norman had short stays in hospital, she was frightened of being alone in the house, especially at night. If she was so afraid, then she had given Norman total power and control over all aspects of her life. I've often wondered how happy she really was or wasn't. In a divorce she could have demanded half of his savings without any problem. And being an intelligent woman, she would have known that.

Did Norman ever once stop and think about his poor relationship with his only son? Doubtful. Norman didn't have relationships with anyone. He had discissions and conversations with his son which were always matter of fact and most certainly always geared around saving or making money. Any so-called fatherly advice was about what bank accounts were giving the best interest rates or reasons for not buying something. I could always feel the awkwardness between the two men when in their company. All conversations were kept very informal and neither seemed to be able to relax like close family members should be able to do. How sad is that? Most fathers are thrilled when they can go for a pint with their son (or daughter) and put the world to rights. Not our Norman.

Grandchildren. Now, normal parents are overjoyed when blessed with a grandchild. Norman was privileged to have three granddaughters! And he was blessed with two great-grandchildren. Did he adore them, love them or be prepared to take a bullet for any one of them? No! He had occasionally carried out what he thought was a grandfather's duty, but it never seemed to be with genuine love or desire.

My parents were eager to babysit for us when they became grandparents. Saturday nights were the most common nights for my parents to come to our home and let us go out for the evening. Not to be outdone, Margaret volunteered her child minding services and of course Norman would be tagging along. After all, he was using our gas and electricity and we had heating in our home, so he couldn't lose, could he?

But the huge difference was that my parents enjoyed spending time with their granddaughters, and it showed in the way our girls behaved towards them. They looked forward to my parents coming to stay with them. But on the alternate weeks when my in-laws arrived, Norman wanted them sending to bed within minutes of him arriving so he could settle down and watch our television. On occasions the girls would plead with me not to leave them. How bad is that? Out of the mouths of babes. . .

And even our two cats would make themselves scarce when Norman and Margaret arrived, obviously sensing that they had no affection for animals in the home. When my parents appeared the cats were cuddled up by the fire or on my mum's knee, safe in the knowledge that they were with animal lovers.

And because Norman had to stay up later than 9.00pm when he was at ours, it would throw him out of his routine. He needed his beauty sleep so he could go to work the following day. That being a Sunday meant Norman got double bubble for his toil. No day of rest for him.

The only genuine affection Norman ever had was for his passbooks. He proved that with his reaction to his son's illness and fight for life. To me, all I saw was an old biscuit tin full of little paper books, all with numbers inked on the pages and a couple of insurance policies. The contents of that tin were precious beyond belief to Norman. There was an occasion in the latter years of his life when he was admitted to hospital with a chest infection caused by Covid. On that occasion I was there when a paramedic told him he would need to be admitted. Norman's first reaction was to reach out for his precious biscuit tin! He was genuinely concerned about what would happen to his passbooks while he was in hospital. In a sarcastic tone of voice, I offered to feed and water the damn things every day if it made him feel better! That day, his immediate reaction to grab his biscuit tin spoke volumes. It said one thing: Norman loved his money above anything or anyone.

In June 2022 inflation was rising in the United Kingdom, and prices were hiked up due to shortages caused by the war in Ukraine, amongst other things. So, when the government decided to refund every household £150, paid by your local council, Norman was thrilled. Not that he needed any financial aid or would be affected by rising costs in any way. But by mid-July Norman was in a flap. He couldn't find any sign of him receiving his £150 into his bank account. One Sunday when Chris called to collect Norman's shopping list, he was greeted by a very agitated father sitting with a mammoth pile of long white envelopes surrounding him.

Norman then pushed a pile of envelopes, each holding a bank statement, into Chris's hand, expecting him to scan through the payment sections of each page in search of the evasive £150. Looking at the dates on the pile of statements there was no way he would find the payment. The statements were dated from 2010 and before! Yes, Norman kept every bank statement, in the same envelope that it had arrived in, for years, not just the past year.

He hadn't disposed of anything regardless of how useless and irrelevant it was. Chris concluded that the £150 would have been paid to Norman but looking for it was like looking for the proverbial needle in a haystack and declined to help him anymore. What is so saddening is the fact that while Norman was having a panic attack about the £150 that he did not need, his son was struggling with the side effects of chemotherapy. This mattered not a jot that his sick son dutifully continued to take care of his father's shopping needs. Norman was losing sleep over £150 but not over his son's health. I think that says it all.

A week or so later, Norman heard that the bungalow he had previously lived in and sold for £152,000 was up for sale for £250,000. That was £98,000 Norman had lost out on by selling when he did, or so he misguidedly believed. This had him spending hours with a pen and paper trying to work out if the £152,000 that he had re-invested had made enough interest to cover the £98,000 difference in the sale prices of the bungalow. Finally, after a lot of sweating and stressing he concluded that it had. But what Norman hadn't considered was the amount of any renovation that had been done on the now more valuable bungalow. Adding a conservatory, garage and modern fixtures and fittings costs money. And what did it matter how much Norman may have made if he'd stayed in his home a few years longer? None! Except to Norman it did matter, really matter. If there was the slightest chance that he had missed out on making a few extra pounds he could not rest easy. Yet he didn't seem to care about the thousands of pounds he had forked out in rent to the council for his flat in Cell Block H.

You reap what you sow. Norman had sowed very little seed in his life. How sad is it when on his 94th birthday only Chris called to visit him? Yes, he went bearing gifts and we had really pushed the boat out to celebrate Norman reaching a ripe old age. Well, I may have exaggerated slightly about the gifts. I'd scoured Home Bargains store until I found a birthday card costing twenty-nine pence! It had just two words on it, "Happy Birthday!" That was all. I added our names to the greeting. No words of affection. And I'd splashed out on a small box of chocolates for him. Job done!

Two of his granddaughters didn't acknowledge his birthday in any way. Our eldest girl had also rummaged about in shops until she had found a card for twenty-five pence! Bargain! Not one of the girls felt the need to see him. Nor did I. The few seeds Norman had sown were harvesting a very poor crop.

It wasn't enough bragging to his family about his wealth. In his final years he became a bit of a pain to anyone he met on his walks about town. I know of one woman who'd asked him how Chris was getting on, knowing he had been so ill. Norman turned their brief conversation around to how he was a millionaire. And on one occasion one of his neighbours stopped Chris to air her concerns about Norman. He had been sitting outside his flat, enjoying the sunshine with other residents and of course he had been prattling on about his money. Dressed in second hand clothing, looking like a tramp, he had gone on and on about his wealth. Well, you can't blame the folk for doubting what he said. And the poor woman looked genuinely shocked when Chris reassured her that Norman wasn't losing the plot. If anyone engaged in a topic of conversation with Norman, it was swifty changed to the same old story: Norman had started out with nothing but was now a millionaire. I would say that he was once a wealthy young man that had a wife and child, a home and a job but seven decades later he had only money in his life.

Rumours were rife in our local watering holes that Norman had given his son £500,000!!!! My neighbour had heard that he had given Chris £380,000! In his dreams perhaps. And I was once referred to as the richest lady in our town! It was Margaret that left her son some money when she died and I'm almost certain that if Norman could have prevented it, he would have, keeping the money in his accounts. And when Chris did receive some cash from an insurance policy that was paid out after Margaret's death, Norman thought Chris should give him a huge chunk of it! It broke his heart to lose control of any money even when it was going to his only child. What other rumours were being spread? Norman just couldn't keep his mouth shut about his wealth. Wealth? No, he had money and that is not wealth!

There were a couple of Christmas's when Norman gave his son a cheque on Christmas Day, which I suspect was Margaret's idea. The cheques were for modest amounts and were never in both our names. No surprise there. I remember one time when Chris passed the cheque to me as I deal with all our banking and finances, Norman was quick to tell me not to lose the cheque as I was folding it to put in my purse! That little piece of paper was precious to him. What he never knew was that by the time we had left his flat I was already texting our girls to tell them to expect a bank transfer into their accounts. We didn't need the money, but they could all make good use of it. Had he ever discovered we were not investing the money into an account there would have never been another grand gesture from Norman. But we were investing the cash wisely in our opinion. We were investing in our children who always put the cash to good use rather than us looking at some figures on a bank statement.

With all his bragging to anyone who would listen I doubt he realised that he may have been putting himself in danger. Gossip runs rife in a small village and who was to say that the rumours about Norman having money wouldn't encourage a certain kind of person to rob him in his home or mug him in the street. They would have found little or no cash on him or in the flat. But who was to know that? My thoughts were. . . be it on his own head!

After Margaret died, it was all left to me to sort out Norman's direct debits and such as he had never got involved with paying the bills before. Then one day he presented me with a form from the Inland Revenue that he wanted filling in. It wasn't too taxing to complete and was all about Norman's state pension and income. But it seemed Norman was under the impression that he could still claim the married man's tax allowance even though his wife was dead! He was reluctant to accept the fact that he was not a married man anymore. As much as I tried to explain why he could not claim the allowance he was adamant I was to fill the form in, including Margaret's name and full details. Well, I did complete the form exactly how Norman wished, but to cover myself, after he'd signed it, I added a small note on the bottom of the form, stating the date Margaret had died. I wonder what the person in the tax office thought when reading the form?

And then I discovered something else that really confused me. While filling in the tax form I had to declare Norman's weekly pension. He gave me a letter from DWP stating the amount he received weekly and an additional allowance. Norman had been granted an allowance for his disability! What disability was that exactly? To my knowledge I'd never heard anyone mention a disability or noticed anything physically wrong with Norman, apart from physically struggling to get his hand in his pocket. Naturally, I asked why the allowance had been given to him. His answer? A doctor once came to Miser Mansion and examined Norman's legs and hands. That was it! I was still no wiser as to what illness he suffered from, and Norman was never forthcoming with an answer. Norman did have Dupuytren's Contracture in two fingers of one hand but that is not a condition that is classed as disabling. I know this to be true as Chris also has the condition and has had two operations performed on both his hands. He has never been able to claim for this and his hands are far worse than Norman's.

To Norman money was everything that mattered. To me personally, money is nothing more than smelly, germ riddled pieces of paper. I realised that back in 1969 when I went to work in a bank. Try counting out hundreds of thousands of bank notes, covered in blood, gunk and God knows what else, that are handed to you over a counter by butchers, market traders and shop keepers. Bank books are little books with numbers in. They don't do anything. Yes, we all like to have a little money in the bank and yes, it's nice to have surplus money put away for rainy days. Who wants to be poor and in debt? Nobody. But Norman was poor and in debt even with all his wealth. He didn't have the love of his family so he was a poor man who was in debt to them all his life for not being the husband, father and grandfather he should have been or could have been.

Chapter 20

A pain in the arse!

While Chris was waiting to have his Whipple operation in 2022 Norman was admitted to hospital with suspected Covid symptoms. We'd already had one incident where I'd had to ring 111 and seek advice which resulted in a paramedic coming to assess him. The second time he spent about a week in hospital which Norman loved! He wasn't too ill and was being fed three times a day and had plenty of company to talk to. When he arrived back home, he told Chris that he wanted to go into the local care home which was only a couple of hundred yards from his flat. I honestly believe Norman thought he could just ask to be admitted and would be able to treat the care home like a hotel, being able to go for a walk on his own whenever he wished. Well, that idea was swiftly dismissed when we told Norman how much the care home fees were if he was self-funding. He probably thought it would cost the same as a cheap Blackpool boarding house.

So, then he decided that he would walk the few hundred yards to one of the local cafes and have a cooked lunch each day. That would save him having to cook. Well, that didn't happen when he realised the true price of a decent meal. Compared to the cost of a boiled onion there was no way he was going to splash out on eating out.

Then in November 2023 it seemed Norman's health had started to deteriorate. He was ninety-four years old, so it was no surprise to us. He was very stubborn, still insisting that he could look after himself in every way which meant he wasn't prepared to pay for any help around his home. And I certainly wasn't prepared to undertake any cleaning of his now very grubby flat. Norman knew best! Nor would he have any form of communication installed in his home. Adamant that he didn't need a landline telephone or a big button mobile that we had previously given him and been thrown in a drawer, never to be used. No way was he prepared to charge a phone or top up a sim card and he was equally adamant that he didn't need to be able to contact us or anyone. This was not open to discussion! But Norman's stubborn, money saving obsession backfired on him big style that November.

On November 2nd we received an early morning call on our landline. I was still in bed with it being around 8am but Chris was up and about. It wasn't one of our usual nuisance calls but a call from Norman's next-door neighbour. Norman was struggling to breath! Apparently, around 4.00am a gasping Norman had struggled to get out of bed, his head spinning with dizziness, thinking he was about to die! What could he do to get help? Nothing! So, he sat in his armchair for four hours, convinced he was about to take his last breath at any moment. Eventually, knowing that his neighbour was usually up and about by 8.00am he managed to drag his disorientated body across the landing to knock on his neighbour's door and beg for help. So much for never needing a telephone!

Being the dutiful son, Chris made a mercy dash to see his ailing and failing father while I rolled over in bed for another hour. After all the occasions that I had been made aware that I wasn't a blood relative, I certainly wasn't going to behave like one when it suited Norman. Anyway, a 999 call had a very quick response, with two paramedics swiftly on the scene, checking Norman's vital signs. His blood pressure reading was sky high and the chesty cough that Norman had been troubled with for weeks, had got much worse. Yes, Norman needed admitting to hospital but strangely, once he had folk fussing over him, his symptoms and panic appeared to subside.

So, what did Norman do? True to form, as the paramedics were checking him over, Norman started telling them how rich he was! "I'm a millionaire!" he proudly announced much to Chris's embarrassment. Well, I'm pretty sure the two female paramedics would have already noticed the state of Norman's flat. It was dirty to say the least and had been for a couple of years. They must have thought Norman was rambling, confused with his high blood pressure and who could blame them? So, even when he was so ill Norman's main concern was that everyone and anyone should know he had a large amount of money. What does that say about him?

The day after Norman had been admitted to hospital Chris wanted to go to his father's flat and clear out any food that may start rotting and to get a good look at the state of the other rooms. Just how well had Norman been looking after himself? Well, we soon found out alright. What we saw that day was stomach churning. Apart from the lounge being grubby and exceptionally dusty, the kitchen was cluttered with opened tins that were partially filled with mouldy food. Cupboards were crammed full of used tin foil, tons of bread wrappers and foil wrappers from individual apple pies. His bedroom was almost as bad. The bedding, whatever it was that was on the bed, hadn't been washed in years. And the bathroom. . . there are no words to describe it. The whole flat was in dire need of an industrial clean. So why didn't we, as Norman's family, get stuck in to cleaning his flat? Most families would have, though normal families wouldn't have allowed this to happen to a loved one. The cruel but truthful answer is. . . we just didn't care!

So, Norman had been constantly pestering the hospital doctors to let him go home and just a week later, on a Tuesday night, he was discharged from hospital and packed off back to his hovel at around 8.00pm. Wasn't this a bit late to send an elderly person home alone to a cold flat? What had he told the hospital staff? We don't know but during a phone call from the hospital, informing us about Norman's looming discharge, Chris made it clear that he wasn't coping on his own. I suspect the medical team may have asked Norman if he needed a home care package arranging or maybe a couple of weeks respite in a care home before finally going home. And I am certain he will have refused all offers of help and told hospital staff that he had a family who would be helping him when he did arrive back home. Wrong! There will have been no mentioning that his son was having chemotherapy or that he wasn't in the best of health. But we did discover that Norman had been told by a doctor he must get a phone, but he'd refused outright!

The morning after Norman arrived back home, again his dutiful son went to see him. He pressed the intercom for the flat.

No reply. He let himself into the block and knocked on Norman's door. No reply. He tried the intercom again. No reply. Finally, he tried to put the spare key onto the lock. Norman had left his key in the other side. Not a wise move. Luckily, Chris managed to jiggle the spare key in the lock and open the door. What did he find?

There was no sign of life in Norman's flat. Chris opened each inner door in turn. Still no sign of his father. With only the bedroom door to open, with bated breath he took a peep round the door. Was he about to find a corpse in bed? No such luck! Tucked up, still wearing the clothes he had worn throughout the previous day, Norman was sleeping soundly. The noise of Chris entering the bedroom woke Norman from his beauty sleep. Confused as to why Chris had come visiting so early in the morning, believing it to be 6.30am, Norman was told it was in fact 10.30am! True to form, Norman hadn't put new batteries in his alarm clock and the ancient relic had stopped! And a day or so later when Chris mentioned the hospital telling Norman to get a phone what do you think his reply was? "That's never going to happen!" Stubborn or what?

As much as I didn't want anything to do with Norman, I drew the short straw of having to go to his GP's surgery and try to arrange for him to have all his medication requested and delivered by the local pharmacy. Well, if I was to say that the nice woman on the surgery reception desk immediately knew who Norman was when I mentioned his name it will come as no surprise that she also knew he was a millionaire! I knew immediately by the look on the receptionist's face that Norman had been bragging to the staff and asked her straight out. Maybe it was a little cruel, but I made it known that he wasn't looking after himself anymore and we hadn't been consulted before his hospital discharge. And to labour the point I showed the receptionist a video of Norman's disgusting bathroom. My hope was that she may mention my concerns to a doctor and arrange a home visit. That would surely have prompted someone to raise the subject of Norman needing help in the home.

My next stop was to the pharmacy to confirm the new prescription arrangements. And yet again as soon as I mentioned his name, I knew the staff had been told about Norman's wealth.

It was agreed that he would receive a weekly dosette box to make sure he didn't get confused with his various tablets. But what did I discover afterwards? Norman had a unique way of taking his pills. He dropped them all into his bowl of porridge each morning! I'm pretty sure this method of pill popping goes against all the different instructions on the various pill packets.

A couple of days later, Chris paid a flying visit to collect Norman's shopping list. Norman was sitting in his chair, legs swollen, wheezing as he drew breath. He hadn't felt well the previous day he claimed. How were we supposed to know? All it would have taken was for the silly old sod to say he wasn't well, and he could have gone back to hospital. From there we could have sorted out what was best for him. Coming home to the flat with carers visiting would have been the only option to going into care. Norman knew this and I am certain he was prepared to suffer rather than be parted from his precious passbooks or have anyone intruding and upsetting his miserable life.

The following day on another flying visit with more shopping for his now failing fast father (or so we thought), what did Chris get greeted with? Wheezing and feeling dizzy as he tried to get up out of the chair our Norman was most concerned about a couple of his ISAs that were coming to fruition. He had received a letter from his building society and was adamant that he must get there on December 4th or his accounts would be changed to a minimum interest rate! He wanted to switch them to higher interest rates in new two-year accounts. Two years??? He was planning on living another two years. Really? Either Norman hadn't grasped the severity of his congestive heart failure, or he was blotting it out of his mind, just like he had chosen to block out the severity of his only son's illness.

True to his word, Norman was not going to let anything stop him from switching his precious ISAs to a better interest rate. So, on a very cold and snowy Monday morning off he set to catch the bus to the building society. He'd slipped and slithered his way to the bus stop only to find the next bus wasn't due for another forty-five minutes. Well, the thought of standing for so long at the bus stop made a breathless Norman think twice and he abandoned his journey. But with a heavy heart, instead of skating his way back home he chose to struggle to his dental surgery and book an appointment for a check-up! Why? It can't have been necessary as the appointment he was given wasn't until April 2024!

After struggling to walk back home he was so exhausted that he couldn't get up the stairs to his flat and had to wait for his body to recover from the strain, supposedly. Eventually, he made it up the stairs and sat in his armchair for over thirty minutes feeling weak, breathless and dizzy. And this was all for what? Norman's desperation to make a few extra pounds in two years' time!

After his stay in hospital, following Norman's bout of high blood pressure and breathing difficulties, he was sent an appointment for an echocardiogram to check out his heart function. So, his dutiful son took him for this appointment a few days after his failed attempt to get his passbooks updated and Chris had even agreed to take Norman to get his ISAs sorted afterwards. Take note that Norman was happy being ferried about in our car even though he thought cars were an unnecessary and expensive possession. So, on arrival at the hospital carpark Norman wasn't going to leave his precious passbooks in the car. Oh no, they had to go with him, so clutching the books wrapped in a carrier bag, off he trotted for his echocardiogram.

Norman just couldn't help himself from telling the medical staff that he was wealthy. Panic had swept over him when he was about to get dressed after his echocardiogram and his carrier bag wasn't with his jacket. Someone had moved the bag! When he was re-united with the love of his life (passbooks) he just had to get the books out to show the young nurse how much money he had invested in ISAs. And of course, he will have told her about his million. What the nurse thought when she saw the scruffy state of Norman and realised that he really wasn't a penniless old tramp, is anybody's guess. Now if the staff had wanted to monitor his heart properly, they should have wired him up clutching his carrier bag and then tried to take it away from him. Being parted from his pass books would have really had his heart racing! And another mystery to me is how could they do an echocardiogram on a man who had no heart?

When Norman did eventually get his precious ISAs updated to the higher interest rate, getting there by being ferried by his son, his first words when getting back in the car were about his ISAs. He warned Chris that if Norman died before the two years was up then he must not cash the ISAs in but must let them continue to accumulate full interest! Well, ISAs can only be passed on to your spouse and then only if the spouse uses the same bank! So, Norman was now worrying about saving money after he died!!!!

And just to emphasise just how much Norman worshipped his passbooks, he had two drawers in a French dresser that were crammed full of old books. Each expired book was carefully stacked into a pile with two rubber bands binding them together. He had dozens of them all neatly stored away. None were of any use to him and could have been shredded or burned but Norman cherished each and every one of them.

And on that journey to get Norman's precious books updated, Chris pointed out some newly built houses that were on the market. When he told his father how much the asking prices were for the houses, Norman was adamant that nobody would be silly enough to pay such ridiculous amounts for a house. He really was living in a different world to the rest of us with no concept of the price of anything. Norman was in his own little world. Because we were getting his shopping for him, he had no clue as to what a normal week's shopping for a family cost or how much an average mortgage repayment was. Margaret had lived without what we all consider the necessities of life and pandered to his strict food rationing for so long, she had allowed Norman to live happily in his own cocoon.

A few days later Norman was ill again with diarrhoea and dizziness. He claimed it was due to eating some cheese that he had kept in the fridge for almost six weeks, but he'd cut the mouldy bits out before devouring it! Again, he couldn't ring us if he needed help, so he had to wait for his son visiting. But when Chris was dropping off his shopping all Norman could talk about was his bloody ISAs and another warning not to cash them in if he died.

But what was a little worrying was something Norman said to Chris when dropping off his shopping. Norman started talking about picking mushrooms as a young lad, in the local woodland area close to his home. Nothing unusual about that until he added that he had to be very careful when picking the mushrooms as Jack the Ripper was prowling the area! Jack the Ripper? He was lurking about in Whitechapel in the 1800's and Norman wasn't born until 1929. Nor did Jack the Ripper ever frequent the North of England as far as we know! Was he going senile?

And then our concerns about Norman's mental state rocketed on Christmas Day. Chris dutifully went to see his father, bearing gifts from us. Well, that is if you consider a bag of Aldi humbugs, a bag of liquorice allsorts and a bar of cheap chocolate a gift. It was an obligatory gesture from us, all be it a very poor one. Chris arrived at Norman's around 11.00am to find him preparing his lunch. When he asked why his father was going to be dining on a small pork pie and a tin of mushy peas and not the sliced beef we had got for him, Norman's answer was. . . "I'm saving the beef for Christmas Day!" He thought it was still Christmas Eve! Well, we can all get a little confused about the days of the week, especially over holiday periods, but how could anyone who watched television not know when it was Christmas Day?

And then Norman announced that he was now saving the paper bags that his prescriptions were delivered in. Why? So that we could put the numerous plates and ornaments Norman had on show in a display cabinet and on various shelves into the bags when he died!!! He didn't want any of them damaging when his flat was being cleared out. Well maybe he didn't want them breaking but why hoard those specific bags? Any box and a newspaper would have sufficed. And another example of unnecessary hoarding was obvious when Chris spotted an old wooden fruit bowl that he had made in secondary school. The bowl was brimming with the foil wrappers from Tunnocks chocolate teacakes, all screwed up and piled in the dish. For what purpose?

Norman also seemed to be obsessed about what was going to happen to his furniture and possessions after his death. It may have been connected to his onset of hoarding, not wanting anything to go to waste or thrown away but anyone thinking rationally would not have expected us or anyone to want his old three-piece suite. It was second hand when he got it over twenty years earlier and by then it was covered in stains and marks so badly that Margaret had new covers made for it before she died. During her decline in health and her mobility being limited I know she had a few accidents on the sofa. And the chair that Norman had spent so much time sat in, adding up his passbooks, was equally as bad. We had already discussed how his furniture and clutter would be disposed of and there was little if anything that any of us wanted to keep.

Was Norman staring to develop some form of dementia? Well, we had to consider it as a warning. It was a very real possibility, yet we didn't have Power of Attorney so that we could have any input into Norman's welfare if it ever came to him needing professional care. He had always believed he would go to bed one night and not wake up. It had never occurred to him that he might end up totally dependent on professional care. And the thought of giving anyone, including his son, access to his bank accounts was his worst nightmare.

Now, as I have previously said, I could not forgive Norman for the comment he made about having to make a new Will if Chris died before him. So, in January 2024, during storm Isha, we received a phone call at 10.00pm from Norman's neighbour asking us to go down to the flat. Norman was having a nosebleed that was showing no signs of stopping after thirty minutes. As he was taking Warfarin to thin his blood any bleeding was dangerous. So, out of duty and to help Chris, I agreed to go to Norman's flat and ring 111 for help. He couldn't have picked a worse night to be ill. The wind was howling and rain lashing down as we drove into the night.

Following instructions from the NHS 111 helpline we took Norman to A & E, leaving a bit of a bloody mess in his flat and Norman's face looking like he had been given a good beating. Thankfully we didn't have long to wait before he was called through to be assessed. As soon as a triage nurse hinted that Norman could be a few hours before he would be seen by an ENT specialist, and to be seen by one he needed to be transferred to another hospital, Chris and I decided we were not hanging about all night. His nose bleed could also have been due to his congestive heart disease, but nobody was saying what they suspected. We could do nothing and were certainly not prepared to have Norman bleeding profusely, feeling weaker by the minute, in our car. We made our excuses and left him there, promising to ring the next day and see what was happening with him. Arriving home at 12.30am I found it difficult to fall asleep, half expecting the hospital to ring us with bad news about Norman. Would it have been bad news? Not for me!

I did reluctantly ring the following day and was told he was on a surgical assessment ward. As Norman refused to have a mobile phone, we were unable to speak to him and vice versa. A second call later in the day and we were told Norman would be coming home later that evening. Could anyone come to take him home? No! I hoped the ambulance team would escort Norman into his cesspit of a flat and possibly report what they saw to Social Services. Apparently, he finally arrived home at 7.00pm by hospital transport. The following day Norman told Chris that the ENT consultant had decided to take a chance on sending him home as the bleeding could start again. Now would the doctor have done that if he'd known Norman lived alone with no phone and no regular visitors? And I wonder how many times Norman told members of the nursing staff that he was a millionaire? And what did they make of his declaration, as he sat like a bag of rags in a wheelchair on the ward? Early onset of dementia probably!

But what was so obvious about Norman's latest emergency was that he proved yet again that he could manage to walk the few feet to his neighbour's flat and ask for help even when he was struggling to breath or bleeding badly. So, why didn't he make the effort to get to his neighbour's flat and ask to use his phone to enquire how his son was before and after his life saving operation? For that I would never forgive him or forget what he'd said.

And it wasn't long before Norman proved yet again that he favoured money over family. Just a week after Norman's nosebleed fiasco Chris went for his routine CT scan on the Sunday lunchtime, expecting it to be a quick appointment. Wrong! The scan showed that he had a blood clot on his left lung and one in his leg. This resulted in him being taken to A & E and anyone who has ever had to go to A& E will know that it is usually a long wait. Six hours later Chris was back home and on blood thinning injections. It wasn't good news, but we'd had far worse. The following day we went to get Norman's shopping as usual and then Chris was off again to deliver it to his father.

Now, on hearing about his son's latest medical emergency how did Norman respond? He was most concerned about. . . Rishi Sunak possibly making a change to the Inheritance Tax laws! Not a word of compassion or concern for his son came from Norman mouth. Yet again, his silence spoke volumes and by now I had an encyclopaedia of Norman's reactions.

Now to say that Norman was becoming a pain in the arse would be an apt description of how we were feeling about his stubborn ways. And just as we thought things were settling down with Norman's health, I got a phone call out of the blue from the hospital. A female doctor from the ward Norman had been on during his nose bleed incident wanted to ask me a few questions. And what did she want to know exactly? Wait for it. . . did I know how long Norman had had a lesion on his buttocks? Now, why would I be privy to such intimate information and why would I want to be? No! But I did know that he had suffered from haemorrhoids in the past.

So, I assumed that when Norman was sitting in a wheelchair for hours with his nosebleed, he must have complained about being in some discomfort on his buttocks. And I can only guess that someone had drawn the short straw and examined Norman's arse cheeks (forgive my crudeness) and taken note that he had a lesion, which I imagine was an open wound of some sort. Anyway, this doctor, having only our telephone number as a contact number, wanted to send a district nurse to give Norman's arse the once over. Could the nurses contact me about going to visit him. Yes! Oh yes!

Was it any wonder Norman had some festering wound or abscess when he didn't use toilet roll, preferring to use the Daily Express for his ablutions. Imagine all the germs on the newspaper after it had been handled by many, not to mention the ink. Add to that the fact that he hadn't had a bath in years and given his nether regions a good soaking, it was no surprise. But for the doctor to want to send a district nurse to examine Norman indicated to me that they were concerned about it, otherwise they could have just given him a prescription for antibiotics or a cream.

As it turned out, when Chris questioned his father about the lesion and why a nurse needed to see him, Norman revealed the possible reason why. When he had been admitted with Covid a few weeks earlier Norman had been checked out for pre-existing pressure sores before he was allowed to get into a hospital bed. The reason being that the hospital trust had received claims for compensation from patients complaining about developing bed sores whilst in their care. To avoid any further possible false claims, patients were being checked on admission. Now it seems Norman at that time must have already been suffering from some kind of lesion and it had been previously recorded in his notes. Why on his admission hadn't the lesion been treated? I suspect Norman will have been told to see his doctor when he was discharged but never had. Yet he had continued to trek up to the surgery every week to put in his prescriptions. So, now our pain in the arse had got a pain in the arse!

Well, someone must have thought that Norman's festering bottom needed urgent attention because no sooner had Chris informed his father about a possible visit from a nurse than one was knocking on Norman's door! That day a nurse caught him off guard, with no time to clean up some of the filth in the flat or for him to get changed out of his usual tatty dressing gown. When Chris dropped off his shopping the following day, Norman told him about the visit and he revealed that he'd had the lesion, wound, sore or whatever it was, for a decade or so and it had now scabbed over! Well, Norman may not have thought it anything to worry about, but a medical team thought differently.

I'd have liked to have been a fly on the wall when the poor nurse entered the flat after being greeted at the door by someone resembling a tramp! And if the grotty surroundings didn't faze her, she had to take several photos of Normans arse! Presumably these were to show a doctor and get advice, but she did show Norman the intimate images she had taken before she left. Her visit lasted about thirty minutes during which time she chatted with him, possibly taking mental notes about her surroundings and Norman's ramblings about how wealthy he was. When I heard about this visit, I was expecting a phone call from the said nurse about Norman's mental state. Surely the nurse would think him deluded about his wealth, or had he got his collection of passbooks out to prove it?

Meanwhile, at this point Norman's congestive heart disease, gave rise to a constant threat of having another heavy nosebleed as well as his pain in the arse. But did it distract him from coming up with penny pinching ways? Not on your nellie! While he sat whiling away the hours sat on his makeshift rubber ring, he decided that he could save a couple of pence more by preparing his breakfast the night before. Soaking his porridge oats in a dish of cold water overnight would allow the oats to absorb the liquid and then the following morning it would take a minute or so less time in the microwave to heat up the bowl of stodge. How much money would he be saving in the process? A few pence per week!

Chapter 21

The vultures are circling!

By the end of February 2024 Norman was struggling to walk any distance especially uphill, or so he claimed. The reality of this must have hit him when he set off to collect his prescription for warfarin. He'd just managed to get to the chemist shop just as his legs were about to buckle. On seeing him gasping for breath, a friendly member of staff brought Norman a chair to rest on while he waited for an elusive prescription. Then it seemed the prescription request that Chris had pushed through Norman's GP surgery letterbox a few days earlier had gone astray. But the pharmacist was very helpful, and the problem was quickly solved. Yet once back home Norman must have forgotten about his failing health because on his next visit from Chris, he pre-warned his son that come the beginning of April another visit to the building society would be on the cards and Chris would have to take Norman to the building society as more ISAs were coming to fruition. Yet again Norman was more concerned about the prospect of losing a few pounds in interest that his declining mobility and poor health.

But by March, Norman was again mulling over the idea of going into a care home. I strongly believed he was slowly realising that he was vulnerable to numerous ailments and his body was failing fast. How lonely had he become? I have no idea as he had never seriously welcomed anyone to spend time with him. He had the means to pay for all the care he needed around the home and much more, but he was never going to do so. Then he mentioned to Chris that he would have all his needs taken care of if he did go into care. The money he wouldn't be spending on household bills would go towards the cost of his stay. Well, the few pounds that he saved from his bills would have paled into insignificance compared with the true cost of care. Nor did Norman realise that he had to be assessed to go into care. He may or may not have qualified for financial aid towards the cost.

He was under the impression he could just knock on the door and move into the home that was just up the road. It never occurred to him that he may not have a real choice in the matter.

By mid-April, Norman had finally succumbed to using a walking stick when he left the flat. One of his neighbours had given him one that he could fold up when not needed. Would he have ever bought himself a stick? Doubtful. And then it seemed like Norman was having weird illusions again. Probably the Charles Bonnet Syndrome kicking in once more. This time Norman was tucked up in bed when he saw a man come out of the wardrobe, jump over the bed and walk out of the door. He told Chris about this but didn't seem concerned at the strange happenings. Charles Bonnet Syndrome isn't a mental health issue just a symptom of deteriorating eyesight. So, I ask, why didn't Norman mention any of this to his doctor? And the problem could have been easily sorted if Norman had got his eyes tested and invested in some prescription spectacles but that was never going to happen if it cost money. Any normal person would have freaked out had they seen someone coming out of the wardrobe but not our Norm.

Now, Norman seemed determined to trek to his GP's surgery at least once a week, come hail, rain or shine, so why wouldn't he tell a receptionist when he needed to see a doctor? On one of Chris's dutiful visits, he revealed that he was having bad bouts of dizziness. He'd mentioned having dizzy spells before, but these must have been more severe, bad enough to have him stumbling about, grasping at anything to stop him keeling over. Any normal person would have wanted to see a doctor but as bad as he said his dizziness was, he still didn't ask his son to make him an appointment. Why?

As much as I wasn't prepared to visit Norman, if asked I would have made a phone call to get him checked out. But he never asked or hinted at wanting medical help. There was only one conclusion I could come to and again it all came down to money. Should a doctor have considered Norman needed to go into hospital and had he eventually needed 24/7 care, then it may well have resulted in him being put into a home. Now, as much as Norman had occasionally mentioned care homes, he certainly wouldn't have wanted to be taken to one that wasn't close to the village. In his tunnel vision he would need to be within a short bus ride to his building society. What would happen to his precious ISAs when they all came to the end of their fixed term? Norman would be thinking of the few lost pounds should he not get his passbooks constantly updated. Where would he keep his pile of passbooks, hundreds of statements and insurance policies for safe keeping. He certainly wouldn't trust carers to look after them. Basically, those piles of paper ruled his life.

Well, it wasn't long after complaining of his dizzy spells that Norman had something else to complain about. He told Chris that he had been having pain in his lower right side for a couple of days. He also added that he'd had a bit of flatulence and been passing wind for a couple of days. He thought the pain was connected to that. Well, in a normal person I would perhaps have made the same assumption. However, this was Norman and Norman parted with nothing! That said, he still didn't ask Chris to contact a doctor or make an appointment for him. But he did ask for a lift to the building society to get two more ISAs updated, again panicking that if he didn't go on a specific date the interest rate would drop. This took priority over his health every time.

So, as we arrived, Norman clutching his passbooks like his life depended on them, he was like a spring chicken trotting from the carpark to the building society! All signs of his unsteadiness in his legs and pain in his abdomen were gone! Norman visiting the building society was akin to a devout Muslim on a homage to Mecca! This really was a place of worship for him. Only he had come at least a week too soon to get his ISAs updated and had to return home without his books being updated. And it had never occurred to Norman to take any ID documents. In his mind he was a very important customer, thinking the staff would be bowing down to him on arrival. He was wrong on all counts and treated like any other customer. This meant he would need another lift a week or so later to get the books updated.

For someone who believed he was savvy when it came to money Norman was anything but. He'd received through the post two boxes of Covid tests. These were free due to him being high risk. So, what did the silly old sod do? He took both boxes of tests back to the local chemist shop to say he didn't want or need them! Apart from the tests being useful to have to hand if Norman ever showed any symptoms that may be Covid, couldn't he have given them to his son who had a low immune system and needed to check if he ever had symptoms? We had to go out and buy a box of tests to keep at hand. Norman could have saved his son some money by passing the tests to him. Knowing he had returned the tests made me even more determined that if Norman was to fall ill with Covid symptoms I would not be making any effort to test him. He was on his own.

A few days before Norman reached the ripe old age of ninety-five Chris called to collect his shopping list. It was around 10.00am and Norman already had his lunch sorted with potatoes and cabbage bubbling in pans. Frozen Yorkshire puddings were also on the menu and a jug sprinkled with gravy granules was at the ready. What was Norman having to go with his veg and puddings? Lamb chop? Pork chop? Sausages? No, Norman was having fish fingers! Well, he was nothing less than inventive, but do fish fingers and Yorkshire puddings covered in gravy really complement each other?

When Norman's birthday dawned, to mark the momentous occasion we really pushed the boat out. Well, it is an achievement to reach the age of ninety-five and we wanted to mark the occasion in true Norman fashion. I had scoured Card Factory for a suitable offering and for the second consecutive year found one for twenty-nine pence! Chris chose a bag of Aldi's best sherbet lemons and a bag of liquorice allsorts. These were hand delivered by Chris, on his way home from his chemotherapy session. I had no desire and felt no remorse for not wanting to visit my father-in-law. And like previous years, none of his three granddaughters marked the occasion in any way.

Now if I am fortunate enough to reach the ripe old age of 95 and am still physically mobile and compos mentis, I will be wanting to celebrate with my family. No expense spared! Reaching such a good age is a privilege and those lucky enough to do so must know they really are on borrowed time. What better time to celebrate and leave a lasting memory for your family and friends? No such thoughts will have passed through Norman's mind.

It was only a good week or so after Norman's birthday that he decided once again that he wanted to go into the local care home. Apparently, he had stubbed his toe on something and when Chris called to collect his shopping list Norman was quick to show off his badly bruised foot and ankle. His foot had swollen so much that he couldn't get one shoe on. He was plodding about in a brown shoe and a very old black one that had no laces. This meant Norman couldn't get out of his flat. He was housebound! Then he admitted that he was struggling to climb the stairs to his flat at the best of times and was now having regular dizzy spells accompanied by shortness of breath.

Did Norman ask his son to contact a doctor or seek any advice about his bruised foot and his dizziness? No! He wanted Chris to make enquiries about going into the care home if he was self-funding! Norman had been doing some calculations and had decided he wouldn't be much worse off financially if he had to pay for his care when he had deducted the running costs of living in his flat. Again, I am sure he had no real concept of the true cost. And hadn't we had this conversation before when he had come out of hospital?

This left me with a personal dilemma. Should I continue to wash my hands of him, ignore his deteriorating health issues and let the miserable old sod suffer? Or should I rise above it, do the decent thing and get Norman some help? I'd been to see his GP surgery once before and sorted it so that he could have home visits. What had he done once he felt better? He'd continued to trot to the surgery at least once a week with his prescription requests. And without a Power of Attorney, we had no authority to act on his behalf, so if Norman was serious about paying for care, then he would have to get his finances in order and cash in some of his ISAs to cover the cost. Could Norman bring himself to do that?

The following day, Chris took Norman his shopping and I suggested he explained to him exactly what he would need to do if he was serious about going into the care home and still wanted us to make enquiries. Chris got an unexpected response. Norman told him that he didn't expect to live much longer and didn't think he would see the year out! He wasn't happy at the thought of losing any interest on his ISAs but seemed to accept that some would have to be cashed in. At this point the bruising in Norman's foot and ankle had faded considerably and was not as swollen.

On hearing the news that my father-in-law wasn't planning on being here much longer, cruelly, I asked if Norman had been precise in when he was going to snuff it. Did he have a month in mind for dropping off this mortal coil so we could be prepared? The vultures were now circling their prey.

Chapter 22

One foot in the grave?

Well, within hours of Chris leaving, thinking that his father's leg was on the mend we got another early morning call. Tuesday morning at 7.45am our landline ringing woke us both up. Instantly I thought it was a call about Norman, and it was. The call was from his neighbour telling us that the awkward old sod had spent all night in pain with his leg and had waited until he knew his neighbour would be up and about to ask him to ring Chris. Being the dutiful son, he agreed to go straight to Norman's rescue. My feelings were to roll over and have another hour in bed, but I knew that Chris would need me to make any phone calls and manoeuvre through the endless options before getting through to a human voice. I was not amused as you can imagine and didn't rush to get myself dressed and ready to go. One thing I was determined to do was make sure my bladder was empty because there was no way I was going to set foot in Norman's bathroom!

What were we greeted with as we entered Norman's hovel? He was sitting in his crusty dressing gown with his pyjama leg rolled up. Not a bonny sight at the best of times. Yes, the redness in his foot and ankle had almost gone but now he had the redness in the calf of his leg which was painful. Norman said he was afraid that he might lose his foot. What should we do?

Well, Chris was due to be at the hospital for his pre chemo blood test that morning, so he decided to take Norman up to the A & E department and leave him there. Chris would then go have his bloods taken then go back and see what was happening to Norman before coming back home. But no way was he prepared to sit for hours in a hospital waiting area. He had seen more than his fair share of hospitals in the past three years. And what good would he be doing by sitting there? Norman was more than capable of explaining what he was suffering from.

Now, I couldn't lose my patience with Norman because I had none to lose! So, when the awkward old sod knew he was going to be going to A & E, he decided he would have a wash and shave, get dressed and have his breakfast! That told me he wasn't in as much pain as he made out and why did we have to rush to his aid so early in the morning when he felt he had time to spare eating and dressing? That was it for me. I left Chris to deal with Norman and walked back home. I knew Chris had no patience with his father and there certainly wasn't any love lost between them, but he would do his duty and drop him at the hospital and leave the medical staff to do the rest.

As for the state of Norman's flat, it was now a real health hazard. It had been a while since I'd last been there but what had been dirty was now filthy. Squalor comes to mind to describe the state of it. The lounge had inches of dust covering everything, cobwebs upon cobwebs, carpets full of crumbs and what appeared to be gravel. No way was I going to look in the bathroom unless absolutely necessary and I already knew the bedroom was a tip from my last visit. Norman was living in squalor. Why? I can't believe his eyesight was so bad that he couldn't see the mess so why didn't he ask for help to keep his home clean? It all came down to the love of his life: Money.

What I didn't expect was for Chris to come storming through our door about 5 hours later, steam coming out of his ears, cursing his father. Why? When he told me I didn't know whether to laugh or swear profusely. So, I did both.

As I had walked out of the flat Norman was having a wash with the hot water he'd boiled in the kettle. Well, it would be more like a wipe round with a wet flannel rather than a wash. So, once he'd tidied himself up, Norman wanted to have his breakfast of porridge oats in water before he left for the hospital. Once he'd shovelled that down his throat, he decided he wanted some toast! Chris waited whilst silently fuming. But then Norman decided that he would have another cup of tea and some ginger biscuits because he didn't know when he would next be eating! Chris couldn't have a cup of tea because Norman didn't have milk in the fridge. This was something he had stopped having delivered after Margaret died. Not a thought was given to his son who had rushed to his father's aid thinking it was an emergency. He hadn't had a thing to eat or drink since the previous evening. It was at this point Chris must have put his foot down and insisted they leave for the hospital at once as it had been two hours since he had arrived at the flat and he had an appointment to have his blood taken which he had to attend.

Norman was duly deposited in the A & E department where thankfully there were only two others waiting to be seen and he was dealt with immediately. What was the diagnosis? Was Norman at risk of losing his foot from infection?

After all the drama, all that was wrong with Norman's leg was a bit of bruising caused by him knocking his foot. Taking warfarin made the bruising look more serious. Paracetamol was suggested for any pain Norman was suffering. He'd supposedly suffered all the previous night. Or had he? Chris then left him and went to get his blood tested. On his return, he went looking for Norman who was waiting for a precautionary x-ray result.

It was a spritely Norman who walked from A & E to the carpark for the journey home, all discomfort in his leg forgotten. He was adamant that he would not be taking any painkillers as he didn't like taking pills! And then he revealed that he hadn't been up all night with pain in his leg as we had been told. Norman had gone to bed at 9.00pm and slept soundly until 4.30am. It was only then his leg started to hurt, allegedly. So, why didn't he get washed, fed and ready during the hours he was waiting for his neighbour to get up? Then, to really annoy Chris, Norman had the bare faced cheek to complain that being at A & E so long had put him behind with his dinner!!!!!! At this point Chris's stomach was aching for food while all Norman could do was moan.

For someone who had been claiming that he couldn't bear weight on his leg, Norman had no problem getting up and down the steps to his flat. And as I suspected, all thoughts of going into care had been put on hold again. Norman had worked out how much interest he would be losing by cashing in some of his ISAs. And then Norman told his son that he had realised something about the money he had saved, the money that had ruled his life and that of his late wife. What as it? "You only really need enough money to get by on!" he proclaimed.

Had Norman finally realised that the tax man, the government and more, would all take a chunk of his savings during his life and especially after his death? Call me sceptical but after a half century of watching him scrimp and scrape to save every possible penny I didn't believe a word he said. But time would tell.

When Chris finally arrived home, angry, frustrated and starving he was adamant that if Norman's neighbour ever rang us again, we would not be running to his aid. At best, I would ring for a home visit from his doctor, or we would ask the concerned neighbour to ring for an ambulance.

Yet again, Norman had proved that he was able to get to his neighbour's flat and get him to ring our number when he felt ill or was in pain. But not once did he make that short walk to ask his neighbour to ring and see how his son was before or after his operation. As you will have realised, this was and would always be a bone of contention with me.

If anyone reading this considers me cold hearted, callous or plain heartless then I must stress that in the couple of days before our farcical phone call about Norman, I had been on one of my regular visits to an elderly couple who lived near me. I'd taken a large cream cake for us to enjoy over coffee while we caught up on our news and had a laugh together. I enjoyed their company and they mine. The following day I visited Margaret's younger sister and her husband who were also friends as well as family. I was helping them with official paperwork they needed to complete but we also had a good natter over a coffee and biscuits. I enjoyed being in their company and am more than happy to help them in any way. But when it came to Norman, I felt nothing only hatred and anger.

Chapter 23

Pie in the sky?

Well, it was only days later that Norman made another life changing decision. Chris had been to collect his father's shopping list on Sunday morning and arrived back home mumbling and shaking his head as he read what was on the list.

Norman had made no comments about his supposedly painful leg and had now decided he was going to start dining out each lunchtime at one of the local cafes. He'd asked his neighbour about the numerous cafes we have in the village because Norman had a desire for a meat and potato pie. So, the plan was that Norman would walk up the road at 11.25am each day for a cooked meal. We both knew that he didn't have a clue about prices in cafes as Norman hadn't bought a meal in one for decades. He probably thought a couple of quid would more than cover the cost of his meal and possibly a nice pudding. He was in for a shock!

Then he handed over his shopping list to Chris. This was nothing like the one he had been giving him for years and when I saw it, I couldn't help but smile. A punnet of English strawberries was the first item followed by British lettuce! Why the sudden demand for British goods? And for the first time in seven years Norman was asking for milk. He had decided that he wanted to start drinking coffee again and insisted on a jar of Nescafe. The last time Norman had bought coffee it was probably only a few pence a jar even for the quality brands. He had a shock coming when he discovered the current price of everything.

The cost of his shopping and dining out was about to rocket but Norman was convinced the extra money he would be spending would save him a lot of tax being paid when he died. What he wasn't realising was the fact that when he snuffed it there would be no tax for him to pay. Any tax owed would come out of his estate, meaning less for any beneficiaries. We waited with bated breath to hear how Norman had got on in the café, if it ever happened.

Well, Monday morning off we trotted to do our shopping and get the stuff on Norman's list. I usually took a backseat when it came to picking Norman's items, letting Chris mumble and moan to himself as he searched the shelves. After scouring three stores we arrived home. English strawberries had been substituted with a tin of mandarin oranges. A jar of Nescafe replaced by a box of Aldi's Latte coffee sachets. Chris had decided he wasn't trailing round the shops for items that Norman would only complain about being so expensive or it could have been that he had lost patience with his father. I'm sure it was the latter.

So, off Chris went to deliver the groceries, mumbling and grumbling. He arrived at Norman's flat only to find it empty. Where was his elusive father? According to a couple of Norman's neighbours, he had set off at 11.25am to have his lunch in a café! So, regardless of him knowing that his son would be dropping off his shopping, he had beggared off out. And being a creature of habit, obsessed with eating at specific times each day, Norman had made sure he was sitting in the cafe for 11.30am on the dot. Curious as to how Norman got on at the café and him not having a phone or any other form of communication, Chris decided to wait for him to arrive back home, spending the time sat out in the sunshine, chatting to Norman's neighbours.

About an hour later Norman arrived back home. How was his dining out experience? Sadly, the café didn't really have anything much to tempt his appetite, so he had settled for egg and chips! There was plenty of choices on the menu but nothing that Norman was prepared to try. Nor was he happy with the mug of tea he had been served. The tea bag had been left in the mug, so it was too strong for Norman's bland palate. After all, one tea bag served four cups of tea in his world.

Would Norman be dining out again? He wasn't sure but I was certain by the time he had worked out the cost of his egg and chip meal compared to making it for himself, it would probably be a great big no!

Chapter 24

Cry wolf!

We've all heard the tale of Peter and the wolf. Well, Norman should have taken note of that story. We had no sooner got over the fiasco of his wasted and unnecessary dash to A & E the previous week when Norman was at it again with his early morning cries for help.

This time it was a Friday morning when we had our young grandson sleeping over. All three of us were enjoying our last hour of peaceful slumber when the landline phone rang. It was 6.30am so probably not a nuisance call, except it was more than just a nuisance call. Once again it was Norman's neighbour ringing. Chris had leaped out of bed to answer the call before he had engaged his brain. I instinctively knew who it was at the other end of the line. Well, I didn't have to be Mystic Meg to work it out.

Apparently, Norman couldn't breathe, and it had taken him ten minutes to walk the six or seven feet across the landing to get to his neighbour's door. Once again being the dutiful son, Chris quickly dressed and was out of the door within minutes. I had an excuse not to go as I had our grandson to get ready for school, not that I would have gone to Norman's rescue anyway.

Fifteen minutes later a very angry and exceptionally annoyed dutiful son was back home. If looks could kill, then Norman would have been on his way to meet his maker that morning. Why was Chris so fired up? Well, on arriving at the flat, Chris was greeted by a very perky suited and booted father, sat waiting with a carrier bag holding his toiletries, ready to get off to the hospital again. Where was the breathless Norman who needed urgent medical attention? There wasn't one! The reason for our early morning call was because. . . Norman had pain in his foot.

It may have been a pain in his foot, but Norman was fast becoming a regular pain in the arse!

On seeing Norman scrubbed up and packed up ready for a trip to A & E just because his foot was hurting had pushed Chris to the limit. He made it clear to his father that no way was he taking him to hospital again and that he would be going straight back home. Then, at 8.00am I would ring the surgery and request a home visit from a doctor.

Apparently, Norman seemed disappointed that he wasn't going to be taxied to hospital. Then he wanted to know what time a doctor would be arriving. Would it be before he had his dinner at 11.30am or later? God forbid Norman didn't get his dinner dead on time. He was told to keep his door unlocked and that a doctor would arrive at some point in the day. But this of course didn't fit in with Norman's strict routine.

I did my duty and at 8.00am requested a home visit, giving a vague description of Norman's symptoms and made it clear that we would not be at the flat when a doctor called. The ball was now in the surgery's court. I'd done my bit and was determined to do no more. There was no reason for anyone to have been disturbed so early that morning, so what was behind Norman's cry for help?

Was Norman now starting to feel vulnerable, lonely and even afraid? It was beginning to feel like he wanted admitting to hospital where he would be cared for, without having to pay. So, if he felt that way, why couldn't he just ask for some kind of home care package or a place in a care home. But of course, it all boiled down to money. Did he think that by going into hospital he could be transferred to a care home at no cost to him? Possibly.

With no way of contacting his father, Chris called back at the flat around 4.00pm after we had been out for a few much-needed drinks in the local pub. I went straight home, more bothered about what to have for my tea than Norman's health.

And after all the early morning fuss, what did the doctor diagnose when he finally arrived at 2.00pm? Gout! Norman had suffered with gout in the past so should have known what the symptoms were. He had taken pills for gout before so should have known it wasn't always deemed serious enough for a hospital admission. The doctor had even arranged for the local chemist to deliver Norman some pills before 6.00pm. But had the young doctor noticed the filth and squalor in the flat and if so, had he acted on it or at least put it in his notes? I was hoping that Norman had told the young doctor about his wealth and judging by what he must have seen in the flat, he would think Norman was now losing the plot. Time would tell. But Norman had now cried wolf too many times. If we got another distress call and ignored it, would it turn out to be a genuine cry for help we ignored?

A couple of days later Chris set off on his weekly trip to collect Norman's shopping list. Would he be feeling better after a couple of days on his gout medication? No! Norman hadn't received the promised pills he had been prescribed or so he claimed. But in conversation with Chris, he let it slip that he had fallen asleep on the Friday afternoon after the doctor's visit. Was he asleep when the chemist's delivery man had called, and Norman hadn't heard him knocking? Chris knew Norman was getting hard of hearing and had previously claimed the warfarin nurse had missed some regular visits. We could only assume that was what had happened. But I would like to know how someone who was in so much pain and distress with gout, who had felt the need to get us up out of our beds at 6.30am, could manage to sleep so soundly once a doctor had visited? Then Norman revealed that the doctor had asked him if he was coping with everyday living. Did he have any help around the flat? The doctor had gone into the kitchen and had a look around. That wasn't surprising considering the doctor must have seen the filth in the lounge. And maybe he had a crafty look in the bathroom on his way out. That would have answered all the doctor's questions.

Norman then revealed he had fallen in the bedroom the previous evening. Again, he complained about his head spinning. But he had never told the doctor about his dizziness or breathing issues. He claimed yet again he wouldn't see the year out and wanted to go into the local care home. But the silly old fool was still reluctant to lose a couple of thousand pounds interest on his ISAs by cashing them in. Again, money came before his welfare. Chris told his father to think seriously about going into care as there was no turning back once he was in a home. That gave Norman something else to think about apart from his gout.

To many it will sound very callous when I say we now hoped Norman could give us a precise date for his demise. We as a family had plans ready to put in place. I personally couldn't wait for Norman to snuff it because the curse would be lifted from us. After half a century of being taunted with money that was coming to him, with endless promises broken, it sometimes felt like Chris was destined to die before he could inherit any of what Norman had promised him. And it wasn't as if we needed Norman's money because if or when Chris inherited any cash, it was far too late for him to get any benefit from it. But he could make sure his family did. And if Norman was to go into care, then he couldn't expect many visitors. Apart from his dutiful son, nobody else would be the slightest bit interested in Norman's welfare. For me, it would be out of sight, out of mind and his granddaughters had never had a desire to visit him.

When my mother was widowed, I was in contact with her every day, be it a phone call when I got home from work or taking her shopping and even taking her out with us to the local club at the weekend. She also had an alarm pendant to wear in her last year so she could always contact me or my sister for help. But then my mother was repaid for the kindness and care she had showered on me and my family.

While all this business with Norman was happening, our eight-year-old grandson was insisting that he came to sleep over at ours at least once a week and said he loved being with us. We were also receiving videos from our fourteen-year-old granddaughter who was on holiday in Rhodes. Our grandchildren knew that they were loved and a very important part of our lives, as they should be. Love for his grandchildren was something Norman never appeared to have and in return he received no love or affection from them.

As callous as Chris and I may have appeared towards Norman, those that knew us well knew how and why we had become so. When my own father was dying of cancer and in his last couple of weeks on this earth, Chris often went to visit him without me, with no prompting or ulterior motive. My parents had a better relationship with Chris than Norman and Margaret had with their only son. Actions really do speak louder than words.

Chapter 25

Give me strength!

Miraculously, the following day, Norman's gout had disappeared! As the late Tommy Cooper would have said, "Just like that!" He hadn't yet received his medication and declared that if or when it arrived, he wasn't going to take it anyway!

At this point Norman's flip flopping about going into care and the early morning phone calls, along with his stubbornness were taking their toll on Chris. Each day he was getting more and more irritable and angrier at his father. Norman never stopped to think that his son was dealing with a life-threatening illness, suffering chemotherapy sessions and attending what seemed to be never ending hospital appointments. For me it was a no brainer. Chris's welfare came first. For years, Norman had often said he would never go into a care home insisting he would go to bed and hold his breath first. I'd reached the point where I was more than happy to go down with a pillow and help him do so!

The following Monday, Chris arrived at the flat to find Norman had got his knickers in a twist. Why? Because we had been later than usual setting off to go shopping for Norman's groceries and had spent longer than usual having a good look round the charity shops for a bargain (who doesn't love a bargain?). Chris was almost thirty minutes later than usual when he arrived with the shopping which meant Norman hadn't been able to have his dinner at 11.30am. This had really upset him. For a man who had nowhere to go and nobody to see why did he have to eat at the exact same time each day? It was all about what Norman wanted.

But then Chris threw a spanner in the works that was going to upset Norman's routine. We had booked to go to Blackpool for five days. This was to be from Sunday to Friday which meant Norman would have to have his shopping delivered a couple of days early and would have to make his groceries last a bit longer. It had been almost five years since we had been away on any kind of holiday. Covid stopped us in 2020 and in 2021 Chris started his battle with cancer. I doubt Norman would have thought it was good news that his son was able to have a holiday, only seeing it as a disruption to the strict timetable that ruled his life.

Well, a few days passed before Chris was getting wound up about Norman yet again. Off he trotted to collect his father's shopping list only to be informed that Norman had started dining at another café. He'd asked his neighbour to check out another café and its menu, which he did. It turned out that the kind café owner had even sent Norman a complimentary dinner for him to try! Which of course with it being free Norman had devoured. He had then gone back on another occasion for a cooked breakfast and was planning to dine out more often. The café also did home deliveries which Norman was interested in. How Norman was going to ring the café and place his order without a phone was anyone's guess. But on his journey back home from the café Norman had fallen in the street and was unable to get himself up from the pavement. A kind and caring man who lived in the flats opposite was quick to go to Norman's rescue and as luck had it, a passing ambulance also stopped to check on Norman, who was none the worse for his tumble.

When Chris saw Norman's shopping list, he aired his concerns that there were not enough items on it to provide Norman with a week's meals. To which Norman was adamant that he would be dining out most days before mentioning that his gout had flared up again. His gout seemed to flare up and miraculously disappear when it suited his plans. But if Norman was adamant that he didn't need much in the line of groceries, then so be it, thought Chris. His patience was stretched to the limit at this point.

Well, what can I say about a man who claimed to have a hiatus hernia, needed to take Lansoprazole and Gaviscon every day for acid reflux and thought it acceptable to have a boiled onion for a main meal? This was a man who for decades rationed himself and his wife to pathetic meals like an egg on a slice of toast after a day's work, insisting that they couldn't eat large amounts. The very same man who was now making regular trips to the local café. I'd always known he could eat for England when it suited him and especially if someone else was paying or doing the cooking.

How long would Norman's new obsession with dining out last? Not long I suspected once he realised exactly how much a week he was spending. That would bring him to his senses. I personally was hoping this sudden surge of energy and desire for food was a lightening before Norman's health took a sudden and fatal nosedive.

Well, Norman dined out a few more times in the first couple of weeks after his bout of gout which surprised me. But then Chris told me what was going on in Norman's head. The silly old fool had convinced himself that for every £7 he spent in the café he was saving £2 in tax! This was how he could bring himself to spend a few pounds. He was convinced he was saving money. Really? Norman would never have any tax to pay on his money as that would only come into effect when he died, then the beneficiary of his Will would have that to deal with. But if Norman could convince himself that he was saving money he could justify the cost of dining out.

Chris and I were able to finally take a much-needed holiday. It was our first break away for five years. He couldn't fly because of his blood clots but we headed off to Blackpool for five days with a couple of friends. I was adamant that my mobile number must not be left as a contact number for Norman. He was on his own and as he was so thrilled with the café, he didn't want much shopping before we set off on our travels. So be it.

The day before we went away, we had spotted Norman sat in the café as we were passing. I pitied the poor woman who was trying to run her small café when Norman had got bedded in for a few hours after his meal. I had no doubts at all that Norman would have told her his life story and how he was a wealthy man. It was all he ever talked about to anyone and everyone. That poor woman may have started out being generous and welcoming to a new, elderly customer but I was certain that it wouldn't be long before she started dreading Norman walking through the café door. He was blinkered enough to think he had found someone who was interested in his life story but after hearing Norman's ramblings a few times it became tedious and boring. And he must have thought that he really had got his legs under the table because later, on a visit to see his father, Chris was shown an orange-coloured casserole dish that Norman had raked out from some cupboard. He was going to give it to the café owner to use until Chris pointed out that the inside of the dish was totally rusty!

So, after our much-needed jolly jaunt to Blackpool, the dutiful son trotted off to see his father. Norman was really pleased to see him! Why? Well, it wasn't because he had missed seeing his only son, it was because he had some more ISAs that were coming to fruition on Thursday 31st July. That was in four days' time. Norman was adamant that he must go to the building society by that date or the interest rate he would be getting paid would drop back to the low standard rate. How often had we heard that? He just couldn't let that happen. And he was expecting Chris to take him to the building society on the Tuesday, two days before the ISAs changed over. Norman just couldn't wait until the due date.

But Norman was not happy on hearing that Chris had a very busy week ahead of him with four hospital appointments to keep in three days. First, he had to be at an eye clinic at 9.40am on Monday morning to see a consultant about a problem that had been detected during a routine eye test. On Tuesday morning he had a blood test appointment and later in the day he was to have a routine CT scan. Then on the Wednesday it was his start of another cycle of chemotherapy. Yet none of this mattered to Norman when it came to money. He just couldn't settle at the thoughts of losing a couple of pounds in interest. Why did he need any more money when he had more than enough? He was never going to benefit from the cash. Yet again Norman was showing us what his priorities were, and it wasn't his son's health! And considering that Norman had recently had problems walking, he was seriously considering getting a bus to the building society to get his ISAs sorted. His overwhelming obsession for more money never faltered.

Norman proved he really did have a swinging brick for a heart just a few days later when Chris took him his shopping. His only son had finally had a bit of good news about his health after seeing a consultant that morning about his eye problem. The collection of fluid in a sac behind his left eye had shrunk in size and was expected to continue doing so. This meant that with a little bit of luck Chris wouldn't need any sort of medical procedure. This eye condition wasn't life threatening but had been yet another problem for us to worry about. I hadn't realised just how much this had affected me until I'd had a call from Chris to say he was on his way home from the hospital and he wouldn't be needing any kind of surgery. When our conversation had ended, I was overcome with relief, tears running down my cheeks as the tension ebbed away. I could only try to imagine Chris's relief. We'd got used to living with cancer and all the fear and stress that comes with it. With the uncertainty of what may lay ahead for us we certainly didn't need any more pressure thrust upon us.

But what was Norman's response to his son's good news? Norman was full of concern and exceptionally anxious but not about his son. That would have been too much to ask. His ISAs needed Norman's immediate attention, and he just had to be at the building society by Thursday at the latest or he would lose some interest. Again, on hearing this it confirmed what I had known for decades. Norman's only love was for his money.

And true to his word, he did get a bus and go to the building society on that Thursday because Chris had declined to take his father days before the official date that the ISA's could be renewed. So, that day we had just left the supermarket carpark ready to do our shopping when Chris spotted his father heading our way, briskly walking up the steep incline towards the building society. I ignored him but Chris suggested Norman wait for us after he had sorted his ISAs, then we could give him a lift home. I was well chuffed at the thought of that! This was the same man who had got both of us and his neighbour out of bed on two occasions due to his painful legs, gout and breathing problems, but had walked very sprightly from the bus stop, then up the steep incline. Never underestimate the healing powers of money! Norman's journey really was like a devout Muslim making a pilgrimage to Mecca.

On the way home in the car, I just couldn't bring myself to speak to Norman. Did he notice? I neither knew nor cared! He had shown me yet again how insensitive he was. What normal parent would seriously think about their bank balance whilst knowing their child was suffering and fighting for their life? Most parents would give their life in return for sparing their child's.

At this point I wasn't at ease with my attitude towards Norman. After over half a century of seeing the repercussions of his penny-pinching ways I had not an ounce of concern or compassion for him. As far as I was concerned Norman couldn't die soon enough and when he did cark it, I was hoping he would be alone, trapped in his filthy flat, with just his passbooks beside him, nobody there to hear his cries for help. If I had heard these comments from anyone else, I would have been shocked and disgusted and rightly so. But there are no words that truly describe how insensitive Norman was or how obsessed with money he had become. Yet at the same time I was upset to find out that an elderly neighbour, a good friend of mine, wasn't long for this earth. Without any hesitation on hearing this news I went to visit her to say our last goodbyes, sickened that I was going to lose her friendship. The genuine sadness I felt at the loss of this lovely lady who I was privileged to have called my friend, reassured me that I wasn't totally heartless after all. It was just Norman that made me feel that way. And when had Norman ever seriously been interested in his son's health or anyone else's health or happiness? Never!

It wasn't long before Norman was becoming a pain in the arse again. He'd made his miraculous recovery from being unable to walk and struggling to breath which just happened to coincide with another couple of his treasured ISAs coming to fruition. And now he was a regular visitor to a local café and becoming a concern for the café owner.

Chris had made one of his routine Sunday morning visits to see Norman when on leaving the flat, Norman's neighbour pulled Chris to one side. The neighbour needed to have a word with him about Norman. As I had suspected, Norman was getting bedded in at the café where he went for his dinner, spending far too long sat at the only table in the café after he had finished dining. He was using the time to tell the café owner, along with any of the other customers who entered the premises, just how wealthy he was. Norman had been at it again, going into detail about his life and how he had amassed his wealth. He just couldn't help himself from bragging about money.

The caring café owner had raised her concerns to Norman's neighbour, worried that if any unscrupulous characters were to hear Norman's bragging about his money, they may cause him some harm. I doubt the poor woman knew that Norman never kept above a few pounds in his flat or on him. She may even have thought he was rambling in old age. Chris made it clear to the neighbour that there was nothing he could say or do to stop his father constantly bragging about his money. Be it on Norman's own head if he was mugged or robbed. Though he did later mention it to Norman, who was not amused that his ramblings about money had not been well received. I pitied the café owner having to listen to Norman's constant droning on about his money. I wouldn't have blamed the woman if she'd thought about pulling the shutters down on the café at 11.25am each day (just as Norman was about to arrive). Then when Norman had turned around to head off home, lift the shutters and carry on as normal. I would have done in her place. Having had to listen to Norman's life story on far too many occasions, the poor woman had my sympathy and empathy.

Had Norman forgotten that a few years prior his wife was mugged on her way home from shopping at the local Co-op store? A young man had followed her back to the flat and just as she reached the communal door to her home, the thug had grabbed her handbag and run off. The contents of Margaret's bag were later found a few hundred yards away, scattered over the pavement. Naturally, Margaret was physically shaken and upset by this, but the thief will not have benefited from the contents of her bag as she would have only had a few pounds in it and little else of any value. Why was she singled out to be mugged? Margaret would not have looked like an affluent shopper, so could it possibly have been related to Norman's incessant bragging about his money? Had someone who Norman had been bragging to mentioned this to others who then thought the couple were worth mugging? We will never know but I personally could not see any other reason to pick on Margaret.

Then as Chris was setting foot out of the communal door, he was stopped by another of Norman's neighbours. This woman was concerned about Norman struggling to climb the communal stairs to his flat. She suggested Chris contacted the council and ask for a ground floor flat. Again, Chris told the concerned neighbour that Norman, under no circumstances would agree to moving. No way would Norman consider moving simply because it would cost money. Any new property allocated to him would have central heating and need new carpets and wardrobes. Central heating was something Norman had refused to have installed when he and Margaret moved into the flat from their lovely bungalow.

And it was marvellous how Norman's neighbours saw him struggling to get about, yet he could get his arse in gear and tackle steps, hills and more if it meant he could get his ISAs updated. Knowing this, I hadn't an ounce of concern for Norman's wellbeing, be it him struggling with steps or him getting mugged. So be it if he was attacked and injured because he would only have himself to blame. I had lost all patience with the man. Just the mention of his name made me want to scream.

But then to really wind me up, we were walking to the pub the following Friday lunchtime when we spotted Norman sat in the café, obviously looking out for us. Within seconds of him clocking us, the café owner was standing at the door shouting, "He can't half eat can't this one!" This was the same man who I will remind you had a hiatus hernia, suffered badly with acid reflux and for decades had insisted that he could only eat meagre portions! Norman may have been enjoying dining out and the company he was keeping but little did any of us know that things were about to drastically change.

Chapter 26

Fact or fiction?

Well, what problem was Norman about to heap upon us next? Just as he appeared to be getting over his many ailments, he told Chris that his doctor had told him he probably had bowel cancer! Supposedly, a nurse unexpectedly visited Norman to take a blood sample. Then he was given more appointments for further blood tests and a doctor's appointment. What had started all this? Had Norman requested an appointment? We had no idea. But my suspicions were that the phone call I had received a few weeks earlier when a doctor was asking about the lesion on Norman's arse, had got the ball rolling. So, he possibly had got cancer. My first thought was, welcome to our world!

Then, out of the blue I received a call on my mobile from Norman's GP surgery. A secretary asked to speak to Norman! On telling her that he didn't live with us, and he had no phone in his flat, she was at a loss as to what to do next. Because of patient confidentiality, she couldn't discuss Norman's condition with me, but I was able to tell her a few home truths and did so. I quickly put her in the picture about Norman's refusal to have a phone and about Chris's poor health, hammering home the fact that we had more than enough to contend with without us having the burden of Norman's needs thrust upon us.

On hearing about Chris's health and Norman's stubborn and ridiculous attitude towards having a phone, the secretary suggested she obtained Norman's written permission for medical staff to put me in the picture about his health issues. But there was a sting in the tail to her suggestion. Apparently, I would end up being responsible for making decisions and would be involved in his future care arrangements. She also mentioned a care package being set up. Can you guess what my response to that suggestion was? Not a chance!

Our phone call ended with the secretary having no choice than to seek further advice from Norman's doctor as to what happened next. Meanwhile, Chris would try and find out what was happening when he next went to visit his father on the forthcoming Sunday when collecting his shopping list.

Steam was coming out of Chris's ears when he returned that Sunday morning from visiting Norman. What could possibly have got him so worked up? I waited with bated breath to have confirmation of Norman's bowel cancer diagnosis. But then I also had steam coming out of my ears after hearing what Norman had just told his son.

Well, according to Norman, who couldn't hear a word Chris was saying unless he shouted every word, there was no bowel cancer diagnosis! All his tests were clear, but he needed more investigation into his platelet count. And he had been prescribed folic acid. Apparently, the only referral Norman needed was to an audiology clinic to get his ears checked out as his doctor was convinced a build-up of wax was the cause of his problem. Really? Ear wax removal does not usually call for a referral to hospital and can be treated at home or by a nurse. Then Chris told his father about the call to my mobile asking for Norman's phone number and the information I had gleaned from my conversation. Norman denied any knowledge of a care package. He then added that he wouldn't allow anyone into his flat if anyone did turn up. He was adamant that he did not need any form of care.

Nothing made any sense. And I doubt that Norman would have given his permission for the surgery to contact me and discuss his health issues. Then he suddenly announced that he was going to visit the local care home and if he liked what he saw, he would cough up the cash and pay for residential care. Yeh, we'd heard it all before.

So, now we hadn't got a clue what was happening with Norman, apart from him handing a form to Chris, expecting me to book him an appointment to investigate his hearing loss. But the more I mulled over my phone conversation with his surgery and what Norman had said days prior to that, about having bowel cancer, I was sure he was lying and hiding something.

The following day, Norman was still winding Chris up when he went to drop off his shopping. Norman said he had a prescription for folic acid which usually ties in with someone being anaemic. And his gout had flared up again! I'd never heard Chris so angry when talking about his father as he was telling me about the claptrap Norman had spouted to him. How were we supposed to know what was true?

As I've previously stated, my anger and hatred for Norman was overwhelming. So, when he sent a self-referral form for me to book him into an audiology clinic, I just saw red. I looked online at the four choices of audiology clinics. Three out of the four were offering appointments within the next three or four days. But our local hospital waiting list was a month at the earliest. So, I deliberately booked Norman an appointment at the hospital with a waiting time of six weeks! If the poor man couldn't hear his television or what anyone was saying to him, it would make his miserable life even more so. Just knowing that fact gave me great pleasure! I was being deliberately cruel, but that man had pushed me and Chris to the limit. Norman could sit and stew in silence, his foot throbbing with gout. Enough was enough.

If anyone who reads this has ever suffered with gout, they will know that it does not flare up for hours and go away just as quickly. Gout sufferers take medication for weeks before their suffering ceases or have preventative medication, but not Norman. Within forty-eight hours of shuffling around his flat with the help of a zimmer frame (it had been his late wife's walking aid), claiming to be in great pain, he was able to walk unaided to the café for his lunch. We saw this miraculous recovery as we passed the café on our way for another much-needed drink. There he was, chatting away to the café owner, not a care in the world. And what happened to Norman's sudden deafness? Did that miraculously clear up just in time for him to get to the café? We were being taken for fools!

She who laughs last, laughs the longest, or so the saying goes. Well, a sudden turn of events had me smirking and I felt sure I would be the one having the last laugh at Norman's expense. Social Services came knocking on Norman's door two days after his second miraculous recovery from gout and this unexpected and unwanted visit really had him rattled.

So, I was right about what the lady from Norman's GP surgery had hinted in her phone call to me. They wanted to arrange a care package for him. And from what Chris was told by Norman a few days later, he was going to be getting a follow up visit. Had someone listened to what we had told them about the squalor and filth in the flat and him not having a bath in years? Well, it seemed so as the uninvited visitors had a good look around the flat, taking notes. When he was asked why he didn't have a telephone, Norman replied by telling them how much he had saved over the years by not having one! I'd like to know how he came to the specific amount he'd saved when he had no idea how much it cost to have a phone of any kind.

Norman was adamant that he was not having anyone coming into his home and he could manage on his own. But he would consider going into a care home. But any thoughts of giving up his flat were swiftly dismissed again. One of Norman's biggest concerns about being in a home was the dinner menu. Did they serve meat and potato pie? No way was he going to eat any foreign muck like pasta. If they didn't serve meat and potato pie he wasn't going in! What can I say except the man was sick in the head. And he'd given a lot of thought about having to cash in an ISA or two to pay for his care. No way would he consider losing a few pounds of interest to sit alongside other care home residents who probably hadn't had to pay a penny towards the cost of their care. It was going to be a big fat "No" to anything that Social Services suggested on their return visit.

As much as Norman was insisting that he could look after himself, on his next visit he showed Chris a saucepan that he had been using to boil potatoes. The pan had no bottom! Somehow the pan had been left to boil dry until the bottom had turned black and fallen out. Had Norman fallen asleep while the pan was on the hob? Probably! Yet he still thought he was safe to be left alone.

Another idea he flirted with was to have Wiltshire Farm foods delivered to his door. I think Norman thought this was a service like the old meals on wheels with a hot meal being delivered to your door every day. He couldn't get his head around the fact that ordering meals was done online or by phone, they were delivered frozen and to have two meals a day plus a dessert would cost him over ten pounds a day. He thought the cost of getting a full day's menu would be less than a fiver! He really was living in cloud cuckoo land!

I was hoping Social Services would insist on Norman having some kind of care but alas, it was not to be. All they did was send him a pack of leaflets to mull over with information about the care homes in the area and their fees. Other services were available at a cost including an SOS pendant. Norman did seem interested in a pendant until he saw it would cost him around ten pounds a month. That thought was swiftly knocked on the head. Well, you can't help those who won't be helped, so as far as I was concerned whatever fate had in store for Norman when it came to his demise it was all down to him. He may have been convinced he would simply go to bed one night and not wake up but the chances of that were slim. For the sake of spending ten pounds a month he could have had some peace of mind but keeping those few pounds in the bank was far more important.

And as for Norman being a regular customer at the café, it was very hit and miss. The café suddenly seemed to be closed more days than it was open, especially in the busiest times when it was our weekly market. Had the poor woman lost the will to live after hours of listening to Norman banging on about how he made his money? She really had my sympathy.

After weeks of drama, being told Norman had bowel cancer, or not as we were later told, and the early morning SOS calls, things settled down. Norman was trotting to the café on a regular basis and his health issues appeared to have been forgotten until Chris called with his shopping one Monday. What was his latest ailment? When he got up from his chair or turned around Norman felt faint. So much so that he had put a dining chair in the middle of his tiny kitchen to grab hold of when he went lightheaded. And what did he want his son to do about it? Ring his GP for advice? Ask for an emergency home visit? Go to the walk-in centre? No, Norman wanted Chris to take him to get his ISAs updated again! Who in their right mind worries about losing a couple of pounds in interest when their head is spinning and is in danger of passing out?

So, because he knew he would be getting to the building society in a few days' time, Norman wanted to wait and see if the light headedness stopped but if it didn't and he did faint then what? If he was to hit his head on the floor or fall awkwardly and break a leg or a hip, how would he get any help? We were back to square one! With no telephone or SOS pendant then he had no way of communicating nor had we any way of contacting him to see if he was ok. He really was his own worst enemy, putting his life in danger when it wasn't necessary. It was only a matter of time before his stupidity and stubborn defiance caused his demise.

Now considering what Norman had told Chris about feeling faint, it came a somewhat of a surprise to learn that the following day our Norman was back dining in the café! He was seen leaving the café mid-afternoon after eating a hearty lunch. Another miraculous recovery! Or was it? Were we really being taken for fools? I was beginning to think the ailments Norman claimed to be having had been grossly exaggerated and just a way of getting his son's attention. If my suspicions were correct, then Norman was wasting his time.

Chapter 27

Scream and scream again!

As I have previously said, Chris was losing all patience with his father but on Monday 30th September 2024, he was pushed to the limit. It was a dreadful morning with rain lashing down and very chilly. We normally went shopping on Mondays because Norman needed food for the week, though with him trotting to the café numerous times a week his list had got smaller. But that morning Norman had insisted he must get some more ISAs updated. With Chris feeling he had no choice than to take him, off we went to pick up Norman who had been told to be ready for 10.00am and we would be there anytime between then and 10.30am.

As you can imagine I was thrilled to be venturing out in appalling weather just to appease Norman and had dawdled when getting ready. We arrived around 10.20am and I waited in the car while Chris went to the flat. And what was Chris greeted with? Well, Norman was suited and booted, anxiously pacing the floor in the communal entrance hall. He'd been there for over twenty minutes, clutching his precious passbooks, annoyed and wanting to know why we were late!

I barely managed a grunt in response to Norman speaking to me, having no desire to engage in a conversation with him. Chris had to shout every word he spoke so that Norman could hear him, which was frustrating, but thankfully it was a short journey before we swiftly dumped him at the building society door. What could go wrong?

After we had trudged around town in the torrential rain, Chris called into the building society to collect Norman and take him back to our car. Just looking at Chris's face and his body language I knew someone had got him wound up and it just had to be Norman. I was right.

Yet again, Norman in his eagerness to get a better interest rate on savings he would never need, never use and never see, had come a day too early to get his books updated. His ISAs expired at midnight 30th September therefore nothing could be done until the following day. The silly old duffer thought that some nice woman would manually update his books like they probably did in the 1960's. No, he had to leave his books behind and was asked to return later in the week.

Well, being parted from his books is Norman's worst nightmare and I knew he would not be able to rest until the love of his life was back in his biscuit tin. Now, Chris already had a very busy week ahead with trips to the hospital on the Wednesday for bloods taking, then Chemotherapy the following day. But he was also having to take Norman to the hospital on the Tuesday to see an audiologist. This didn't stop Norman assuming that Chris would be happy to take him to the hospital and then straight on to the building society to collect his books! Not a single thought for his son and the stress he was living with every day. All that mattered to Norman was him getting a better interest rate and being able to clutch and caress the passbooks that he showered with love.

As we strolled up and down the aisles at Aldi, leaving Norman in the car, sulking, Chris was spitting venom about his father. He had refused to take him back to the building society the following day insisting he would make him wait a week or so. Naturally, I was in full agreement, knowing that Norman really would lose sleep and not be able to settle without those books back in his care. On our journey home I never uttered a word to Norman. Did he notice? Did he care? Doubtful. He really was pushing Chris and me to the limit where we both wanted to scream with frustration.

But I did take note of one comment Norman made on the journey home. He said in a "Oh woe is me" tone of voice that he would go home and watch the news on the television. Was he hinting that he was lonely and perhaps we might invite him to stay at our house for an hour or two and perhaps offer him a spot of lunch? Or was he just feeling down at heart because of being separated from his passbooks? Either way it made no difference as there was no way I wanted to spend another second in his company.

The following day I thought Chris was about to blow a gasket when he arrived home from Norman's trip to the audiology clinic. When he told me what had happened, I couldn't help laughing. It had been typical Norman behaviour. When they had arrived at the hospital Chris asked if Norman had brought the letter with his appointment details. Most folk would have had the letter to hand, but this was Norman and not normal folk. What had he brought along? Clutched in his hand, Norman had brought along a large envelope full of letters from his GP, hospital and more, some being years old. The relevant letter was in the envelope, but Chris had to look at and flick through the pile to find what he needed. More hoarding by Norman!

Then, as Norman was waiting to be seen in the clinic, in a very loud voice he began making comments about the staff who were there. He wasn't amused that all the staff were Asian, only he used a more derogatory word to describe them, making Chris cringe with embarrassment. Thankfully the clinic wasn't busy, so Norman was seen quickly. And what was the reason for his deafness? Ear wax! His lugholes were packed solid. Well, I knew he didn't like to part with anything, so this didn't surprise me! Would he ask for the wax they removed to be given back to him so he could make a candle and save a bit more on the cost of lighting?

But what we couldn't understand was why Norman's GP didn't look in his lugholes and prescribe olive oil drops before referring him elsewhere. Or did he and Norman didn't hear or understand what he should do? Because all the staff at the clinic could do was tell him to do just that and then he could make another appointment to have the wax removed. It had been a waste of everyone's time and a bind for Chris who had two more visits to the hospital lined up for that week.

On arriving back home, Norman couldn't get out of the car. After numerous attempts to get out of the front passenger seat, Chris got out and walked round to see if he could lever Norman out of the car only to see that his seat belt was still fastened! Then to add insult to injury, Norman didn't have any money on him to buy some olive oil. He'd only brought with him the exact amount he needed to have dinner in the café. A typical example of how Norman's mind worked. You only take out exactly what you need. Guess who paid for the olive oil by giving Norman a fiver?

That weekend I saw a Facebook post from the lady that owned the café where Norman had become a regular visitor. It was Saturday night, and she was advertising her Sunday lunch menu and taking orders online. Yet when Chris went to get his father's shopping list the day after, Norman mentioned that he wasn't having his Sunday lunch at the cafe as it wasn't opening. The café owner had told him so! Had the poor woman got fed up with Norman loitering in her café for hours, churning out his life story and hindering from getting on with her work? I thought so.

And just when I thought Chris had been pushed to the limit with his father's antics, on the Sunday, he pushed him a little further! Norman could not get it into his head that it was not a matter of great urgency to get his passbooks updated. And then he revealed that he hadn't left his books at the building society the previous week, so that was another lie he had told us. After twenty minutes of trying to hammer home that we were having to change our usual day for shopping, due to us having a plumber calling on the Monday, Norman still thought we were going to take him to the building society the following morning at 10.00am on the dot! He either couldn't hear what Chris had been saying due to the wax in his ears or he didn't want to hear. Nothing was as important in life as him needing to get a couple of percent more interest. Hence, Chris arrived back home full of anger and frustration yet again.

Now exactly what Chris said to his father that Sunday or just how angry he got with him I do not know. But true to form, Norman had got up very early on Monday morning to catch the bus. He just couldn't wait any longer to get his ISAs sorted. I'd already told Chris that I suspected Norman would get the bus rather than wait a minute longer. I knew him well. So, when Chris called at lunchtime that day with his shopping, Norman was all smiles again. He'd finally got the new interest rate he craved. But while he was at the building society, he must have had a pang of guilt about his recent behaviour and how badly he had upset up his son because he presented Chris with a cheque! He'd withdrawn some of his beloved money and given it to his long-suffering son.

The cheque was a small token gesture and only made out to Chris and not both of us. No change there then. What was Chris supposed to do with this money? Nothing! There was no suggestion from Norman that the money should be used for enjoyment of any kind. It was unsaid but expected that he paid the cheque back into an account, never to be withdrawn. Well, that was what Norman wanted but we had other ideas. How could we put the money to good use? Within 30 seconds of Chris handing me the cheque I was texting my daughters, telling them to expect a payment going into their bank accounts.

As far as we were concerned, we were investing the cash into worthwhile projects, knowing the money would be spent wisely by our daughters' either on their homes or future holidays. Either way we were happy to hand over the money, knowing it would bring our three girls some pleasure. Depositing the cash into our bank account would bring no pleasure to anyone apart from Norman. What he didn't know about wouldn't hurt him. And if he thought that handing his son a piece of paper with numbers on made up for anything, he was wrong. Were we being ungrateful? As my name was not on the cheque, I had nothing to be grateful for. For me, the simple omission of my name on the cheque was yet another reminder that I was not blood and never would be. And though Norman in his warped mind probably thought he was being generous to his son, to me it was just a totally meaningless act. When was there any financial help when we had a family to raise or when Chris was being forced out on strike back in 1979? Back then Margaret was happy to loan us money! Maybe she wouldn't have asked for us to repay it, but her choice of words, "If you need to borrow any money" had said it all and I'd never forgotten that.

Handing Chris a cheque, forty-five years later, that may have been considered a lot of money by Norman, would make no difference to our lives. Those years had long gone but I would never forget those who had helped us in any way when we needed it. And until his dying day I would never forgive Norman for showing no compassion or concern for his son when he had suffered numerous bouts of sepsis, chemotherapy and was fighting for his life.

Chapter 28

Taking the biscuit!

Just as we thought the early morning alarm calls about Norman were over with, we were wrong! Norman was at it again. After his visit to hospital to clean out his bunged-up lugholes, Norman received an appointment date to attend an out of hours local surgery. For reasons that evaded us, he had to be at the surgery on the coming Tuesday evening at 7.00pm. And as removing wax is not an emergency, we couldn't fathom out why he had been allocated such a late time slot.

And another mystery was Norman's unexpected visit from two women who had turned up at his door supposedly to help him with his hearing problem. Headphones that connected to the television were brought for him to use. One of the women was using sign language! Why? Who had sent them with the headphones when Norman was due to have his ears cleaned out just days later? Norman had no idea who they were or where they were from, or so he claimed. So, On the Tuesday evening, Chris did his duty and picked up Norman, who was coughing and wheezing, and off they went to the late-night surgery. Thankfully, Chris didn't have to wait long for his father to get sorted.

The following morning at 6.15am our landline ringing woke us up and I immediately knew it was about Norman. His long-suffering neighbour had been disturbed from his slumber so he could ring for Chris to go to Norman's aid. On listening to the neighbour, I picked up on something he said. "Norman has got breathing problems, apparently!" Apparently! So, the neighbour wasn't convinced that Norman was as ill as he was claiming and probably fed up with being got out of bed to be used as a go between. Norman claimed he didn't need a phone of any kind but was happy to be a nuisance when he needed one!

I did my duty and rolled over to enjoy another couple of hours in bed while Chris set off on yet another mercy dash. And what did he find when he arrived at Norman's? It was another unnecessary visit! Norman was sitting in his chair, feeling much better and about to have his breakfast!

Breathing fire down his nose, Chris arrived back home about fifteen minutes later. Annoyed is a very mild way of describing how he was feeling. As he'd left the flat, he had told his father that I would ring for a home visit from his doctor. Well, no way was I getting up early to ring the surgery! I eventually made the call at 9.15am and made it clear that I had no idea what was going on with Norman and he only ever told us what he wanted to.

That afternoon a doctor rang me saying that Norman needed a chest x-ray to confirm that he had fluid on his lungs, and it needed to be done within the following couple of days. In a polite but firm manner I made it clear that Chris and I were not able to be at Norman's beck and call and often unable to take him to appointments because Chris had more than enough appointments to keep with his chemotherapy sessions and more. I was on a roll! I hammered home the fact that we had done our best to get Norman to have a phone, but he was a stubborn, silly and selfish old man. I added that we had been told by him that he had got bowel cancer only to deny it all a few days later! Then for good measure, I mentioned something Norman had said to Chris that morning. Apparently, the previous evening, a woman's face had come through Norman's bedroom wall, where he had been sat on a horse with a sword in his hand, fending her off! I got the impression when I'd finished speaking that the doctor had got the message. Chris did take Norman for his x-ray the following morning but only because he had a chemotherapy session to attend and the Xray department was only a few yards down the corridor.

Just when I thought my anger at Norman had peaked, I received a phone call about him that sent me into overdrive! About eight days after having his x-ray, Norman was claiming he had gout again. Now we had to assume he wasn't lying because as we were on our way to a lunchtime drink (or two) the café owner collared us as we passed to ask where Norman was, as he hadn't been to the café for a couple of days. Later that day when we arrived back home there was a phone message waiting for me. Could I ring the warfarin clinic?

On two earlier occasions I had told staff at the warfarin clinic not to leave us any messages about Norman. If he needed a change in dosage, then they should write to him and not expect Chris to run down at the drop of a hat. So, I waited until the following day before returning the call. And what was the problem? The warfarin nurse had called as planned, to see Norman but had not been able to see him. After ringing his doorbell and knocking on his door she got no response. So, could I tell Norman she would be visiting him the following Wednesday? Then something inside me snapped!

I apologised in advance to the poor woman on the receiving end of my call, but I was determined to put her in the picture. In no uncertain terms I made it clear that they must never use our landline number as a point of contact for Norman ever again and exactly why. If he was adamant that telephones were unnecessary items, then he should not need the use of ours! I told her everything about the farce we had to deal with all because he refused a phone. And the reasons for him not answering his door to the nurse were either he had fallen asleep and didn't hear her knocking, he'd gone out and forgotten a nurse was calling or he was dead. We knew he hadn't been out to the café, so he probably was in his flat. And if he was dead, Chris would find out when he went to collect his shopping list. I apologised again for my ranting and our call ended amicably. How callous and cruel had I become?

This brought back a memory of my once ringing my own mother and it being engaged for over an hour. Worried that something was seriously wrong I dropped everything and drove to her home with a knot in my stomach. She was shocked to see me on her doorstep after I'd hammered frantically on her door. Her phone hadn't been put back on the hook correctly, nothing more than a simple error on her part but it was enough to give me palpitations! Yet I was being so vindictive towards Norman.

Well, more drama was waiting for Chris when he paid his dutiful call to collect Norman's shopping list on Sunday morning. When he arrived, the flat door was unlocked and no sign of Norman until he opened the bedroom door and thought he'd found a corpse! We should have been so lucky!

Norman had got up in the middle of the night and stumbled to the bathroom and fallen into the bath before being sick. Then he couldn't stand upright, feeling dizzy with a severe pain in his head. Even with a zimmer frame he couldn't keep his balance and had fallen a couple of times trying to get back into bed, where he stayed until Chris arrived. So much for not needing a mobile phone or an SOS pendant. Norman struggled to get out of bed as Chris rang for an ambulance that arrived relatively quickly. And what was Norman wearing? Pink boxer shorts! Where the hell had he got those from? He certainly won't have bought them.

Then as usual, while they were taking his blood pressure and other tests, Norman had to tell the paramedics that he was a millionaire! This was followed by him rambling on about his late wife being a high-ranking nurse. Same old, same old. Chris had no intentions of going with his father to hospital before Norman insisted that he didn't go with him. So, this left Chris alone in the flat, able to have a good look around. What he saw made up his mind that Norman could no longer live alone in that flat. He needed to go into care. The bath was covered in cobwebs as were walls. Dust was in abundance everywhere and the flat was now smelling awful. But as Chris had no power of attorney, he didn't have any legal control over Norman's welfare or finances.

It was over twenty-four hours before we were able to get any information about Norman. Eventually, we were told he needed a CT scan and would be seen by social services about how he was coping at home. This was our cue to say he wasn't coping. Then, the following day we got a call from a physiotherapist who was assessing Norman's ability to walk unaided. It seemed Norman couldn't remember things or answer a lot of her questions which I thought was convenient. The lady suggested he had strip washes and not take baths anymore due to him being unstable on his feet. He had told her he bathed regularly when he hadn't had a bath or shower since 2017 if not longer! I put the record straight.

Norman may have been able to cope with the stairs to his flat but would be needing a zimmer frame to walk about, this lady informed us. That meant if he wanted to leave his flat, he would need someone to carry the zimmer up and down the stairs for him. How practical was that? We took the opportunity to tell her a few home truths about Norman's dizzy spells and falls and how he was no longer able to stand for more than a minute or so when trying to cook his meals and much more. We ended our conversation telling this lady that Norman was no longer fit to live alone and needed to go into care. She didn't disagree and told us social services would be in touch about what would or could happened next. But our minds were made up. Norman was going into care!

What we didn't know was that we would have an emergency visit to hospital for Chris a couple of days later making Norman's problems the last thing on our minds.

Chapter 29

Home from Home!

Norman had been in hospital for four days when we had a medical drama of our own to contend with. Chris had suddenly developed a severe abdominal pain which had woken him up in the middle of Monday night and had him bent over in agony. This was just what I needed! But the following morning, after dosing him up with paracetamol, the pain had eased, and he was able to drive to his three-monthly routine CT scan at 10.00am.

But over the next twenty-four hours the pain returned just as intense and had spread to his back. After numerous phone calls to the emergency helpline that cancer patients must contact and after an appointment with a GP, Chris had to go to the Acute Oncology unit to be checked out thoroughly.

After being treated for his pain, and as he was already on the premises, Chris decided to visit his father and finally tracked him down to a discharge ward where he was tucked up in bed. Norman seemed to think he was going home later in the day but mentioned that he had suffered another of his dizzy spells and fallen that morning, unable to walk properly. His hospital bed had an alarm that warned the nursing staff if he tried to get out of it. So, the chances of him going home were less than slim but it was possible that Norman would be discharged to our local hospital whenever a bed became free. He'd found Norman in bed still wearing the shirt he'd been wearing when admitted four days earlier, unshaven and looking scruffy. Just looking at him anyone would have thought he was a tramp. Did he still have on the pink boxer shorts? So, what did the medical staff think when Norman told them he was a millionaire and as sure as hell he will have mentioned it many times? Maybe they thought he was confused and who could have blamed them? But on a positive note, our Norman was quite happy with the situation because the hospital food was good. Three meals a day plus drinks and not a penny to pay. And better still, he wasn't using any electricity in the process!

On numerous other occasions when we'd had the early morning distress calls from Norman's neighbour and Chris had taken his father to A & E or for an x-ray, Norman had been ready to go with a bag packed full of clean undies and toiletries. Yet when he knew he was likely to be admitted, he took with him just a comb! That was it, no change of underwear or pyjamas and not a penny in his pocket. What was he thinking? But what did I care as for me it was out of sight out of mind.

Now, Norman had insisted when they hauled him off in the ambulance that Chris should not visit him. Not a problem as neither of us intended to. But when Chris did eventually visit his father, the chap in the next bed told him that Norman had been wondering when his son would come and visit him! This from a man who never once thought about visiting his seriously ill son.

Well, the following week Chris had more hospital appointments to attend as the cause of his back pain was causing some head scratching amongst medical staff. But while he was at the Acute Oncology clinic on another occasion, he took Norman more clean shirts and underpants, thinking he may be needing them. Wrong! Norman's pink boxer shorts had been discarded, and he was trussed up in a nappy (Norman's description of it). Not wishing to ask the specific reason for the nappy, we could only assume Norman, for numerous reasons, probably wasn't getting to the toilet in time. So, there was no way that he could go home to the flat, yet nobody seemed to know what plans were being put in place for him.

Then we heard the news that the little café Norman had been frequenting had ceased trading! Was it a mere coincidence that trade had suddenly dropped off or was it that the poor woman had lost the will to live? Well, who wouldn't have after a few weeks of listening to Norman's incessant spouting about his money?

Now you can call me evil, spiteful and any other name but when we had an unexpected phone call from Norman, I couldn't help but feel somewhat amused. He had got a nurse to ring our number then hand the phone over to him. I answered the call, but he asked to speak to Chris. I duly passed the phone over, which was on speaker so I could hear the conversation, but I never asked how my father-in-law was. He wasn't happy. The food wasn't up to much he claimed, unlike the previous week when he was saying how good it was. He wanted to go into care and seemed to think Chris could wave a magic wand and get him immediately moved into a care home. Just like that! When asked if the medical staff had mentioned Norman's discharge, he had no idea what was happening. Nor did we, but I hoped he wasn't thinking of discharging himself. No way were we taking any responsibility for him. As a parting thought to end his conversation with Norman, Chris mentioned that we had no authority to get involved with any financial commitments and that the council or social services would need access to his money to pay the care home fees. That will have given our Norm food for thought.

As for Chris and me, we were going to wait and see if anyone contacted us about discharging Norman or moving him into care. After all, Norman had always claimed that telephones were unnecessary so he could hardly expect us to use our landline and pay for the calls, could he? And as usual, when Chris had told his father that he wasn't well and he had attended five hospital appointments in the previous week, Norman made no comment. No change there then. His callous attitude towards his son simply made me more determined not to help Norman get the care he needed.

Thankfully, at this point Chris's health was improving. The discomfort in his back and often down his side had turned to a more niggling pain as opposed to being severe enough to have him bent double. He hadn't been able to lay flat on the sofa or in our bed so had spent over a week sleeping upright on the sofa, but finally he was able to get some proper bed rest, and a few hours of sleep each night. Calm had been restored to our lives or so we thought until we received a phone call the following day from the hospital informing us that Norman would be getting discharged later that day!

The medical staff and whoever else who had got involved in Norman's case had decided he was fit and able enough to go home. This had both Chris and me firing on all cylinders as we told the nurse on the other end of the line why we knew Norman couldn't take care of himself. We held nothing back about the state of his flat, his personal hygiene and his total obsession with saving money and how only the day before he had asked if Chris had found a suitable care home for him to go to. Our revelations were falling on deaf ears, but the nurse agreed to speak to someone else about what we had told her and would ring us back. How could they send him home knowing what we had told them?

Unbelievable! No other word describes what we were told when we received another call from the ward nurse. Norman was sitting beside her, listening to our conversation, mumbling that he was fine and wanted to go home. The fact that the flat would be cold and there was no food in his fridge or freezer was irrelevant because someone from Age UK would be at the flat to get him sorted with some shopping and a care package had been arranged to start the following day. Norman was being sent home regardless of anything we said. Great!

Determined that he was not going to be at his father's beck and call, Chris waited until the following afternoon to visit the flat and get a shopping list from Norman. But the flat was empty when he arrived. The only sign that Norman had been there was a pair of red hospital socks left on the lounge carpet. So where was he? With no phone to contact his father on Chris rang me and said he was off for a pint and would call back at the flat an hour later. When he returned there was Norman sat in his chair, wearing his old crusty dressing gown. He'd been to a different local café for lunch! And in their brief conversation, Norman revealed that he had had another dizzy spell while in there.

For his supper the previous evening he had made a fried egg butty with the bread that was in his cupboard. That bread had been in the cupboard for over three weeks, yet Norman claimed it wasn't mouldy. Strewn on the sofa was a pile of documents that Chris looked through with information about carers from the local council. But then he spotted something written in bold letters. It was a warning to all carers that they must wear gloves and a protective apron before touching Norman! If this was normal procedure, I found it odd, but had someone been to the flat when he arrived home and seen the filthy bathroom and disgusting state of the whole place? That would make sense and would prove that we had not been lying to stop Norman coming home. But the best was yet to come!

Now, what I'm going to reveal next is not meant to be any kind of racial slur or disparaging remark. It is merely what Norman told Chris when he asked why his father was so desperate to leave hospital. Apparently, Norman was in the hospital ward when a group of black doctors and nurses, dressed in tribal clothing, began to circle him, chanting as they danced around. He was then rescued by a young German speaking woman with long blonde hair who whisked him away to a party at a bungalow. The bungalow was owned by a chap who had a market garden and off Norman went to see it. But he was convinced that everyone was just after his money. So, Norman went to the manager's office and refused to leave until he was discharged from hospital. Well of course he did! And no way would Norman accept that he may have been dreaming or hallucinating.

The following day, Norman had trotted off again even though Chris had told him he would be delivering his shopping around noon. So, he left the shopping on the kitchen worktop for Norman to find. But somehow when we had been packing the groceries into a bag, we had omitted a tin of red salmon that Norman had on his list. A very disgruntled Chris called back later in the day to the flat, making a detour on his way back from having another blood test taken at the hospital. A very anxious Norman was home from the café and sat in his chair. What was the cause of so much anxiety?

Well, Norman had arrived home from the café and thought he had lost a five-pound note from his pocket on the short journey home. Desperate to find it, he had walked back and forth numerous times, retracing his route home, in search of the missing fiver. He'd even asked in the café if anyone had found his missing money. It was only when Chris asked how much money Norman had taken with him that the mystery was solved. Norman had taken just a £10 note to the café and spent £5.50 on his meal. That left him with £4.50 change and not a fiver as he thought. No money had been lost but it took some explaining to Norman before he accepted that he wasn't a fiver out of pocket.

Had Norman lost the plot? Well, it seemed so when he started asking Chris weird questions. Basically, Norman couldn't remember anything that had been said to him just a couple of minutes earlier and wasn't making any sense of what was being said to him. Did this sound like a man who was of sound mind and able to decide that he could live alone? We had no idea what Norman had been treated for, what tests had been carried out or what medication he was on, nothing! Were carers calling in to see Norman and if so, how often? As much as I didn't want to see Norman, for Chris's sanity I agreed to go to the flat and try and make sense of some paperwork that had been thrown on the sofa and left there.

Reluctantly, I went to the flat with Chris on the Monday lunchtime. We were greeted by a woman we assumed was from Social Services (she never made her position clear) who must have been there quite some time. And it seemed that she had arrived just in time to avoid a fire in Norman's flat! The silly old fool had put a pan on the hob, presumably with some water in and then he'd fallen asleep. This was the second time he had let a pan boil dry and burn the bottom out that we knew of.

But no matter what we told the woman she was adamant that Norman was mentally stable enough to make his own decisions. Norman had also refused to have an SOS wristband that the woman had offered him. Why wouldn't he want one? Well, the answer is obvious. He would have to pay for one. That fact would always override his safety issues or peace of mind. What do they say? You can't help those who won't help themselves!

Then Chris made the announcement that changed everything. He made it clear that Norman could not live alone any longer and he must go into care. He also told Norman he would be self-funding his care and this idea was supported by the social worker. Thankfully Norman seemed to think it may be a good idea at that point.

Then it was my turn to break some sad news. I made it clear that Norman would have to free up some of his cash before he got a place in a care home and that meant going to cash in his precious ISAs that week. We needed a special bank account opening with sufficient funds to cover his fees for at least two years. Not that I expected or wanted him to live that long.

Norman agreed to do as we had told him, but I could see the cogs going round in his head as he contemplated what this would mean to his treasured million. He wasn't thrilled at the prospect of losing a year's interest, but he would have no option in the matter.

Chris revealed to the woman that Norman was worth a million pounds or more and I wouldn't have blamed her for thinking he was lying. The flat and Norman were both in a disgusting state. It was then that Norman once again made it clear that I was and never would be family to him in one short comment. "It's all going to *him*!" Yes, Chris was the beneficiary of the Will, which I knew, but it was the emphasis on the word, "Him" and not "Them" that hammered home the point. Even after fifty-three years I was still not considered family.

We left Norman, without me speaking a word to him other than explaining the financial situation, then we headed off to the local care home to make enquiries about getting him a place. After a quick look around, Norman's name was fourth on the waiting list for a room. Now all we had to do was get him to free up the money. Would he go back on his word when he'd had time to think about the money he would be parting with? Would the thought of losing interest on his cash bring about another dizzy spell and cause him to fall again or maybe a heart attack? Could we be so lucky?

Well, wonders will never cease, as they say. Norman finally saw the light! He must have realised that he was a danger to himself and others living in the block of flats as well as admitting to himself that he was getting weaker by the day. With no resistance he cashed in four of his precious ISAs expecting to lose a year's interest, but he was a happy chap when the cashier at the building society told him he wouldn't be penalised for withdrawing his money early because he had told them he was using the cash to go into residential care!

Then off we trotted to the bank to deposit the four cheques into an account that was to be used only for paying his care home fees. And while we were there it was agreed that my name would be added to Norman's current account, giving me full access to it. I'd been keeping and using Norman's debit card on a weekly basis to get his shopping or any cash he required and purchase any large items he or Margaret had needed. It just meant that when Norman was given a room in the care home he could move in at once, leaving me to settle all his utility bills, rent and much more. But before my name was added it took over an hour of me having to give many personal details about my own financial status. Had I got a mortgage, credit card debt, loans, savings and more. I was a customer there so was sorely tempted to ask the bank clerk if he wanted my bra size into the bargain! But it was job done and Norman could go into care as soon as possible. We could manage whatever happened without it costing us a penny. After all, it had been Chris who ultimately footed the bill for Margaret's funeral. We were not prepared to cough up for Norman's.

The Universe must have been listening and watching over us because our prayers were answered just a few days later. I got a call from the care home to say they had a room free. Did Norman still want to take up residence there. Yes! Yes! Oh Yes! I'd received the call on my mobile as we were driving to Aldi. We practically danced around the store as we pushed the trolley down the aisles, grinning from cheek to cheek.

Within days we were to have Norman packed up, signed up and taking up residence in the care home. A date and time were set for him to become the new kid on the block. With bated breath we counted down the hours.

Chapter 31

God's waiting room!

Yes! Friday 6th December was the day that Norman packed his tatty vests and underpants, his best suit and a few other items and off he went to pastures new. I was quick to get all the paperwork filled in and sorted then it was job done. Norman had gone into care, out of sight and out of mind as far as I was concerned. And the irony of Norman's insistence many years before that I wasn't allowed to be an executor of their Wills, yet it was me who would be taking care of all his finances, just like I had for Margaret.

Norman had five days to think about what he wanted to take with him, but he'd left it all until the final morning. He said that he had been packing since 8.00am but by 11.00am he still wasn't organised. And the reason for all the chaos was? Instead of sorting out what clothing, photos and personal items to take with him, he'd asked his neighbour to get the lady who ran the local antique shop to visit the flat and look at his furniture and all the clutter he had accumulated. The flat had decorative plates, statues, mirrors and endless knick-knacks cluttering every flat surface. Mixed in with the general clutter it made it hard to get organised. Norman had known that Chris had already been to see the antique dealer about viewing Norman's furniture and ornaments, but this was to be after Norman had left and we had had a chance to tidy up the mess. But Norman just couldn't wait to find out how much his clutter was worth, but it turned out that the dealer wasn't prepared to make any impulsive decisions.

Anyway, once Norman was no longer living in Cell block H and settled into God's waiting room, Chris and I were able to go back to the flat and assess what needed doing. We found cupboards full of rubbish, drawers full of even more rubbish intermingled with old photos and personal items. His kitchen cupboards had tins of stale food, covered with mould that had obviously been there a while. His worktops had more stale food in tins and wrappers. The kitchen was a real health hazard and how Norman hadn't died of food poisoning was a mystery. Who has a drawer full to brimming with torn up envelopes and letters? Norman had, because nothing was ever wasted. The bits of scrap paper were used to put his shopping list on and any notes he needed to make. But did he need to keep stuff from the 1990's? The flat was a perfect home for vermin of every kind. How he hadn't got rats living with him is another mystery.

Then there was the bathroom, still in a disgusting state that nobody would want to tackle without a Hazchem suit and breathing apparatus. But there was something just as gross waiting for us in the bedroom. Norman had been put on pills to reduce water retention claiming he had to get up to the toilet four or five times a night. What he didn't mention was that he had been weeing in a plastic bucket that was kept on the floor under the bedroom window. Knowing he had asked the antique dealer to visit his flat why wouldn't he have emptied the bucket and hidden it out of view? But he hadn't and we were greeted with a bucket brimming with stale wee!

I'd never been a regular visitor to the flat and not paid any attention to the bathroom for quite a while. But that day something I saw really struck me as odd. Who has a "Vacant" sign on their bathroom door, just like the ones you see in public toilets? Had Norman been responsible for fitting this? Was he charging for visitors to use the toilet? That wouldn't have shocked me, but I know I wouldn't want my bathroom door resembling a public loo!

We also found a smoke alarm, still wrapped, unused and complete with new batteries to fit, supplied by the council. Why hadn't Norman put the alarm to good use, especially as he was prone to letting pans boil dry? We knew the existing smoke alarm wasn't working when Norman had last let a pan boil dry and was only awakened from his sleep by the social worker knocking on his door. It wasn't going to cost him a penny to have it fitted and working plus he had a duty to not endanger the other residents in the block of flats. How his mind worked was becoming more of a mystery.

After about an hour of rummaging about in the filth and clutter we called it a day. My skin was itching at the thought of what may be crawling about in the muck and dust. We'd managed to find some family photos and stuff that were not for chucking out. The rent for December had just been taken out of Norman's bank account so we had no rush to hand back the keys to the council.

Amongst Margaret's possessions I found Christmas and birthday cards that our girls had sent her when they were much younger. A note that had been sent to her from one of our girls, many years ago had also been kept. And there were many old newspaper cuttings about Melanie when she had appeared in some of her shows and many more cuttings that featured the dozens of letters Margaret had published.

But one thing I found summed up what a sad life she had lived. Margaret had kept an old birthday card that someone had probably sent her many years ago and she'd ripped out the inner sheets of paper that would have had the birthday greeting. On the inside of the card she had written, "To my wife, Many Happy Returns, lots of love, Norman XX". So, she had created a card to give herself that was supposedly from her husband. Why? Was it so important to her that she got a card from Norman even when it wasn't? A pointless exercise in my opinion.

The following morning Chris went back to the flat to remove small pieces of furniture to take to the antique shop and collect some more of Norman's clothing. When he got to Norman's new home it seemed he had settled in and was happy with the food being served to him. But he couldn't find his wallet that he had supposedly take with him when he moved. He claimed there was four hundred pounds in his wallet, yet to our knowledge Norman never carried money or had more than a few pounds at his disposal. And wasn't it rather a lot to take with him as all his needs were going to be taken care of? Then he said he couldn't find the bags of sweets we had left for him which were still where I had put them, in plain sight. Nor could he remember what he had done that morning up to Chris arriving. We could only assume that Norman really was losing the plot and had gone into care just in time. But he wasn't our problem anymore and his wallet did turn up in the disgusting old dressing gown pocket that Norman had discarded on the floor of the flat.

Chris brought back some more legal documents so I could start cancelling direct debits and the manuscript of Margaret's novel that she had written years ago. I have mentioned this in an earlier chapter and that I was the only person to have read it because she had sent me every chapter to look over as she completed them. And then some years ago, with her permission, I transferred the novel to a Word document. So, as I scanned through the synopsis and dedication she had written for the novel, I was surprised to see one sentence that hammered home a couple of points I have been making throughout this story. Her book was dedicated to her three granddaughters but especially to Melanie, who had supposedly proofread every chapter and supported her every step of the way. Well, it was me who had read every chapter and not my daughter! So, once again she was going to show her favouritism towards one granddaughter while dismissing my contribution to her book, reminding me that I was never considered family or worthy of a mention. And I was surprised that Margaret omitting my name could hurt me after over fifty years of feeling rejected, but it did.

While Norman was lapping up all the attention he was getting in the care home, he had found his huge and hearty appetite once more. Proving once again that he chose to eat meagre morsels to keep the cost down and not because he didn't have an appetite. Meanwhile, Chris and I were losing the will to live at the amount of trash and squalor we were finding each day. It was jaw dropping and made much worse because we were finding important documents stuffed in envelopes along with old newspaper cuttings, greetings cards and more. Everything had to be examined and sorted. And some envelopes were tucked away in drawers housing Margarets underwear! She had been dead since April 2017 and Norman had made no effort to clear out her clothing.

I'm sure that if it had been a legitimate challenge, Norman would have won the Guiness Book of Records title for collecting plastic bags. He had hundreds stashed in every nook and cranny. It was the same with his collection of screws, nails, paper clips, buttons, bits of wood and more. He had tins full of these tucked away in every cupboard, inside ornamental pots and his large collection of biscuit tins! I really can't accurately describe the state of the flat.

But I did find a few interesting items in and amongst the mammoth pile of papers. In 2010 Margaret had written a letter to a financial advisor asking for advice on how she could help her son to be able to retire early. She wanted to give him money to cover all his household expenses, stating that Chris had a hard job and worked long hours. But she didn't want to break any laws in doing so. Well, obviously the letter was never posted, or it was intercepted by Norman. Maybe she had a heart when it came to her son but why didn't she insist on helping Chris in any way she could? After all it was her fat NHS pension and wages that had helped Norman to save so much money. And take note that my name wasn't mentioned in Margaret's letter. And I doubt that Margaret had any concept of what the average household bills came to after living with Norman.

If I had ever needed proof of Norman's obsession with money then it was confirmed by the number of notebooks and sheets of paper he had saved, all with his calculations on. He couldn't add up for toffee, as my late mum would say, but he must have spent hour upon hour, year after year, pouring over his passbooks and letters from insurance companies, listing each amount on old envelopes or in old diaries. His poor writing skills stopped him from lining the figures up neatly so when he added them up, he was hundreds out. I checked a few to prove the point. Why? Why did he feel compelled to keep adding up the figures. It wasn't as if he was spending any of his cash and needed to check what had gone out of his bank account so that proves to me that Norman had a mental illness comparable to alcoholism and gambling addiction. He may have even been on the autistic spectrum.

Then in and amongst some old photos I turned up a couple of surprises. Margaret had two photos of her with a well-known celebrity of that time. It was none other than Jimmy Saville! These were probably taken at some nursing event she had attended. I was discovering quite a few secrets as I rummaged through the rubbish. And one little gem I found in and amongst a drawer full of rubbish was a book about how to be a good mother-in-law! I can only assume she never read it.

And then I found another couple of Margaret's letters that were never sent. One was to the script writers of Coronation Street! She wanted those who wrote the storylines to include a character having his or her home taken from them to pay for care home fees. It was quite a lengthy, detailed letter and I suspect that Margaret secretly hoped someone would pick up on her vast knowledge and reach out to her for advice when writing the storyline. The other letter was a complaint to her MP, written about twenty years earlier, about the discontinuation of having a warden on call for tenants of the flat they had just moved into. This was at a time when the council were putting much younger tenants into the flats and not just the elderly. But what Margaret's bone of contention was the optional implementation of installing a Carephone in each flat. This was a cheaper alternative to paying a warden's salary but still giving tenants instant access to emergency help. But there was a small fee to be paid by each tenant who had such a phone. That was the real reason for Margaret's rant in her letter. The cost was minimal to have peace of mind but not in Margaret and Norman's opinion.

Chapter 32

The end is nigh.

Well, only five days had passed before we were again having problems with Norman. Chris had gone to take him some more clothes and was told by Norman that he had lost his balance whilst in his en-suite washroom that morning. He'd fallen backwards and supposedly hit his head on the wall. Staff had swiftly attended to him and Norman appeared to be fine. But a couple of hours later, I got a call from a staff member who had just met Norman for the first time. There appeared to be some discrepancy about the funny turn Norman had and his injuries, so a phone call had been made to 111 asking for advice. That was fine by me as I had washed my hands of him!

When Chris called the following day with more clothes, Norman revealed that three paramedics had examined him, but he was injury free. Then he claimed that money was missing from his wallet! This was not true. When Chris counted the notes in the wallet there was nothing missing but Norman wouldn't accept that fact. Slowly, as Chris counted out the notes all became clear. Some twenty-pound notes had been counted as fivers by Norman!

And then a day or so later I got another call from the home. Norman was incontinent! That was news to me. But the young carer told me that Norman's bed was wet every morning, and he was even wetting himself when supposedly using the toilet. He wasn't our problem anymore and I was thankful we had got him into care before Norman had become incontinent. But when someone had taken his soggy trousers to be laundered, the person responsible had found Norman's wallet tucked in the back pocket and handed it in to the manager to put in the safe. It had only taken a few days before Norman was causing chaos in his new home.

On the Wednesday, Chris had called in to see Norman on his journey home from having pre-chemo blood tests. We needed to know what Norman wanted to do about changing his address on his precious policies and passbooks. He was greeted by a very confused father who couldn't stand or walk unaided and supposedly had been sick numerous times. Norman was rambling when he spoke to his son, telling him that he had been for a walk round the village earlier that morning and whilst on his walk he had come across a body on the pavement. On further observation, Norman recognised the body as being. . . himself!

The following day I had yet another call from a staff member at the home informing us that Norman wasn't responding to antibiotics he'd been prescribed for a suspected UTI. Now his bed wetting had stopped he wasn't passing any urine, so he was going to be taken to hospital to be checked out. That was fine by me, not our problem anymore. As far as I was concerned the £1100 weekly fee more than paid for any special care he needed. But I did make it clear that if Norman appeared to be talking gibberish this had been going on for weeks and not a sudden onset.

It was three days before we decided to make a phone call and find out if Norman was still in hospital. He was but had been transferred to another hospital. Through gritted teeth I rang the ward and with fake compassion asked about my father-in-law. He was waiting to have a scan of some kind and being treated for de-hydration. I was quick to throw into our conversation that Norman had told us he had bowel cancer just weeks earlier but then denied it. I got no response about that but was asked if we would be visiting that afternoon. No!

After days of wading through muck and clutter in the flat we had all the carpets and furniture on the rubbish remover's truck. Piles of cushions, tons of coat hangers along with endless bags of useless stuff were thrown out of the first-floor bedroom window to save the two removal men from trekking up and down the stairs to the flat endless times. The furnishings and décor that Margaret and Norman had cherished were now nothing more than a pile of rubbish, all worthless. I'd contacted a company that accepted second hand furnishings attaching images of various items but had no reply. A different antique shop owner had been to look at the contents of the flat and turned his nose up at everything. So much for Norman thinking everything he owned was worth something. It wasn't! But what I didn't find amongst all the clutter was the present I had given them for their silver wedding anniversary. I'd really pushed the boat out and bought a silver coated tray that held six sherry glasses. It had been put out on display initially but then disappeared. I'd gone to great lengths in buying that present. It was Littlewoods catalogue's finest silver coated bit of tat that cost me about a fiver! After Margaret had given me a couple of pre-washed hand towels, I wasn't prepared to splash the cash either.

So, everything Norman had treasured was nothing more than trash to be disposed of and had been taken away. For us it was a blessed relief. We could finally relax for a few days and enjoy Christmas. But we still had the dreadful task of cleaning up the revolting grime, grease and whatever it was that was covering a large part of the bathroom.

But something had caught my attention when I'd braced myself to look in the bathroom that day. It just didn't make sense that the white tiled walls surrounding the bath were in pristine condition. Nobody has a shower or even a bath without getting soap suds on the tiling. After twenty years the grouting was still spotless. So, if Norman couldn't be bothered cleaning the toilet, then he certainly hadn't bothered to scrub the tiles. Then the penny dropped!

If Norman didn't allow Margaret to have the hot water tank on to fill the washing machine, which was a hot water fill, then I can only surmise that also applied to heating up the tank to have a bath or shower. If you were trying to save on the electricity, then it would make sense that if you were heating up the tank to have a bath then you would do a load of washing with the remaining hot water or vice versa. So, no hot water meant no bath or shower, hence the tiles never got covered in soapy water. Suddenly it made sense! I felt sure that neither Margaret or Norman had taken a bath or a shower since moving into the flat twenty years earlier. Thinking back, when I had to live in Miser Mansion when I married Chris, even back then hot water was rationed to one bath a week and we all had to bathe on a Saturday using just one tank of hot water! I suspect Norman had just taken things a step further.

Another weird item I noticed in the bathroom was the light switch. For obvious reasons they do not put normal wall light switches in bathrooms because of the moisture and danger of wet hands touching them. We all have a cord to pull with a little bobble of some kind to grasp. This is also hygienic as the bobble can be wiped clean of germs. So, what did Norman have in his shithole (sorry but it's the only word to describe it)? He had replaced the cord with what looked like an elaborate silk tie back for a curtain, complete with a tassel on the end. Waste not want not! Apart from it harbouring germs it looked ridiculous. A room drenched in urine and daubed up with faeces (that's a posh word for shit) had a cord that resembled something used by Gentry to summon their servants. Why?

Also, in and amongst the clutter, I found a pile of photos that were of the bungalow Norman had foolishly sold to become a prisoner in Cell Block H. It was obvious from looking through them that they were very proud of their home as photos were of the couple proudly standing in both front and back gardens. I could see changes that they had made to the lounge to accommodate the second-hand suite they had given, and the once room length feature fireplace had been changed to a much small one. This was probably due to Norman, in a fit of temper, smashing part of the fireplace with a hammer as I've mentioned previously. It was obvious that they had spent money on sprucing up their home, so why would any sane person then want to give all that up to start paying rent for a bog standard, small council flat?

At this point it was Christmas 2024 and goodwill towards all men wasn't on our agenda. I'd begrudgingly made a couple of calls to the hospital to see if Norman was likely to be going back to the care home for Christmas. I didn't get an answer, just told that it was up to the doctors. We still had no idea what Norman was being treated for but reckoned that sooner or later someone would inform us if he was being discharged or had snuffed it. Chris had no desire to visit Norman, and I certainly wasn't going to, so we carried on as normal. After all, Norman had said numerous times that he didn't want visitors and of course he had never shown any interest in visiting his son. I'm sure you will have already realised that I keep harping back to that fact.

We waited until 28th December to ring the hospital again and see if Norman was still breathing. He was, but with difficulty it seemed. He was on oxygen and an intravenous drip to put fluids in his body. And he was refusing to take any pills offered. Had he finally had enough and decided not to prolong his miserable life? Was he bothered that his only son hadn't bothered to visit him and had been reluctant to even make enquiries about him? Well, if he was then maybe he should have given more thought to visiting his son in his time of need. What goes around comes round!

New Years Eve 2024 we made our last attempt to clean the flat. Chris, complete with Marigold gloves, attacked the disgusting toilet bowl. Bleach and a scrubbing brush made little impact. A hammer and chisel may have had a better effect! Meanwhile I had ripped up the bathroom floorcovering, with rubber gloves on, and cut the urine drenched vinyl covering into small pieces to deposit in the wheelie bin. After thirty minutes the toilet looked only marginally better, but then we discovered the toilet wouldn't flush properly. Was this anything to do with the wooden sticks that Norman had kept in the bathroom? Was he ashamed to ask the council to repair his toilet when it was in such a state? At this point we'd both had enough and decided to do no more.

I'd had a quick run around with a sweeping brush, trying to make the rooms look a little less of a disaster area. Then I spotted Norman's vacuum cleaner, hidden at the back of the utility room that we had overlooked. It was a Dyson but a very early model and didn't look to be in good condition. Then I remembered something I'd been told years earlier. Margaret and Norman had been out on one of their daily walks when Norman had spotted a discarded vacuum cleaner amongst a pile of rubbish that had been fly tipped. Yes, true to form he had taken the vacuum home and bodged it up! Owt for nowt! And Margaret was as bad as her husband for allowing him to get away with his antics. Did she not deserve a new vacuum cleaner? Just what was it that made her succumb to all his stupid ideas? I sincerely hope it wasn't the threat of physical violence. Norman had a vicious temper though

I doubt he would have harmed his wife. But he may have behaved like a bear with a sore head if he didn't get his own way when it came to spending or saving money. He had smashed up the fireplace in their bungalow in a fit of temper and may well have had other similar outbursts.

On New Year's Day we had a call from a doctor at the hospital with an update about Norman. He was having problems swallowing and had been seen by a specialist team about it. He was to be given a softer diet but if he struggled with that then the next step was to be a feeding tube through his nose! Nice! But then things began to make sense. I Googled the symptoms of a hiatus hernia and how they often got bigger and more protruding, especially in the elderly. They matched what Norman was suffering from. He had internal bleeding, chest pains, breathing problems, difficulty swallowing and more. And it accounted for the large number of pillows and cushions Norman always had in his bed. I'd read that there was a certain position to sleep in for someone with a hiatus hernia to prevent acid reflux, so those dirty pillows in his bed had been used to keep him from rolling over in his sleep. Norman had refused treatment way back in 1997 when he was first diagnosed, opting for pills and potions to ease the symptoms of acid reflux. Twenty-seven years later the hernia had probably got much bigger and become a serious problem. It had only taken five days of sleeping in the care home bed, without his extra pillows supporting his body, for Norman's hernia to start causing him serious problems. It all fitted with the symptoms he had suddenly developed.

On January 4th Norman's health was rapidly deteriorating giving medical staff cause for concern. I took a phone call from a doctor who explained a little about Norman's condition and mentioned that he hadn't had any visitors. She then asked if his son would be coming to visit Norman. No! I didn't have to lie because Chris was at another hospital at that moment having his weekly chemotherapy session. I politely mentioned that he may not feel well after his treatment, as cancer patients will know. But Chris was coping well with his treatment. Should he have wished to visit his father he would have been well enough to do so. However, it had only been a few days prior that visiting in all our local hospitals had been forbidden due to a Norovirus outbreak and the usual Covid and flu viruses. Anyone having chemotherapy has a low immune system so should keep away from anyone infected by these and other germs doing the rounds. The doctor couldn't argue with that!

The following morning, we had a call at 8.00am to say Norman was failing fast and would Chris be visiting him. No! The elements had been in our favour by covering most of the country with heavy snow. We genuinely couldn't have got out of our drive, never mind travel on the roads. We had vehicles abandoned on the road causing even more problems for those who did try to travel. Then a few hours later we got another call. Norman had Pneumonia and Sepsis and was not responding to any treatment. He was on 60% Oxygen to help him breath but there was an option to move him to another ward and administer 100% Oxygen. However, the doctor didn't think Norman would survive this so was Chris in agreement to just keeping him comfortable and letting nature take its course. Yes! Norman was barely conscious, and it was only going to be a matter of hours before his body gave up the battle with his infections. So, we carried on as normal, expecting another call later in the day to say Norman had snuffed it.

Now as callous as it may sound, there was no way we were going to sit at Norman's bedside watching him die. He had refused to stay with Margaret in her last hours and I could never forgive or forget how he had prattled on to me about inheritance tax and probate, while he was sitting at her bedside. He was more concerned about the thoughts of having to part with his cash than losing his wife. That was callous! And in his final hours, did Norman realise that passbooks he treasured don't hold your hand as you slip away or shed any tears when you have?

Monday 6th January brought us the news that Norman had shuffled off this mortal coil. The first phone call was around 9.00am to say he was fading fast and probably wouldn't survive until lunchtime. If we were wanting to be by his side, we had to go straight away. No, we did not! The next call was about an hour later. Norman had gasped his last breath, could we go collect his possessions from the hospital? No! Chris casually told the chap to throw Norman's possessions away. What exactly were these? All he had was a cheap wristwatch that had cost one pound in a charity shop. He had no rings or any other jewellery to his name and as for wanting to collect Norman's second-hand clothing, why would we want that back?

So, that was it, Norman hadn't outlived his son, a fact that Norman never gave any thought to. It hadn't fit into his plans. How many tears were shed by any member of our family on hearing of Norman's demise? Not one single tear. That was sad but Norman's passing wasn't. Nobody had any kind of bond with him. The only bond Norman had ever formed was with his money and that couldn't shed a tear for him.

I'd always said I would dance naked through the village when Norman died, but sadly we were having below zero temperatures and heavy snow falls. I wasn't going to risk hyperthermia so had a little jig around our kitchen celebrating a huge weight being lifted from our shoulders, especially Chris's.

Were we thrilled at the thought of Chris inheriting Norman's million? Was there even a million to inherit? We only had Norman's word about how much his long-term investments were worth. And the tax man would be clawing a huge chunk of Norman's money before the solicitor got a chance to deduct a few thousand for her fees. At some point in the future, we would have to decide what to do with the balance. The days of putting cash under the floorboards were long gone. And no matter how much money Norman had left to his son it wouldn't restore Chris back to his previous good health.

Did Norman ever stop and think just what he was doing with his money? Instead of thinking he was saving money, perhaps he should have looked at it from a different angle. He had given thousands of pounds to insurance companies, banks and building societies for them to invest and make huge profits. In return, Norman was given yearly interest or a bonus. But the amount Norman received was peanuts in comparison. He had lived a life of poverty to give his cash for others to benefit from. Well, that's how I saw it. And as though it was a bind to us that Norman never had a phone, it may have been a blessing in one way. I am sure that if an unscrupulous fraudster had contacted Norman, inviting him to invest his money for a huge profit in the future, he would have. Norman really would have fallen victim to scammers with his greed for more money.

So, when Chris did inherit Norman's estate, what could we buy that we couldn't already afford? Nothing that we wanted or desired. And there are regulations to follow before you can give money to other family members. But what we would all have liked was a proper loving relationship with Norman that didn't revolve around saving money. I would have liked to have been accepted as a member of Norman's family. Margaret's siblings accepted me as into their families and we all became friends into the bargain. Therefore, I can only assume it was Norman and Margaret who had issues with forming friendships or relationships.

On Friday 10th January we were finally able to hand over the keys to the flat. A chap from the housing department came to inspect the property and we were bracing ourselves for being told there would be a charge for leaving the flat in such a poor state. But he informed us that the flat would be completely gutted before a new resident was put in and there would be no penalty to pay. He did however tell us something we didn't know about Norman. The young man revealed that he had visited Norman about a year earlier to discuss him moving into local sheltered accommodation. We had no idea that Norman was thinking of moving at that time. But after chatting to the young man, Norman just wanted information, and the matter was never mentioned again. So, he must have realised he wasn't coping and was making himself vulnerable by not having any form of communicating in an emergency, but he continued to be stubborn about it.

So, just as we were handing over the keys, ready to leave Cell Block H for the last time, Chris decided he would take a brass light fitting that had been in the kitchen and give it to the local antique dealer. He carefully placed the light fitting into a carrier bag, with a pack of antibacterial wipes we had been using and an almost full bottle of Aldi's best washing up liquid taken from Norman's kitchen cupboard. The bag was placed in the boot of our car for the short journey home but must have fallen over at some point. When Chris picked up the bag from the boot, the light fitting was covered in a green gooey substance. Norman had struck again!

Only on very close inspection did we discover a very tiny hole had been pierced into the top of the washing up bottle. Norman had made the hole to restrict the flow and ration the liquid, making sure he never used more than a thimble full! If this wasn't confirmation that Norman really was mentally sick, then what was? What normal person would ever think of doing such a thing?

Friday, 17th January we were able to get death certificates and any necessary paperwork to allow Norman to be cremated. We had no idea what day or date this would take place, and the truth was that we were not remotely interested. The curse we had lived under for decades was slowly lifting!

What can I say? Even after he'd died Norman was still causing problems. After days of wading through his pile of treasured passbooks and policy documents, I'd managed to get all the paperwork into some order to hand over to a solicitor. As I handed over the documents and Norman's Will, the young woman began sifting through the pile. Then I saw her facial expression change. Did we know that Norman had been writing on the actual Will document? No! The silly old fool had been highlighting sections of the Will and making comments on it which could have deemed it void. Thankfully the solicitor was of the opinion it would still be acceptable. What was Norman thinking of?

After doing some rough calculations, we were told how much inheritance tax would have to be paid. Again, Norman had got it all wrong when working out his figures. I'd been expecting the sum due to be at least six figures and it was, plus a whole lot more. We didn't care about that having to be paid but it did mean the money Norman had received from the sale of his bungalow was going to be clawed back by the tax man and more. And there was the rent he had paid for twenty years. The reality was that he would have been financially better off in the end if he had stayed in the bungalow that Margaret loved. They money raised from the bungalow would have been exempt from inheritance tax. So much for thinking he was a genius with money. What do they say? Penny wise and pound foolish! That just about summed up Norman and how he had spent his life.

Then finally, Norman was cremated on Friday 24th January. We didn't ask nor were we told what time of day it would be. But that night I felt the relief as the curse of Norman was silently ebbing away.

Chapter 33

Rich man, Poor man, Beggar man, Thief

I know I've stated it many times, but I cannot emphasise enough the power that those passbooks and policies had over Norman. It was seriously disturbing. His love for money, though he only ever saw numbers on a piece of paper and didn't have any of the cash physically in his possession, always came before anything and anyone else.

And I had asked myself one question numerous times. What did Norman think would happen to all his wealth when he died? Well, that should read, what would happen to his money when he died, because he had no wealth! And the one certainty in life is that we all die eventually. Oh, if it had been possible for Norman to take it with him, I'm sure he would have. Was he silly enough to think any beneficiaries in his Will would think twice about splashing his cash about?

Imagine knowing you are in your final year, months or even your last few days on this earth and it's time to take stock of the life you have lived. Perhaps starting with being able to reminisce about holidays and the experiences of the places you've visited, along with the many characters met whilst on your travels. Then you can remember the many friends you've made, smiling at the fun you have shared with them over the years. And of course, the comfort of knowing you are loved by your family and the love you have for them. Remembering the overwhelming love that comes when holding your babies in your arms and later your grandchildren. The joy spent sitting beside your child or grandchild enjoying the closeness and the bond between you. Margaret and Norman never had the privilege of having a grandchild sleeping over, telling them bedtime stories because our girls never asked to sleep there, and they were never invited to. Nor would Norman have bought spare beds to accommodate them. These are simple pleasures that cost nothing but are beyond priceless and must surely bring the satisfaction of having no regrets when your time comes to leave this world. That is true wealth that you can take with you into the afterlife.

Margaret and Norman never had any real friends only neighbours or work colleagues. At Margaret's funeral there were only a handful of mourners. These were family members who felt duty bound to attend and a couple of neighbours. Just what happy memories did she have to mull over in the last of her eighty-seven years? Take away her working life and exactly what had she achieved as a person? Next to nothing! The couple had lived a miserable and practically noneventful life. And the big mystery for me is how Norman got Margaret to agree to sell her much-treasured bungalow and take up residence in a council flat. Norman may have thought he had made a killing when he received £152,000 in the bank, but for the next twenty years he had to pay rent! And what became obvious to me when we had the task of clearing out the flat was that Norman had tried to replicate the same décor that the bungalow had. Was this to appease Margaret? But he hadn't and could never have done so. There was no comparison between the two properties. Selling their bungalow must have hurt Margaret but for whatever reason, she had succumbed to Norman's ridiculous idea.

I wonder whose idea it was to forsake a few days in Blackpool for a joint of beef at Christmas. Who made the decision to return home the same day as they had arrived in Skegness for a holiday? Margaret had been happy to pontificate about everything and anything, hurling verbal abuse at anyone she disagreed with, but maybe she should have directed some of her anger and criticism closer to home!

I'm certain that in her dying days Margaret had many regrets about her life. During one of our last visits to the hospital I saw it in her eyes when she said unexpectedly and with regret and anger in her voice, "We should have helped those girls more!" This statement was made while she was looking directly at Norman. Had the reality of the emotional distance between her and her family finally dawned on her, almost seven decades too late.

Did Margaret ever realise that over the years her son had formed very amicable relationships with her siblings and their families? I became good friends with Margaret's mother. We hadn't seen eye to eye when we first announced that our wedding would take place in a C of E church and her being a devout Roman Catholic, but that was all forgotten once we were married. And when we had our first child, I would go visit his grandma every couple of weeks, taking with me her great granddaughter. She always made me welcome, and I enjoyed her company. When the dear old lady died, I was genuinely saddened. Had Margaret genuinely not known that it was her and Norman who were not able to have any kind of normal family relationship?

Was she ever envious of the foreign holidays her siblings had enjoyed and the nice clothes they wore, unlike the second-hand items she had in her wardrobe and her penny-pinching trips to Blackpool? Did she regret not making a stand against Norman's strict regimes? I think she did. Why didn't she tell Norman she wanted a better life especially as it was her earnings that had made him a wealthy man? She should have refused to toe the line and if Norman didn't like what she had to say then she could have told him to get on his bike and take a hike, then taken half of the money they had accumulated!

In her last few months nobody wanted to see Margaret suffer and her passing was a relief not just for her but for us. But sadly, it was no big upset. I do think that had she still been alive when Chris was first taken ill, she would have acted quite differently to Norman. Maybe her maternal instinct would have finally surfaced on realising that her son was seriously ill. And as any mother knows, the instinct to protect your child supersedes anything else. Perhaps she would have turned on Norman, insisting that they paid for their son to jump the queue and see a consultant privately. But we will never know.

And I wonder if before he went into care, in his last weeks, as Norman sat in his self-inflicted cold and darkness, did he have any regrets about how his life had panned out? His only visitor being his son who felt duty bound to do so once a week, apart from the warfarin nurse making a call of duty.

I know he once told Chris that if he had his time all over again, he wouldn't change anything. But did he really mean it? To sit alone through those long, lonely hours, day after day, week after week, did he really get comfort from his precious passbooks? My guess is. . . yes, he did! And forgive my crudeness, but him loving money so much I'm surprised that Norman didn't have the letters M O N E Y tattooed on his manhood, then when he was bored, he could have played with it and watched his money grow!

Because there were only a handful of mourners at Margaret's funeral and Norman's lifelong obsession with saving money, we decided he would not be having a funeral. His body was taken from the hospital and then cremated. He should have been proud of us saving hundreds of pounds.

So, there you have it. It is possible for someone to become a millionaire without having to rely on Lady Luck being on their side. The late Viv Nicholson became famous for saying she was going to "Spend, spend, spend!" when her husband won £152,319 on the football pools in 1961. That equates to £3.6 million in today's money and spend, spend, spend she did. But having all that money didn't bring her or her family any happiness in life. It brought them anything but. Her husband was killed in a car accident and after having four unsuccessful marriages, in later life Viv sought solace by becoming a Jehovah's Witness. What does that tell you?

As a young man, Norman silently vowed he would be rich and that he would "Save, save, save," to be so! And in later life he saved even more! But that didn't bring his family any happiness. It begs the question, is money the root of all evil? No, it's not, but it can be the root cause of sadness and heartache. I've only recounted the eccentric behaviour that I witnessed or was told by other family members but I'm sure there will have been many more money saving tricks that only Margaret was privy to.

So, was it worth it? I would say a very definite No! Norman had once been a rich man but died a poor man. He was always a beggar man and most definitely a thief! Why? Well, Norman was a rich man when he had a wife, a child, a home and a job. He died a poor man with just his passbooks for company. Beggar man? He was always happy to beg for free stuff. Thief? Well, I would say that his son and grandchildren were robbed of fatherly and grandfatherly love and affection. He also stole Margaret's right to live a different life, a more normal family life. She was robbed of a normal loving relationship with her son and grandchildren and denied home comforts like the rest of us enjoy. She was robbed of a chance to pursue other interests other than just her nursing career. Norman's obsession robbed his wife of the right to be herself, a loving mother and grandma and not the obedient wife she became.

Norman was also a very stupid man who had come full circle in his life. He came into this world with nothing and as an old man he left with less! He'd had everything in the palm of his hand as a young man with a wife, son, a job and a home. In his final years he had lost his family, lovely bungalow and was living in a council flat then later in a care home with nothing of any real value, just a pile of papers with numbers on.

I personally held a grudge with Norman for making me behave so callously towards him, yet I have many friends and relatives who are much older than me who I wouldn't hesitated to help. It isn't my nature to be so cruel towards anyone who is genuinely vulnerable, but Norman made me feel that way because of his uncaring, selfish attitude to life and his overwhelming love of money.

So, the next time you catch yourself wishing for big a win on the premium bonds or a lottery win, take a moment to reflect. Wealth isn't having a mansion, a flash car or a wardrobe full of designer clothing, they are possessions. If you have good health and love in your life, be it from a husband, wife, partner, children or just good friends, then you are wealthy. Even to have loved and been loved by a pet cat or dog is a gift to treasure. It's not what you have in the bank, it's what you have in your heart and the people you have in your life that makes you rich, truly rich. And when everyone says, 'You can't take it with you!' I beg to differ. You must leave your money and material possessions behind, but you can take love and memories with you into your next life.

www.ingramcontent.com/pod-product-compliance
Ingram Content Group UK Ltd.
Pitfield, Milton Keynes, MK11 3LW, UK
UKHW022117030425
5313UKWH00011B/547

9 781917 7781